Passion for Action
in Child and Family Services
Voices from the Prairies

To Bob

With thanks for
your steady dedication
& significant contributions
to the well-being
of Saskatchewan
children & families.

All best wishes
in your new role
as Children's Advocate.

Sincerely,
Sharon McKay
& the students
of social work 414
Winter, 2011

Passion for Action in Child and Family Services

Voices from the Prairies

Editors

Sharon McKay
Faculty of Social Work, University of Regina
& Prairie Child Welfare Consortium

Don Fuchs
Faculty of Social Work, University of Manitoba
& Prairie Child Welfare Consortium

Ivan Brown
Centre of Excellence for Child Welfare, Factor-Inwentash Faculty
of Social Work, University of Toronto

2009

Production of *Passion for Action in Child and Family Services: Voices from the Prairies* has been made possible through funding from the Public Health Agency of Canada. The views expressed herein do not necessarily represent the views of the Public Health Agency of Canada or those of the editors. Every reasonable effort has been made to secure necessary permissions, but errors or omissions should be brought to the attention of Sharon McKay at sharon.mckay@uregina.ca.

Suggested Citation: McKay, S., Fuchs, D. & Brown, I. (Eds.). (2009). *Passion for Action in Child and Family Services: Voices from the Prairies.* Regina, SK: Canadian Plains Research Center.

Mixed Sources
Cert no. SW-COC-001271
© 1996 FSC
FSC

Printed and bound in Canada by Friesens. This book is printed on 100% post-consumer recycled paper.

Cover design: Duncan Campbell, CPRC
Text design: Donna Grant, CPRC

Library and Archives Canada Cataloguing in Publication

Prairie Child Welfare Consortium. Symposium (4th : 2007 : Regina, Sask.)
Passion for action in child and family services : voices from the prairies /
editors Sharon McKay, Don Fuchs, Ivan Brown.

(University of Regina publications, ISSN 1480-0004 ; 23)
Selection of some presentations made at the Prairie Child Welfare Consortium's fourth biannual symposium, held in Regina, Saskatchewan, on Sept. 12-14, 2007. Joint publication of the Prairie Child Welfare Consortium and the Centre of Excellence for Child Welfare. Includes bibliographical references and index.
ISBN 978-0-88977-213-7

1. Child welfare--Canada--Congresses. 2. Child welfare--Prairie Provinces--Congresses. 3. Indian children--Services for--Canada--Congresses. 4. Problem children--Services for--Canada--Congresses. 5. Problem youth--Services for--Canada--Congresses. 6. Refugees--Services for--Canada--Congresses. I. McKay, Sharon, date II. Fuchs, Don, 1948- III. Brown, Ivan, 1947- IV. University of Regina. Canadian Plains Research Center V. Centre of Excellence for Child Welfare VI. Title. VII. Series: University of Regina publications ; 23

HV745.P37 2009   362.70971   C2009-904469-2

Canadian Plains Research Center, University of Regina
Regina, Saskatchewan S4S 0A2   Canada
Tel: (306) 585-4758 • Fax: (306) 585-4699
E-mail: canadian.plains@uregina.ca • http://www.cprc.uregina.ca

Canadian Plains Research Center acknowledges the financial support of the Government of Canada through the Book Publishing Industry Development Program (BPIDP) for our publishing activities. We also acknowledge the support of the Canada Council for the Arts for our publishing program.

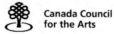

Canada Council   Conseil des Arts
for the Arts   du Canada

Dedication

To those whose passion for action is strengthening and
enriching the lives of our children and youth and their families

Contents

Foreword

The child welfare system is rightfully the focus of close public scrutiny regarding how it protects children, and the supports given to families who may be struggling for a variety of reasons. In the Prairie context, the imposition of this system on Aboriginal families and communities has resulted in immense difficulty and distress for many, and attracted increased attention from scholars and practitioners.

Greater analysis and understanding, and particularly hearing the voices of Aboriginal children, youth and their families, have caused the paradigm of child welfare to slowly shift. Is the harm we are protecting children from perhaps the very harm society has created through its disempowerment, exclusion and forced removal of successive generations of Aboriginal children to denominational residential schools? What are the broader ecological factors that contribute to the conditions of potential harm to children? Is the child welfare system a response to this or a continuation of it?

We know most incidents of Aboriginal child maltreatment that are substantiated pertain to neglect and exposure to domestic violence; the roots of these concerns are in poverty, social exclusion, and limited social serving systems in Aboriginal communities (health, education and family justice systems).

It is only recently that the need to invest adequately in supports for better child development conditions has been considered as applicable in equal measure to Aboriginal communities and families. These essential supports include maternal-fetal support, early infant development, early childhood education, education, parenting instruction and other support programs. The lens is shifting in this system. Better examination of the inequities in social systems and the neglectful level of support to Aboriginal child serving agencies has caused many to rethink the policy framework for Aboriginal child safety, health and well-being.

Amidst this paradigm shift, or perhaps propelling it, is the *Reconciliation in Child Welfare Touchstones of Hope for Indigenous Children, Youth and Families* document, which is both ground-breaking and widely supported.

Touchstones calls for better systemic support for Aboriginal families, children and communities. It also highlights the need for greater recognition that when Aboriginal children enter the system of care, their outcomes may not end up being better than they may have been if they did not go into care. As well, the lack of stability of their placements and the disconnect they experience from their families and communities seriously compromise the outcomes for these children.

The *United Nations Convention on the Rights of the Child* reminds us that all children have the right to be safe, supported and educated. It also acknowledges that the right of indigenous children to be connected to their community is not only a component of their human right to development, it also provides for the sharing of culture from generation to generation.

Focusing on the human rights of the child, new examinations of the paradigm of child welfare, and better understandings of the impact of these systems on the lives and opportunities of those being served propels us in new directions in the Prairies.

There is much to be done. In some instances, the work seems more like arranging for a fleet of ambulances at a cliff-bottom, while waiting for people to fall, instead of doing something at the top of that cliff to prevent what is happening in the first place. This book, and the thoughtful work of the authors and editors in grappling with these issues, will contribute to better understandings and practice. From this, I am renewed with hope that the future will be so much better for my grandchildren than it was for the grandparents of my children. There is passion, action and strength in these essays that will resonate with experienced practitioners and newcomers to this area. I hope it will inspire even more scholarship, and shifts in practice to better respect Aboriginal peoples, cultures and traditions, and especially the children.

Mary Ellen Turpel-Lafond
British Columbia's Representative for Children and Youth

From the Editors

We are very pleased to bring you this book, *Passion for Action in Child and Family Services: Voices from the Prairies*. The book is the second joint publication of the Prairie Child Welfare Consortium (PCWC) and the Centre of Excellence for Child Welfare (CECW). The book is strongly supported by the Social Policy Research Unit (SPR) of the Faculty of Social Work, University of Regina, and the Centre of Excellence for Child Welfare, administered through the Faculty of Social Work, University of Toronto, and supported financially by the Public Health Agency of Canada.

The chapters in the book represent a selection of some of the excellent presentations made at the Prairie Child Welfare Consortium's fourth bi-annual symposium, *Passion for Action: Building on Strength and Innovative Changes in Child and Family Services*, held in Regina, Saskatchewan, on September 12-14, 2007. Individuals attending previous PCWC Symposia (Saskatoon, 2001, Winnipeg, 2003, and Edmonton, 2005) emphasized the great importance of sharing information about programs, policies, and initiatives found to be supportive and effective when working with at-risk children and families. Building on this recommendation, the Call for Papers for the 2007 Symposium encouraged potential presenters to speak to their own 'passions' respecting work that is being done, and new and emerging policies, programs, and initiatives that hold promise for more effectively meeting the needs of at risk children, youth, and their families. Holding to this idea, the day preceding the conference opening was dedicated to one-half and full-day training workshops for participants wishing to learn more about specific programs, interventive approaches and skills. Together the three conference days stimulated numerous informative, enthusiastic, and passionate exchanges between and amongst participants and presenters.

Consistent with the mandates of both the PCWC and the CECW, this book is intended to convey the work of presenters who were able to dedicate time and energy to the hard task of presenting their experiences, ideas, and research in print form for publication purposes. The outstanding contributions that have resulted reflect the dedication, commitment, and passionate zeal of the authors. The introductory chapter, titled *Passion for Action; Fundamental Principles and Values,* places the chapters in the context of two fundamental documents guiding the planning of the symposium: the U.N. *Convention on the Rights of the Child,* and *Reconciliation in Child Welfare: Touchstones of Hope for Indigenous Children, Youth and Families.* Readers are encouraged to begin the book with this chapter, which points to the complex and challenging task of holding to fundamental principles and values conveyed in these two documents in a rapidly changing and troubling social environment. Our contention is that "passion for action" is the necessary and integral driving force that will bring about transformative change in child and family serving systems. Such change is essential if Canada's children, youth and families are to truly thrive and enjoy well-being.

The PCWC is a tri-provincial and northern multi-sector, cross-cultural child and family services network representing university educators, government, First Nations and Métis in-service training and service delivery administrators. Members of the network are dedicated to working together collaboratively for the purpose of strengthening and advancing education and training, policy, service delivery, and research in aid of children and families in need across the prairies and the Northwest Territories. The development of the PCWC has been powerfully and fundamentally influenced by the urgent voices of Aboriginal people deeply concerned with the escalating numbers of their children and youth in the care of the state. This influence permeates the Consortium's vision, mission and goals, which are directed towards ensuring that child and family services in the prairie provinces and the north meet the needs of the children, families, and communities they support. Respect for the needs of Aboriginal communities in the delivery of child welfare services is fundamental. Readers interested in the history and development of the Consortium are encouraged to look up the introductory chapter of the first joint PCWC/CECW publication, *Putting a Human Face on Child Welfare: Voices from the Prairies* (McKay, 2007).

The CECW was established in early 2001 with a mandate to help develop child welfare research across Canada; to disseminate child welfare knowledge broadly among researchers, service providers, policy makers, and other stakeholders; to provide policy advice to governments and service providers; and to build networks of child welfare professionals and other stakeholders across Canada. In addressing this mandate, the CECW has attempted to bridge gaps that existed among provinces and territories; among researchers, policymakers, and practitioners; between those who speak French and English; and between Canada's Aboriginal and non-Aboriginal peoples. The focus on child welfare within Aboriginal communities has been a special area of emphasis. The CECW worked collaboratively with the PCWC over several years as one way of making child welfare a truly national community in Canada.

It is the intention of the editors and authors of this book to help develop this community by adding to the exciting body of Canadian child welfare knowledge that has been emerging in recent years. Further, it is our hope that the perspectives contained within these covers will help readers to move toward expressing their own "passion for action" in a wide variety of ways to address child and family service needs.

Sharon McKay
Don Fuchs
Ivan Brown

REFERENCE

McKay, S. (2007). Introduction: Development of the Prairie Child Welfare Consortium and this book. In I. Brown, F. Chaze, D. Fuchs, J. Lafrance, S. McKay, & S. Thomas Prokop (Eds.), *Putting a human face on child welfare: Voices from the prairies* (pp. xv-xxxvi). Prairie Child Welfare Consortium, www.uregina.ca/spr/prairiechild/index.html/ Centre of Excellence for Child Welfare, www.cecw-cepb.ca

Acknowledgements

Many people have contributed to the creation of this book and, as editors, we would like to thank each of them for their hard work and their support of the book project. We must begin by acknowledging the outstanding contributions of the chapter authors, whose expertise and wisdom and patience with the editing process have created a product that will benefit the field of child welfare research and practice. The chapters reflect the authors' very considerable experiences as practitioners, program planners, and academics. Readers can learn more about the chapter authors in the Contributors section of the book.

The following persons provided feedback and suggestions on the chapters. Their comments helped sharpen the focus and message of the chapters and we thank them for their input: Dorothy Badry, Jason Brown, Keith Brownlee, Katherine Covell, Joan Durrant, Arielle Dylan, David Este, Judy Finlay, Michael Hart, Jean Lafrance, Karl Mack, Brad McKenzie, Raymond Neckoway, Nitza Perlman, Cheryl Regehr, Aron Shlonsky, Hans Skott-Myhre, Karen Swift, Shelley Thomas Prokop, Chris Wekerle, and Fred Wien.

Fiona Douglas, acting director of the University of Regina Social Policy Research Unit (SPR), and Merle Mills, SPR secretary, have provided invaluable administrative assistance throughout the process of putting the book together.

We extend our thanks also to the editors and authors of the first joint PCWC publication, *Putting a Human Face on Child Welfare: Voices from the Prairies* (http://www.cecw-cepb.ca/pubs/books_e.html). The work put into that publication made our efforts this time around all that much easier. Special thanks to Ferzana Chaze who worked alongside the editorial team for this book until her March 2008 departure from the CECW for doctoral studies.

We are grateful to Brian Mlazgar, publications manager at the Canadian Plains Research Center (CPRC), who agreed to publish and distribute the hard copies of the book. For the considerable work in copyediting and designing the book's interior we are grateful to Donna Grant and we acknowledge the fine work of Duncan Campbell for the cover design. Together, the two staff members from CPRC Press meticulously corrected all the inconsistencies across the chapter formats and contributed substantially to the overall quality of the book.

We wish to acknowledge the time and commitment of planning committee members for the PCWC's 4th Biannual Symposium, held in Regina September 12-14, 2007: Dexter Kinequon, Kyla MacKenzie, Derald Dubois, Dr. Geoff Pawson, Dr. Karl Mack, Janet Farnell and Shelley Thomas Prokop, then PCWC project coordinator, and Danny Musqua, who participated as Elder.

We wish to thank the Faculty of Social Work, University of Regina, and the Centre of Excellence for Child Welfare, for providing us with the encouragement and infrastructure support to carry out much of the work of this book.

Finally, we would like to thank the Public Health Agency of Canada, which provided funding support through the Centre for Excellence for Child Welfare. As well, we would like to thank the core partners of the Prairie Child Welfare Consortium and the Centre of Excellence for Child Welfare, listed below, for their cooperation and support.

PRAIRIE CHILD WELFARE CONSORTIUM

University of Regina, Faculty of Social Work
First Nations University of Canada, School of Indian Social Work
University of Calgary, Faculty of Social Work
University of Manitoba, Faculty of Social Work
Alberta Children's Services
Saskatchewan Social Services
Manitoba Family Services and Housing, Health and Social Services
Government of the Northwest Territories, Health and Social Services
Federation of Saskatchewan Indian Nations
Metis Association of Alberta

CENTRE OF EXCELLENCE FOR CHILD WELFARE

Factor-Inwentash Faculty of Social Work, University of Toronto
École de service social, Université de Montréal
Child Welfare League of Canada
First Nations Child & Family Caring Society of Canada
School of Social Work, McGill University

INTRODUCTION

Voices of Passion, Voices of Hope

Sharon McKay

"We need 'Passion for Action'—we need to build with our strengths—we cannot wait for policy and funding decisions," asserted Dexter Kinequon, emphatically summing up discussion of possible themes for the fourth Prairie Child Welfare Consortium (PCWC) Child and Family Services Symposium, held in Regina, Saskatchewan, September 12-14, 2007. Dexter's declaration gave voice to the sentiments of hundreds of participants at PCWC symposia held biannually since 2001. It reflected the frustration of front line workers, service delivery administrators, in-service trainers, child welfare educators and researchers in the field. It served as a call for action, a focus on "what works" and an eloquent reminder of the fundamental passion that drives so many individuals and groups in the prairies, across Canada, and, indeed, around the world to work for the betterment of disadvantaged and at-risk children, youth, their families and communities.

Stories of harm and cruelty to children and youth are seen daily in the press; family and community issues underlying these stories are complex, multi-layered, and seemingly intractable; agency resources are severely under-funded; innovative and promising policy initiatives can

SUGGESTED CITATION: McKay, S. (2009). Introduction: Voices of passion, voices of hope. In S. McKay, D. Fuchs, & I. Brown (Eds.), *Passion for action in child and family services: Voices from the prairies* (pp. xvi-xxiv). Regina, SK: Canadian Plains Research Center.

be seriously undermined by inordinate bureaucratic layers; and front-line workers may not have the training or education or the supervisory support to ensure best practices. Yet the story is not all negative. Numerous initiatives have been undertaken, particularly in the past decade, to try and turn around the individual, family, and community circumstances that have led to an escalating number of children in care.

This book introduces some of these initiatives, beginning with Dexter Kinequon's own personal story as a young Aboriginal boy dealing with his own troubled life circumstances as best he knew how. These experiences led Dexter to enter the field as a social worker and, ultimately, to become the highly respected agency director and nationally recognized advocate that he is today. His passionately delivered opening address to the 2007 PCWC symposia eloquently marries passion for action with positive, practical, and doable policy initiatives at the national level. We consider this address so important that it is placed, intact, following the introduction to this book.

Passion for Action in Child and Family Services: Voices from the Prairies is the second book to be produced by the PCWC. All but one of the chapters (Carriere/Richardson) are based on presentations made at the 2007 symposium. The chapters resoundingly echo the theme of the 2007 PCWC symposium: *Passion for action: Building on strength and innovative change in child and family services.* They reflect a consistent theme of the importance of "giving voice" to the issues and concerns, the ideas and experience, and the policy and practice recommendations that are proving to be effective and offer hope to the field.

"Giving voice" is a clear message contained in the two fundamental documents guiding the planning of the symposia: the U.N. *Convention on the Rights of the Child* (http://www.unhchr.ch/html/menu3/b/k2crc. htm), and *Reconciliation in Child Welfare: Touchstones of Hope for Indigenous Children, Youth and Families* (http://www.reconciliationmovement. org). An essential lesson learned from our four biannual symposia is that giving voice is a circular process. One needs to listen, to return to fundamentals, and to listen again. New and recurring voices need to be heard again and again. The fundamentals contained in the U.N. *Convention on the Rights of the Child* and in *Reconciliation in Child Welfare* need to be consistently revisited.

In brief, the Convention calls attention to universal, legally binding children's rights, namely, the right to: survival; develop to the fullest;

protection from harmful influences, abuse and exploitation; and partici-pate fully in family, cultural and social life. The four core principles of the Convention are non-discrimination; devotion to the best interests of the child; the right to life, survival and development; and respect for the views of the child (see http://www.unicef.org/crc). Initiated in 2002 by the executive directors of the National Indian Child Welfare Association (NICWA) and the First Nations Child and Family Caring Society of Can-ada (FNCFCSC), the *Reconciliation in Child Welfare* document is intended to address the lack of understanding between indigenous and non-in-digenous peoples that is a barrier to improving child welfare services for indigenous peoples in Canada and the U.S. As a first step, the two organizations, supported by the Canadian Centre of Excellence for Child Welfare and the Child Welfare League of America, invited 200 indigenous and non-indigenous leaders in the field from the U.S. and Canada to a three-day meeting in Niagara Falls, Canada, to launch the reconciliation movement in child welfare. At this meeting, the Phases of Reconciliation were exclaimed: *Truth-telling*—engage in courageous conversations about the history of child welfare and indigenous people; *Acknowledging*—ac-knowledge and learn from the harm that has occurred through mistakes in the past; *Restoring*—address the problems of the past; and *Relating*—work together in support of indigenous people taking care of their own children and youth. Alongside these, five guiding values, identified as "Touchstones of Hope," were articulated: *Self-determination*—leadership from and by indigenous peoples; *Culture and Language*—culturally appro-priate child welfare; *Holistic approach* —a lifelong approach, considering all cultural, social, environmental factors influencing the child's develop-ment; *Structural interventions*—addressing known structural risks such as poverty and lack of economic opportunities; and *Non-discrimination*—ensuring equal opportunity in all aspects of the child's life.

Together, the two documents provide fundamental principles and values to guide child welfare policy and practice throughout Canada and elsewhere in the world. The documents call attention to the urgent need to transform the child welfare system as we know it. Transformation re-quires innovative changes and capacity building through strengthening of policies and practices that we know are supportive of child and family well-being and that are effective in bringing about change. The challenge of transformation calls each of us to participate in visionary, troublesome, courageous conversations about child welfare—to do our part to bring about necessary change in practices and policies that create barriers to quality service.[1] *Passion for Action in Child and Family Services: Voices from the Prairies* re-asserts the 2007 symposia theme. Best practices cannot wait for policy and funding decisions. The book reflects the intention of the Symposium to facilitate, strengthen and stimulate *passion for action*.

Following Dexter Kinequon's opening address, the book leads off with Bernstein and Schury's chapter specific to the United Nations Convention on the Rights of the Child followed by three chapters that, while not referring specifically to the Reconciliation Movement, call our attention to the distinctive needs of indigenous children and youth and their families, needs that are frequently unrecognized by mainstream agencies, practitioners, and policy-makers (Carriere and Richardson; Bennett; Goulet, Episkenew, Linds and Arnason). In the same spirit of truth-telling, acknowledging and relating, four of the six remaining chapters speak to distinctive needs of special populations served by child welfare: high-risk youth (Smyth and Eaton-Erickson), refugee children, youth and their families (White, Franklin, Gruber, Hanke, Holzer, Javed, et al.), the children and families of those providing foster care (Twigg) and the needs of children with FASD (Fuchs, Burnside, Marchenski, and Mudry). Watkinson returns our attention to the United Nations Convention on the Rights of the Child, illustrating how she used the Convention and the Canadian Charter of Human Rights to launch a Supreme Court Challenge respecting children's right to legal protection from corporal punishment. The final chapter of the book "tells the truth" and "acknowledges the harm" resulting in the dire living conditions of children and families subsisting in deeply entrenched "spacially concentrated, racialized poverty" in the heart of two major Prairie cities, Winnipeg and Saskatoon (Silver). Aboriginal and visible minority families predominate in these inner-city neighbourhoods. The chapter documents pragmatic, locally based initiatives that hold promise for effectively addressing some of these living conditions and ends with a strong and forceful plea for a long-term

---

1   These words were spoken by Cindy Blackstock, Executive Director, First Nations Caring Society of Canada, in her keynote address to participants gathering at the "Reconciliation: Looking Back; Reaching Forward" event held in Niagara Falls, Ontario, October 26-28, 2005.

government strategy to invest in the infrastructure that supports these "home grown" solutions to inner city despair. This plea evokes Reconciliation principles of "Restoring" and "Relating."

The first five chapters passionately argue for changes that, to some degree, may be viewed as contradictory to one another. A key issue is interpretation of the "best interests" of the child, a fundamental precept of the U.N. Convention, yet a right that two of the chapters demand be considered in the context of families and communities that have been seriously damaged by historic and modern-day injustices (Carriere and Richardson; Bennett). On this question, Bernstein and Schury emphasize that the Convention should not be viewed as an international treaty that sets children's rights against parental rights, but rather as a treaty that "identifies the special/specific rights of children related to their developmental needs and complementing their basic human rights." Related to this point, the authors note that Canada's Standing Senate Committee on Human Rights recognizes that the protection of Aboriginal children's rights is intricately related to the protection of Aboriginal communities' future. Yet, from the Children's Advocate Office view, Saskatchewan's family-centered philosophy has had "devastating and life limiting" effects on children. A clear "children and youth first" philosophy and principles to guide policy, practice and legislation in the province is strongly recommended. A family-centered philosophy "at all costs" is condemned. A sustained focus on child-centered permanency planning is strongly recommended.

Bernstein and Schury acknowledge that decisions made in child welfare work are complex and often highly contested, and that "there is no one simple answer when it comes to the rights, best interests and care of children who have experienced abuse and neglect." The *Reconciliation in Child Welfare* document augments our understanding of the complexity of such decision-making. Aboriginal children, youth, families and communities across Canada experience daily the effects of historical traumas enacted upon Aboriginal peoples. Present-day child welfare policies and practice continue to fuel historical harms by failing to understand the significance of culture and community to indigenous identity and well-being. Along with other social/political/legal systems in the country, child and family serving systems are called upon to redirect their efforts in such a way that indigenous people are treated respectfully and in the context of their own cultural practices and identity. Only in this way will

Aboriginal communities and their families be assured of restoration to a healthy state of well-being. It is imperative for the very survival of many communities that this work be done.

Bennett, Carriere and Richardson, Silver, and Goulet, Episkenew, Linds and Arnason situate their chapters in the context of past and present colonizing practices. Doing so places the chapters in the truth-telling and acknowledging phase of reconciliation. Carriere and Richardson expand our understanding of the significance of connectedness to culture and history as part of Aboriginal children and youth's developing personal identities. The authors challenge traditional application of attachment theory in child welfare decision-making, arguing strongly that practitioners must ensure that children know their family and history and that "retaining kinship ties is part of overall community health and strength."

Speaking of the intimate relationships between Aboriginal children and their mothers, Bennett asserts that the rights of Aboriginal parents are being ignored and that this state of affairs is leading to a further undermining of the confidence and capacity of Aboriginal people to raise their children. Rebuilding parental capacity is essential to the healthy development of children and youth and the rebuilding of communities devastated by social ills. In Bennett's words,

> current child welfare practices too often contribute to intergenerational traumas that have been forced upon and experienced by Aboriginal families since early contact with Europeans. There is an urgent need for a new response system that seeks to ensure the safety of children and also ensures that balance in the family is restored as quickly and painlessly as possible in times of crisis. The need for healing for both children and their families as a result of their experience with the child welfare system is paramount but to date little attention has been paid to this aspect.

Goulet, Episkenew, Linds and Arnason pay attention to the prevention side of child welfare work, exploring the theory and application of drama and Forum Theatre to First Nations youth and their communities. The authors document their experiences using Forum Theatre workshops as the foundation of their research with Aboriginal youth whom they describe as being "embedded in community and family systems damaged by colonialism and, consequently, find[ing] it difficult to see themselves as agents of change." This chapter discusses the potential for drama to be used as an approach with youth, the process and methods used in their own workshops, and lessons learned. The authors conclude that drama is one way to engage youth in examining the potential of healthy choices for leading to different, healthier realities.

While *Reconciliation in Child Welfare* focuses specifically on Aboriginal children and youth, their families and communities, the guiding values outlined in the document, along with recognition of the Rights of the Child, apply universally to all children and youth, whatever their personal ethnic and cultural background. White, Franklin, Gruber, Hanke, Holzer, Javed et al. speak of the challenges encountered in their work with refugee families, due to the strong influence of their own "Western ways of doing and thinking." Their project, designed, in part to assist with reducing the impact of post-traumatic stress disorder, became one of "creating safe spaces, nurturing relationships, community building, and having fun." The project team met the challenges of working with several different languages, diverse cultural practices, and lack of literacy skills in reading and writing by paying close attention over the project to respecting the voices of participants, parents and children. In a sense, the project became self-determining, which the Reconciliation Movement describes as involving leadership from and by indigenous leaders.

Self-determination is a key factor in Smyth and Eaton-Erickson's work with high-risk youth in Edmonton, whom they portray as the "disconnected" youth, whose connections with supportive others are fragile at best. Members of this population frequently live on the streets, are seen as defiant and manipulative, tend to engage in behaviours that seriously jeopardize their safety, and exhibit extreme distrust towards social workers and other helpers. Yet, the authors believe strongly that underlying these difficulties, the youth want connection. The High Risk Youth Unit is a project developed for the purpose of reaching out to such youth in Edmonton. Case studies and guiding principles offered in the chapter reflect the authors' strong belief that, given respect, the opportunity to express their own opinions and ideas, and the steady commitment of the practitioner and the agency, the needs of these young people can be better met. Of particular importance is the belief that through innovative engagement strategies high-risk youth can be given hope for the future.

Twigg points to the serious lack of attention paid to the needs of foster carers' own children and families. His chapter places the current crisis in foster care (shortage of placements, inadequately trained foster parents, changing needs of children being fostered) in the context of child welfare history and the slowly evolving recognition that the chronic lack of carers is a systemic issue urgently in need of redress. He argues that recruitment and retention of future foster carers is highly dependent on provision of support, recognition, training, and adequate financial compensation.

A startling finding from the 2005 research of Fuchs, Burnside, Marchenski, and Mudry is that one-third of children in care in Manitoba fall within a broad definition of disability. This finding exposes a previously overlooked feature of child welfare, one that is in all likelihood similar to that of other provinces and territories. The researchers focus on the 17 percent of this population who are diagnosed or suspected of Fetal Alcohol Spectrum Disorder (FASD). As background context for a second phase of the original research, their chapter discusses the disabling effects of FASD, and significant care responsibility of child welfare agencies in Manitoba for these children. The chapter discusses implications for policy, practice and research and puts forward some directions for further research.

Children's right to legal protection from corporal punishment is not fully protected in Canada. Watkinson, through her own research, was successful in obtaining funding from the federal Court Challenges Program to research the constitutionality of Section 43 of the Criminal Code as it relates to the equality rights of children. She discusses how the Canadian Charter of Human Rights and the United Nations Convention on the Rights of the Child were subsequently used to launch a Supreme Court challenge to Section 43. The challenge was not without controversy, and the decision of the Supreme Court was only partially successful, but it did result in a significant limitation to the scope of Section 43. Watkinson discusses further research respecting the public's knowledge of the case and suggests actions social workers can take to interrupt the "normativeness" of physical punishment.

Jim Silver's chapter draws our attention to one of the single most disturbing factors affecting the quality of life for Canadian children and families—that of deeply entrenched "spatially concentrated racialized poverty." His extensive research places such poverty in the context of historical factors that have progressively led to the vacating of inner-city neighbourhoods except for those people who cannot afford to live elsewhere, primarily those of Aboriginal and marginalized ethnic populations. Four broad socio-economic forces—suburbanization, de-industrialization, in-migration and colonization—have had long-lasting effects on the development of these neighbourhoods. Silver effectively argues that this situation has resulted in a largely unrecognized segregation of populations in our larger cities. Yet, there are reasons for hope. Taking Winnipeg and Saskatoon as examples, Silver points to new forms of development, indigenous to the inner city. He describes numerous small community-based organizations, led by highly skilled and passionate inner-city people who are building an anti-poverty infrastructure using many diverse and creative ways and means. But if this work is to be truly transformative, stronger, more long-standing support is needed. Silver concludes with four suggestions as to where we can go from here.

Returning to the theme of our symposium, *Passion for Action in Child and Family Services,* the chapter authors have written "from the heart," reflecting their passion and sense of urgency for action about issues near and dear to them. Based on thorough research, each chapter expands our understanding of child and family needs across the prairies and beyond our borders. Importantly, each chapter points to actions that are being taken, need to be taken, and can be taken towards transforming current approaches and policies to better serve vulnerable and at-risk children, youth and their families in our part of the world. *Passion for Action* is the driving force required to bring about such transformation. It is our hope that the voices of this book will fuel such passion in each of our readers. For this reason, we follow this introduction with Dexter Kinequon's powerful opening address to our fourth PCWC Symposium. In his own modest, humble way, Dexter relays the factors that drive his own passion to commit his talents and skills ceaselessly towards bettering the future for today's children and their families.

CHAPTER 1

Passion within the First Nations Social Work Profession

Keynote Presentation, Prairie Child Welfare Symposium, September 12, 2007

Dexter Kinequon

Good evening, ladies and gentlemen, Elders, guests and colleagues. I am very pleased and honoured to provide the opening keynote address for this year's Prairie Child Welfare Symposium. I am aware of the amount of work the symposium organizers have put into this event in order to make it a memorable and useful experience for each of you, so in keeping with that effort, I will try and do my part and give you a thought-provoking and interesting presentation. When I was asked last year to make this presentation, I thought it was an excellent opportunity to discuss something that is important to me, and that is the concept of passion, and the role it plays in the delivery of human services, specifically in the context of the First Nations social work profession.

As I reviewed my material for this presentation, I thought I would

SUGGESTED CITATION: Kinequon, D. (2009). Passion within the First Nations social work profession. In S. McKay, D. Fuchs, & I. Brown (Eds.), *Passion for action in child and family services: Voices from the prairies* (pp. 1-13). Regina, SK: Canadian Plains Research Center.

provide some insight into my own personal experiences growing up, in order that you may begin to understand passion as I see it from my perspective and how those experiences molded the passion I feel today. It's not always easy speaking of a difficult past, but sometimes it is necessary and beneficial that we do look at what has made us the people that we are, and why we sometimes act in the way we do, and of course to learn from each other's experience as well. It's also equally important to respect the experiences of others, and in this regard I had asked the symposium organizers not to record my presentation. I am not concerned that my words would be heard elsewhere, my reasons are rather that I came here to speak directly to those of you present this evening.[1]

One of the objectives of my presentation here this evening is to lead each of you to think about your own passion and what it personally means to you. How were you influenced to be doing the work that each of you are involved in, and what goals have you set for yourselves with respect to that passion? When we consider passion in the abstract sense, we have to begin with our own simple understanding of it. According to the literal written meaning in Webster's dictionary, passion is described as an emotional response. The English word "passion" itself comes from the Greek word "pathos" and this word means something that happens to you, either good or bad, usually something bad or something you suffer. From this interpretation the word more commonly came to mean a feeling that you suffer or "a passionate desire."

Over the course of this past year, since I agreed to speak here this evening, I have given much thought to interpreting my own passion, and how that passion has motivated me in my own social work career. When I begin to reflect on my own passion, I begin by looking at my own life and how I have been transformed into the person I am based on the experiences I had as a child, and later in adulthood as an educated First Nations human services professional.

For the purposes of this presentation I begin by reaching back in time to an incident that occurred in the summer of 1975. In the summer of that year, I was twelve years old and my home, like many First Nations

---

1   EDITOR'S NOTE: While Mr. Kinequon's request that his presentation not be recorded was honoured, he did agree to provide his speaking notes so that they could appear here in this publication.

homes, was devastated by the impacts of the residential school system. Although there had always been violence in my home I was probably considered too young to be directly involved in the physical aspect of the violence in our home.

However, that all changed in 1975, as I was almost a teenager. I believe the perception was that I had become old enough to be a combatant and would directly participate in the violent altercations that were part of my family life. Finally, the violence in my home escalated to the point that I felt I had to flee, fearing for my own safety.

Although I had left my home I had not left my town. At first, I continued to go play with my friends at their houses, and hung out like nothing was going on. I had concealed my circumstances well enough from my friends and their families that they were totally unaware that anything was wrong. I continued to act like I always did and played with my friends and stayed at their houses on sleepovers just as I had always done. I was usually careful not to spend more than a day or two at each friend's home. After I left, I would then move on to the next friend's house. Since my friends' parents very seldom spoke to each other about us kids, no one was aware of my circumstances and I drew no attention, until eventually the sleepovers became too frequent and the parents of my friends became suspicious and said I could not sleepover for awhile and would have to go home.

Since I had run out of places to stay in my hometown, I then walked to another town close to ours that was eight miles away. I had a cousin who lived there, and also several other friends. So just as I had done in my hometown, I followed the same procedure and began sleeping at their houses until eventually that caught up to me as well. One by one each of their parents said I could not play at their house anymore and would have to go home. I remember the first evening I had no place to stay. I had been walking around town and was very hungry since I had not eaten that day. I contemplated my situation and knew I needed to take drastic action to deal with my present circumstances.

Finally, after some confusing deliberation, I made a fateful decision to commit a crime, get some money and skip town. In the town I was in, I had seen a small shop that had a window that faced the back of a dark alley. Once that I thought everyone in town had gone to bed, I approached the back of the building, keeping to the shadows as much as I could, then when I reached the window, I took a big breath to calm myself, and then as quietly as I could, I broke the window with a rock, climbed through, found the money drawer and took what was in it.

As I ran from the scene of the crime, I had overwhelming feelings of fear, guilt and shame, which were only later abated by my miserable set of circumstances. As I walked around that night thinking of what I done, I shook not only from the fear I felt over my previous actions, but also from the cold. Since it was getting later in the summer, it was becoming colder at night. So, needing a place to hide and keep warm I went from building to building until I found a door open and huddled in the entrance way until morning.

That next morning I immediately went to the café and ordered the biggest breakfast they had on the menu. Later on, I went walking around town trying to come up with a plan of what I was going to do and where I could go next. Suddenly a car drove up beside me and it was the police. I instantly froze, paralyzed by fear. The officer told me to get in and upon sitting down he said he wanted to see the bottom of my shoes. I showed him my shoes and he compared my runner print to a Polaroid photograph in his hand. As he showed me the matching prints, I knew I was busted. Of course he asked me why I had broke into the store, and I said because I needed the money to buy food. I thought since I was caught there was no point in trying to lie.

The officer then drove back to the shop where I saw the storeowner and his wife standing outside looking at the window. As I approached the owner, I could see that he was absolutely furious. I walked up to him and extended my hand with the remaining money I had taken. The storeowner snatched the money from my hand and I could see he was so angry I thought he was going to strike me right there where I stood.

And his wife—the poor woman was crying so hard she almost could not speak. She then came over to me and kneeled down in front of me and took my face in her hands and in a begging manner asked "Why? Why would you steal from us? Why?" When she continued to plead for an answer, I finally could not take it any longer and with a lump in my throat and tears welling up in my eyes, I pushed myself away from her and in the most defiant voice I could muster, I said, "Because you have everything and I have nothing." *Because I have nothing!* Ladies and gentlemen, that was a defining moment in my life. This situation I found myself in seemed to crystallize the difference between me as an Indian kid and the three white people beside me, and the different worlds we existed in.

After that, I went to the police officer's car and jumped in and sat there with my head against the window, crying at the experience I just had. Eventually, the officer came and got into the car and began driving away from the store. At this point, I thought I was being taken to jail or to wherever they take kids who commit crimes. Instead, the officer asked me if there was someplace he could take me to. In a barely audible whisper, I said, "Nowhere," I said, "I have no place left to go."

I think that because the officer was not sure what to do, he started driving back to my hometown. Along the way, the officer asked me if I would like to go and see someone about my situation. I said, "Sure." It sounded optimistic and I had no other options. The officer then said there was a person who came to our town once a week for two hours. He said she was a social worker and she may be able to help me. He went on to say that although she had been at our town earlier that day and was now gone, she would be back the following week. He said if I wanted, he would go with me to see her. As this sounded fairly positive, I agreed to the idea. Once again the officer asked me where he could take me, and I said to take me out to the highway and I would hitchhike to Saskatoon for the week and then meet him back in town next week.

The officer then drove me to the highway, and as we said good-bye I once again affirmed that I would see him in one week. As I started walking down the highway, I turned to look back over my shoulder as the officer drove back to town, and I wondered, "If I had been a white child, would he still have left me on that road?" This occurrence seemed to confirm that we did live in different worlds, and that there were different police for Indians than for everyone else.

I began walking and eventually hitchhiked to Saskatoon, which was about 150 miles from my hometown. Ladies and gentlemen, I can say without a doubt that the next seven days were the longest days I will probably ever live through. I remember one night lying in some tall grass curled up like an unborn child and crying so hard I felt inconsolable.

And I probably would have been except for some things that I noticed. I noticed the ground was keeping me warm from the previous day's sun, and the wind was blowing like someone would when they are breathing. That wind would blow the grass in a way that would be indicative of taking in a breath, and then the wind would almost exhale and each time this occurred, the long grass would bend covering me one way and then covering me up when it went the other way. In this way the grass kept me concealed, and I felt protected from the dangers that were all around me. I suppose you could say this is one of those moments where I thought I felt and experienced a physical relationship between myself and Mother Earth, and I was thankful for it.

Ladies and gentlemen, I have not told you this story this evening to make you sad, or to bring about any ill feelings to any people. You may think this story involves a unique situation, or an extraordinary set of circumstances, but it does not. If you were to ask almost any First Nations person here if they knew of a story like this one, they would probably be able to say yes.

When I spoke to the store owner's wife about having nothing, I was not just talking about having no food, shelter or basic necessities. I was talking about having a home that had love, nurturing, security and especially hope for the future for me as an Indian kid. This is a part of where my passion comes from. Having lived through that experience was so difficult, sometimes I just want to leave it as far away as possible. But I am unable to because this is one of the experiences that has molded my own sense of passion.

I believe there are numerous kinds of passion in this world. I think some people have a form of intellectual passion which is based on what they think is a good thing, and they educate themselves into positions where they can work with disadvantaged people and they are fulfilled by this type of work. There is nothing wrong with this kind of passion because we need helpers and leaders of all kinds, and disadvantaged children need all the help each of us is willing to give them. Another kind of passion, which is not better, just different, is the emotional kind of passion, where you feel it from your heart and the core of your soul, and is based on experiences you have had and drives you to make every effort you can to help children. The emotional passion is the passion I live with, and is the motivating factor in my day-to-day social work practice. I see children who come from abusive homes and I understand their pain, and the fearful anxiety they are experiencing, and I know what they are going through.

If we fast-track to today, here, right now, you would probably think life is different for me now. As a successful, working First Nations professional, I should have a strong sense of personal security and well-being. And I do, most times. However, there are times when this does not occur. For example there was a series of national events over the past years that have led me to continue feeling like I had when I was twelve years old.

It began with a September 2006 presentation I made to the Standing Senate Committee on Human Rights on behalf of Saskatchewan Native Child Welfare. I had conducted research for this presentation and when I had completed the presentation, I felt uneasy with what I saw. In my report, I stated that First Nations people had initially been optimistic when the Canadian government ratified the United Nations Convention on the Rights of the Child. This meant that First Nations *thought* that there would be some recognition finally, that the involuntary and disproportionate removal of thousands of First Nations children from their homes was unacceptable—and they thought this recognition would pave the way for new initiatives to deal with First Nations issues. But nothing meaningful occurred as a result of the ratification.

And then subsequent to the United Nations Ratification, the Royal Commission on Aboriginal Peoples was completed in November 1996. Upon review, I found that the completed report had been exhaustive and thorough; however, I found very little of the Commission Report's recommendations were ever followed through. And then more recently in 2006, there were commitments made to First Nations people by the federal government through the Kelowna Accord. This would have meant much needed funding for capacity building in First Nations communities across Canada. Once again First Nations hopes were raised in futility.

When the new federal government came into power, all commitments, including the Kelowna Accord, were withdrawn and that government said they would make their own plan and they would have their own strategies on how to deal with the First Nations people of Canada. Earlier this spring, the federal government displayed their new initiatives for First Nations people in the federal budget.

I remember listening to the budget attentively, and was more than dismayed when I heard the investment amount the government was putting into First Nations communities. After the budget was announced, I searched newspapers, newscasts and other media to find the moral outrage that the citizens of Canada would express at the slap in the face First Nations people had just received from the federal government.

As I searched I found no response. Instead, all I could find was a deafening silence and quiet acceptance by the people of Canada. Considering that nothing was being said about the inadequate funding to First Nations across Canada, I then thought I would turn to one of my non-native friends and see if there was support at the local level. When I spoke to my friend and expressed my issue with the funding inequity for Indian and Northern Affairs, my friend made no comment, and instead said, "Well, it's good for the middle-class family," and he said nothing more and did not look at me after he said it. Then all of a sudden my words from 1975 came back to me, "because I have nothing."

You see, even though my own needs have been met by my career, the needs of my people, have not, and therefore I continue to suffer the passion of my people. This is one of those situations that can work at diminishing a First Nations professional's passion for the work they are trying to do. We go to school to become educated in child welfare and then begin applying our skills, only to find we often feel like we are working with one hand tied behind our backs. Tied there by an arrogant federal government unwilling to effectively deal with the social issues facing First Nations people.

Then to add insult to injury, I watched as the Minister of Indian Affairs defended his government's budget by standing up in parliament and yelling that the problem for First Nations was not inadequate funding, but it was what the First Nations were doing with the money they were getting in the first place, that was the problem. Unfortunately, this is the same minister who publicly threatened First Nations people by saying if any First Nations used any federal funds to stage a protest against the Government on June 21, Aboriginal Day, they would have their books audited.

We are currently faced with a federal government today that continues to treat First Nations people as second-class citizens in our own country. Earlier this year I was reading a section of Canada's draft *Military Counterinsurgency Manual,* where it states that, "despite its specific and limited aims, the First Nations rebellions in Canada are nevertheless insurgencies because they are animated by the goal of altering political relationships with both the Canadian government and at the local level—within reservations themselves—through the threat of or use of violence." So, it appears that First Nations people are to be considered potential terrorists in our own country if we stand up too tall for our rights.

What does this have to do with passion for child welfare, you may be thinking? Well, this continued federal oppression weakens the First Nations professional and the organizations they work for. I truly believe, and I told this to the Standing Senate Committee on Human Rights, that I genuinely believe the federal government has no vision for First Nations people, let alone First Nations child welfare. I think they would just like to see the Indian problem disappear.

I see First Nations social workers come into this social work environment, and they come with fire in their eyes and a passionate desire to make changes for First Nations children. Over time you see the passion begin to fade as they struggle within the bureaucracy and become consumed by a system that will not allow First Nations to build the capacity they need to improve child welfare. Eventually, the flame fades and it's difficult to watch as people leave First Nations social work tired and burnt out.

However, I must qualify my statements on the federal government, though, by saying that not all people within the Department of Indian Affairs are at the root cause of the issue. I know many that I believe really do want to help First Nations make positive changes, but most times their system will simply not allow them to.

I believe the federal government is capable of developing more supportive policies and should consider more partnership opportunities with the provincial governments. When you consider both levels of government are involved in on-reserve child welfare services you would think there would be more joint initiatives. Unfortunately, it seems that the federal and provincial governments continue to debate child welfare responsibility and would rather point fingers at each other than try to work more closely.

Speaking of the provincial government, I would say that over the past several years, I have come to consider the provincial Department of Community Resources [now the Ministry of Social Services] as a partner in the delivery of First Nations child welfare services in Saskatchewan. Of course there is still much work we need to do together. I sometimes get the impression that the Saskatchewan provincial government does not know what to do with the First Nations in this province.

My perceptions lead me to believe that the Department wants to get out of First Nations child welfare as quickly as possible in order to eliminate the liability associated with on-reserve child welfare services. However, until that day comes we need to work together in the best interest of children, and I think we have begun moving in that direction. Some examples of supportive initiatives from the Department of Community Resources include much-needed service training for the agencies; another extraordinary example is the current funding arrangement for the newly established Saskatchewan First Nations Family and Community Institute.

The list goes on, but I think I can say that I like the direction we are moving with Community Resources and the partnerships we have made, and if in the end, First Nations become totally responsible for their own child welfare, through self-government agreements, then so be it. But the province needs to relinquish its authority in an appropriate manner over time by laying the framework right now with the necessary resources to allow First Nations success in the future.

I also want to mention the third level of government here, and that is the First Nations governments in Saskatchewan. Unfortunately, this is also a level of government that can be sometimes equally frustrating for First Nations professionals. We have situations where agencies and their directors and boards come into conflict with the political leadership. We take the heat when we apprehend a child, and we take the heat when we do not apprehend children. I have seen directors fight battles with their own political leaders and either give in, leave, or they are cast aside. I would think that these leaders would want to support their professionals to every extent that they could, to ensure the programs and services the agencies are responsible for are supported and of the highest quality.

So with all these examples of situations that can impact on a First Nations professional's passion, you can see how the current child welfare system can deteriorate and reduce the feelings of accomplishment and self-fulfillment in the careers of First Nations professionals. So when we begin to get dragged down by the situations we deal with on an ongoing basis, how do we go about recharging our passion? I think each person is different, and you have to explore within yourself how you will go about doing this, and what will work for you.

From my own past experience in social work, I know that when I get involved in projects or initiatives that directly improve children's services, I find hope for the future of child welfare and that adds value to my passion and allows me to continue working and pressing on.

As you listen here this evening, I think it is important that you understand that I do not pretend to stand up here and lead you to believe I know all the problems and issues in child welfare services. I do not have all the answers. I think I have some of the answers, but I also think that with all of us working together we can find the solutions to problems we are experiencing within First Nations child welfare, which essentially is one of the reasons why were are at this symposium.

Whenever I get a chance I like to discuss possible solutions to some of the issues we face today. I believe Canadian children need a federal children's commissioner. I believe if there was a national position that could look at how the federal government deals with children's issues, I think all children would have a stronger voice in this country, and would ensure that their rights and freedoms would be protected, and that the legislation, policies and program developments that pertains to them would contain the elements of the United Nations Convention on the Rights of the Child. Additionally, I think we need to have a federal children's commissioner to ensure that all children living on-reserve receive comparable services as those children living off-reserve.

Also I think there needs to be an inter-governmental forum that is charged with the responsibility of establishing a ten-year child welfare plan of action. I see this as a national think tank that could provide thoughtful recommendations on the future of child welfare to whatever government is in power.

There needs to be more thought given to the development of preventative programming and how we can intervene with families without removing children from their homes. We all know the success rate in family reunification programs goes down the longer children remain in care.

We also need to have some work conducted in the area of dispute resolution between the federal and provincial governments and the First Nations. Unfortunately, there have been incidents where children have suffered and died as a result of jurisdictional issues between governments. The issue appears to involve who is responsible for paying for services for any child whose jurisdiction has not been immediately determined.

A tragic example of this is based on an incident that has led to First Nations lobbying for federal and provincial approval of Jordan's Principle.[2] This is an incident that occurred in Manitoba and involved the death of a child named Jordan. Apparently, the federal and Manitoba provincial governments were in the middle of a funding dispute for two years, each saying the other was responsible for the high costs associated with this child's care upon his return to his home community. As the two levels of government disputed, Jordan could not be returned home because his high cost of care was not approved by either of the governments; therefore, Jordan languished in the hospital, waiting to go home. In the two years the federal and Manitoba provincial governments were arguing with each other, Jordan died, and although Jordan did eventually make it home, it was to be buried.

On the home front here, you may feel you are helpless to do anything about national issues that may seem out of your realm of influence. But if you look at the concept of passion for action which this symposium is focused on, you should look within yourselves and ask, "Am I doing all that I personally can for child welfare in this country, or am I doing only enough to make myself feel relatively comfortable?"

As citizens of Canada we each have a moral obligation to educate ourselves on social issues so we may be challenged to exercise our social responsibilities for the disadvantaged children that live among us, regardless of where they live. I often hear, mostly politicians, say that children are our future, and this is true, but I also believe that we are our children's future as well, and what we do right now will determine their futures.

As I conclude my remarks here this evening, I want to revisit the concept of passion that I have been using in my presentation. I say to each of you to look within yourselves and find what inspires you to be passionate about child welfare and to think, "What can I do today to improve the life of a child?" As I said previously, I do not know all the answers, but

---

2   EDITORS NOTE: Jordan's Principle, a child-first principle to resolving jurisdictional disputes, was approved unanimously by the House of Commons on December 12, 2007. The principle requires the provincial and federal governments to pay for the government services a child needs first and resolve the jurisdictional dispute later (Blackstock, 2007).

I know when I do respond to questions on child welfare, I provide all of my answers with passion.

I want to leave you this evening with a passage I read somewhere. These are not my words but those of a writer that I thought eloquently summarized my own feelings on passion. This writer wrote, "Passion is a gift of the spirit combined with the totality of all our experiences we've lived through. It endows each of us with the power to live and communicate with unbridled enthusiasm. Passion is most evident when the mind, body and spirit work together to create, develop and articulate or make manifest our feelings, ideas and most sacred values" (Norris, 2000).

Thank you, ladies and gentlemen, for listening to me this evening. I feel honored and privileged that you would find any of my words worthy of sitting and hearing publicly. I wish each of you all the best. And I bid you good evening.

REFERENCES

Blackstock, C. (2007). Speaking notes on the occasion of the vote in the House of Commons on the Private Member's Motion in Support of Jordan's Principle. http://www.fncfcs.com/docs/JP_Speaking_Notes_Dec12_2007.pdf, accessed June 1, 2009.

Norris, B. (2000). What is Passion? http://www.briannorris.com/passion/what-is-passion.html, accessed September 2007.

CHAPTER 2

Passion, Action, Strength and Innovative Change: The Experience of the Saskatchewan Children's Advocate's Office in Establishing Rights-Based "Children and Youth First" Principles

Marvin M. Bernstein and Roxane A. Schury

> There can be no keener revelation of a society's soul than the way it treats its children.
>
> — *Nelson Mandela*

Passion, Action, Strength and Innovative Change. This is the precise terminology needed when considering changes in the delivery of child welfare services to children and their families. Although there are many dedicated staff and much good and innovative work that occurs within child welfare systems, there is also a desperate need for a fundamental change. It is the contention of this chapter's authors that child welfare

SUGGESTED CITATION: Bernstein, M. M., & Schury, R. A. (2009). Passion, action, strength and innovative change: The experience of the Saskatchewan Children's Advocate's Office in establishing rights-based "Children and Youth First" principles. In S. McKay, D. Fuchs, & I. Brown (Eds.), *Passion for action in child and family services: Voices from the prairies* (pp. 15-47). Regina, SK: Canadian Plains Research Center.

services and the children and families they serve would greatly benefit from a change that would entrench child rights as a foundation for
services and put children and youth at the centre of these services. Unfortunately, much child welfare legislation, policy, and practice has deviated
from the concept of the child as the primary client. This has left many jurisdictions, including Saskatchewan, in need of rights-based review and
child-centred change to better serve children and their families.

This chapter explores the importance and relevance of child rights,
as articulated within the United Nations *Convention on the Rights of the
Child* (hereafter, UN *CRC* or *Convention*), the definitive international treaty regarding child rights. The term "child" is used in accordance with
the definition of "child" as set out in Article 1 of the *Convention*, which
means "every human being below the age of eighteen years ..." (Canadian Heritage, 1989). The connection between the *Convention* and the
Saskatchewan Children's Advocate Office is clarified, and the work of
the Office is described. Actual children's case studies that exemplify a
lack of child rights and child-centred legislation, policy and practice in
child welfare are provided to illustrate the strong need for such principles and the action that should follow from them. A practical list of child
rights-based child welfare practice is also provided, leading into the Saskatchewan Children's Advocate "Children and Youth First" Principles.
A call to action is followed by the conclusion, which stresses the need to
move from children's "paper rights" to "lived rights."

UNITED NATIONS *CONVENTION*
ON THE RIGHTS OF THE CHILD

The UN *CRC* is the most widely endorsed international treaty in history, ratified by 193 States Parties,[1] clearly reflecting the commitment
of those signatory nations to respect and promote the positive development of their children and youth. "By its almost universal ratification,
by its comprehensiveness and by its legally binding character, it is ... a
never seen global binding social contract" (Verhellen, 1996, p. 43). All but
two States Parties signed and ratified this treaty, and this was completed
more quickly than any other international treaty developed.[2] It was met

---

1   States Parties is the term used by international treaties including the *Convention
     on the Rights of the Child* to represent nations or countries.

2   The United Nations *Convention on the Rights of the Child* was the most quickly

positively on a global level and "[c]learly, the *Convention* has become the most important international legal instrument on the rights of the child. It has also acquired considerable political importance, being repeatedly cited as the most authoritative standard-setting instrument on children's rights" (Leblanc, 1996, p. 357).

The UN Office of the High Commissioner for Human Rights (OH-CHR) has identified four general principles within the 54 articles: non-discrimination; best interests of the child; right to life, survival and development; and respect for the views of the child. These four general principles are meant to guide national programs of implementation (OH-CHR, 1996).

The UN *CRC* states that children are entitled to the same basic human rights that all citizens of the world enjoy. "The rights-based approach means describing situations … in terms of the obligation to respond to the rights of individuals. This empowers people to demand justice as a right, not as a charity" (UNICEF, 1999, p. iv). This is a very important distinction—whereas charity work reflects a generosity of spirit and can contribute to positive outcomes, only rights-based work entrenches both the rights and obligations of all involved. In addition, the *Convention* entitles children to special rights, due to their developmental vulnerabilities. Thus, signing and ratifying the *Convention* legally obligates Canada[3] and Saskatchewan[4] to:

> ensure that all children—without discrimination in any form—benefit from special protection measures and assistance; have access to services such as education and health care; can develop their personalities, abilities and talents to the fullest potential; grow up in an environment of happiness, love and understanding; and are informed about and participate in their rights in an accessible and active manner. (UNICEF, 2005)

---

signed and ratified treaty in the history of the United Nations. Only the United States and Somalia have failed to ratify this treaty, although each has signed.

3   Canada signed the *Convention on the Rights of the Child* on May 28, 1990, and ratified it on December 13, 1991.

4   Saskatchewan signed the *Convention on the Rights of the Child* on December 11, 1991.

Saskatchewan's and Canada's Commitment

In 1994, Saskatchewan created an Action Plan for Children, which developed a number of programs and services to support and enhance the care and protection of our children. The Plan was based on the belief that "Children have rights and entitlements as defined by the United Nations *Convention on the Rights of the Child*" and on such positive principles as "Wherever decisions are made that may affect the child, the safety and best interests of the child must be the primary consideration" (Legislative Assembly of Saskatchewan, 1994, p. 1). The Plan also established the Children's Advocate Office and was the foundation for the excellent work later achieved by the non-partisan Provincial Legislative Committee on the Sexual Exploitation of Children (Legislative Assembly of Saskatchewan, 2001). The Plan was a good beginning. As a province, we must now take the necessary next steps to ensure that the fundamental human rights of children and youth under the *Convention* are given sufficient priority and are integrated within government legislation, policy, and practice. We must take the "paper rights" of the *Convention* and make them "lived rights" for Saskatchewan's children and youth.

November 20th of each year has been designated as National Child Day in many countries around the globe. Proclaimed by the government of Canada in 1993 (Howe & Covell, 2007), National Child Day celebrates two historic events for children: the adoption of the United Nations *Declaration on the Rights of the Child* in 1959 and the UN *CRC*, adopted by the United Nations General Assembly in 1989 (Howe & Covell, 2007). Canada signed the UN *CRC* on May 28, 1990, and ratified it on December 13, 1991 (Senate of Canada, 2007). Likewise, the Saskatchewan legislature confirmed its support two days earlier on December 11, 1991, with the provincial government stating:

> Support for the Convention is essential because it reaffirms our responsibility for the care and well-being of all children in our society. The Convention also serves as a reminder that as long as there are still children in this province who are not receiving the care and protection to which they are entitled, there is more which must be done. (Legislative Assembly of Saskatchewan, 1991)

The United Nations Committee on the Rights of the Child, in a General Comment in 2002 regarding the need for a National Human Rights

Institution (NHRI) for children in all countries (something Canada is lacking), summarizes succinctly the need for offices such as the Saskatchewan Children's Advocate:

> While adults and children alike need independent NHRIs to protect their human rights, additional justifications exist for ensuring that children's human rights are given special attention. These include the facts that children's developmental state makes them particularly vulnerable to human rights violations; their opinions are still rarely taken into account; most children have no vote and cannot play a meaningful role in the political process that determines Governments' response to human rights; children encounter significant problems in using the judicial system to protect their rights or to seek remedies for violations of their rights; and children's access to organizations that may protect their rights is generally limited. (Committee on the Rights of the Child, 2002, p. 2)

In 2007, National Child Day had special significance, as the UN *CRC* turned eighteen. Consequently, Saskatchewan and Canadian youth reaching the age of eighteen on or after November 20, 2007, became the first children born with universal rights under the *Convention*. Although Canada and Saskatchewan have made some progress in protecting the rights and promoting the well-being of this first generation, to a great extent these entitlements have not been sufficiently implemented and have been largely relegated to mere "paper rights." Howe and Covell have described Canada's level of commitment in the following terms:

> The overall evidence … suggests that Canada's level of commitment is—at best—characterized as wavering …. What the record shows … is an overall pattern of vacillation, sporadic or halting efforts and spotty and uneven policy and legal developments. The CRC [Convention on the Rights of the Child] has rarely even been mentioned in legislation and child-related policy, and this reflects the lack of political concern or even awareness of the rights of the child. (Howe & Covell, 2007, p. 397)

As this vital and eminent international treaty comes of age, there is still much to be achieved by all state governments—including Canada and its thirteen provinces and territories—in order to meet their legally binding international obligations. Both Canada and Saskatchewan must commit to ensuring that the next generation of children and youth will have their rights upheld more stringently and vigorously than their predecessors, and in total conformity with the UN *CRC*. By doing so, they will be taking a lead role in setting standards of care, advancing best practices and ensuring that all children and youth have services and programs that will support their well-being.

ADVANCES BY THE SASKATCHEWAN CHILDREN'S ADVOCATE OFFICE

The Saskatchewan Children's Advocate Office is a rights-based office with foundations firmly entrenched in the UN *CRC*. The Office endeavours to serve the children and youth of Saskatchewan from a rights perspective to ensure not only that they receive the services to which they are entitled but also that they have a voice in all decisions that affect their lives. Our Office continues to be guided by the African expression, "Say Nothing about Me without Me," a constant reminder that children and young people ought to be included and invited to participate in all matters affecting them.

At times we are challenged with queries regarding our rights-based work for children—questions such as, "Don't rights for children erode parental rights?" and "Is rights-based work even needed in a privileged country such as Canada?" In response to the first question, the UN *CRC* is a very parent- and family-friendly[5] international treaty that identifies the special/specific rights of children related to their developmental needs and complementing their basic human rights. "To construct an artificial conflict in the public discourse between parental rights and children's rights is therefore a reactionary position that could be, and sometimes is, used as a justification for repressing children" (Hammarberg, 2007,

---

5   The UN *CRC* Preamble as well as twenty-three of the forty-one Articles pertaining to rights in the *Convention on the Rights of the Child* refer to family, parents or guardians. These are Articles: 2, 3, 5, 7, 8, 9, 10, 14, 16, 18, 19, 20, 21, 22, 23, 24, 26, 27, 29, 30, 31, 37, and 40.

p. 115). As retired Canadian Senator Landon Pearson wrote in the Foreword to *A Question of Commitment*:

> The standards set by the Convention should not be seen as entitlements that set the child against the adult world. On the contrary, they represent the highest norms of civilized behaviour. Because they are vulnerable, children have the right to our protection. But at the same time, they also have the right to be treated with respect. And it is only within a culture of respect that constructive social responsibility is able to emerge. (in Howe & Covell, 2007, p. x)

With regard to the second question, even in a privileged country such as Canada, rights violations can occur. Historically, we are not so far removed from the adoption of earlier European practices. Myriam Denov, in her chapter titled "Youth Justice and Children's Rights," describes three principal stages in Canadian history identified by Covell and Howe as a way to understand the evolution of our perception of children and their rights from chattels to objects of protection to rights holders. "In the first stage, Canadian children were perceived largely as objects under the direct control of parental authority. In the second stage, children were considered a highly vulnerable population in need of state protection. In the final stage, children [are to be] regarded as subjects with inherent rights of their own" (Howe & Covell, 2007, p. 156).

It is imperative that child serving systems, in particular child welfare services, embrace the final evolutionary stage of child rights. To do so would be to recognize children and youth as genuine rights holders who are entitled to service and protection, rather than as vulnerable individuals eligible for charity.

There are still many rights issues that have not been adequately addressed in Canada. For example, full participation by children is far from being recognized, especially when it comes to child welfare proceedings in Saskatchewan. In these court cases, although their lives and futures are being decided, children do not have standing as participants. As our Office has previously submitted to the UN *CRC:*

> In Canada, every province has its own statute dealing with child protection as "child welfare" falls under the

provincial head of constitutional powers. Most provincial child welfare statutes recognize that a child is entitled to separate legal representation where it is deemed to be in the child's best interests; where it will allow a child's perspective to be put forth; where the child has capacity to instruct counsel; or where the child's specific interests differ from those of the parent or state. It is noteworthy that Saskatchewan is the only province that expressly denies a child the right to participate. (Bernstein, St. Onge, & Schury, 2006, p. 5)

A review of the Saskatchewan Children's Advocate Office's advocacy and investigation files indicated that the views and best interests of children and youth were not being routinely represented in child welfare proceedings. Given the vulnerability and disadvantage experienced by youth in general, and especially by those youth who are subject to child welfare proceedings, it is particularly important that they have independent legal representation. In order to address this concern, the Saskatchewan Children's Advocate Office has partnered with Pam Kovacs, Executive Director, Pro Bono Law Saskatchewan, in developing a child and youth representation *pro bono* panel. This panel provides children and youth with a separate voice in the court process:

While the *pro bono* program is an interim measure, it functions to fill the gap until such time as the Government of Saskatchewan changes legislation and implements a permanent, supported program of legal representation for children and youth in appropriate cases. (Saskatchewan Children's Advocate Office, 2008, p. 28)

The Saskatchewan Children's Advocate has also forwarded the following four systemic recommendations to the provincial government, which have not been acted upon as of the time of the writing of this chapter:

06-10840
That the Minister of Community Resources introduce proposed amendments to *The Child and Family Services Act* enabling children to obtain full status as a party in child welfare proceedings.

06-10841

That the Minister of Community Resources introduce proposed amendments to *The Child and Family Services Act* authorizing judges at all court levels in Saskatchewan to appoint independent legal representation for children in child welfare proceedings.

06-10842

That the Minister of Community Resources introduce proposed amendments to *The Child and Family Services Act* setting out prescribed criteria by which a court will determine whether a child requires independent legal representation in child welfare proceedings.

06-10844

That the Minister of Community Resources and Justice, in collaboration with relevant stakeholders, develop, fund and implement a legal program, with sufficient training and administrative oversight, that would provide children with access to independent legal representation in child welfare proceedings.

A second rights issue that has not been adequately addressed for children in Canada is that of the corporal or physical punishment of children. As recently as January 30, 2004, the Supreme Court of Canada upheld the constitutionality of section 43 of the *Criminal Code of Canada*. This confirmation to parents and the public that it is acceptable to use corporal punishment "where the force is reasonable under the circumstances and is administered for the purpose of correction" (Bernstein, 2004, p. 2) appears to be unacceptable under the UN CRC. This would not be acceptable for any other group of rights holders, yet it is included in law in Canada. For example, Turpel-Lafond (2007) claimed that "[t]he legality of spanking certainly raises fundamental issues regarding whether children are truly free from domestic violence on the same par as their parents" (p. 46), and the Saskatchewan Children's Advocate Office (2006b) stated that "[i]t is time for Canada to step up to the plate or risk significant embarrassment on the international stage" (p. 17).

At the writing of this chapter, Bill S-209, *An Act to amend the Criminal*

Code, has received third reading in the Senate and has been referred to the House of Commons for further examination and consideration.[6] While it was hoped by many children's advocates that this Bill would enact a total repeal of section 43 of the *Criminal Code*, the Bill merely amends section 43 and substitutes wording that is too broad, is not rights-based and does not sufficiently protect children. Specifically, the proposed amendment would allow reasonable force, other than corporal punishment towards a child, to be used by a parent, caregiver or teacher for the purpose of, among other things, "preventing the child from engaging or continuing to engage in excessively offensive or disruptive behaviour."

The decision to maintain the legality of corporal punishment is out of step with international developments, the direction many rights-based countries have taken, and Canadian public opinion (Bernstein, 2004). Furthermore, it has been noted that this decision has implications for child welfare workers. They are in the untenable position of working with legal guidelines that allow certain kinds of hitting, at certain ages, on certain areas of the body with children at risk of abuse.

Allowing for children to be physically punished has been shown to be the wrong approach clinically and from a rights perspective, yet it continues. Opposition to corporal punishment is further supported by both the UN Committee on the Rights of the Child and more recently the Senate of Canada. In October 2003, the Committee on the Rights of the Child, in response to the Canadian presentation, stated:

> [T]he Committee is deeply concerned that the State party has not enacted legislation explicitly prohibiting all forms of corporal punishment and has taken no action to remove section 43 of the Criminal Code, which allows corporal punishment. The Committee recommends that the State party adopt legislation to remove the existing authorization of the use of "reasonable force" in disciplining children and explicitly prohibit all forms of violence against children, however light, within the

---

6   On June 22, 2009, Senator Hervieux-Payette's Bill S-209, amending section 43 of the Criminal Code, received second reading and was referred to the Senate Justice Committee for further study (after being re-introduced again after the earlier version died when Federal Parliament was prorogued in December 2008).

family, in schools and in other institutions where children may be placed. (Committee on the Rights of the Child, 2003, p. 32)

The Saskatchewan Children's Advocate has done much work in this area, culminating in three systemic recommendations :

CAO.SYS.1 (05)
That the Department of Learning amend *The Education Act* to prohibit the use of corporal punishment in Saskatchewan schools.

CAO.SYS.2 (05)
That all government departments and agencies who provide services to children and families incorporate the judicial interpretation provided by the Supreme Court of Canada with regard to Section 43 into policy.

CAO.SYS.3 (05)
That education about positive non-violent methods of disciplining children be made widely available to parents by all government departments and agencies responsible for services to children and families.

CAO.SYS.1 (05) and CAO.SYS.2 (05) have both been closed with the Saskatchewan Children's Advocate Office as accepted and implemented. CAO.SYS.3 (05) was reviewed by our Office and archived.

Another argument that has been put forward is that children's rights are a non-issue, as children already have basic human rights and are protected by their parents' authority. On the other hand, Paulo Pinheiro, the Independent Expert for the United Nations Secretary-General's *Study on Violence against Children*, has astutely stated:

Children are not mini-human beings with mini-human rights. As long as adults continue to regard children as mini-human beings, violence against children will persist. Every boy and girl, as any human being, must have their rights completely respected to develop with dignity. Any form of violence can only undermine their development. (Pinheiro, 2005, p. 6)

The United Nations *Convention on the Rights of the Child*, a document meant to be used in pursuit of rights at a large systemic level as well as basic practical rights at the state level, was written to entrench child rights at both the international and state (country) level. The *Convention* was written for *all* children, and clearly, while most children in Canada (let us be clear—*not all*) live a more comfortable life than many children around the world, rights are a fundamental entitlement and protection, even when life is good, and life is certainly not always good for *all* children in Canada. If anything, the statistical information suggests an under-reporting of the extent of intra-familial violence inflicted upon children:

> Official statistics in both the US and Canada indicate that children are over-represented as victims of physical violence in the family, and researchers and practitioners point out that the actual rates of violence and child deaths that result are much higher than those in official reports. (UNICEF Canada, 2005, p. 9)

The track records of both Canada and Saskatchewan are less than stellar when one examines child rights in regard to new Canadians, but especially with regard to indigenous children. As stated by the Standing Senate Committee on Human Rights:

> Aboriginal children are disproportionately living in poverty and involved in the youth criminal justice and child protection systems. Aboriginal children also face significant health problems in comparison with other children in Canada, such as higher rates of malnutrition, disabilities, drug and alcohol abuse and suicide.
>
> ... The Committee recognizes that the protection of Aboriginal children's rights—and thus the protection of Aboriginal communities' future—is an issue of primary importance for all Canadians and an issue of fundamental concern with respect to the *Convention on the Rights of the Child*. Aboriginal and non-Aboriginal communities are destined to live "in perpetuity." For all the lives at stake, the cost of doing nothing ... is enormous. Cindy Blackstock reiterated the point, telling our Committee that "[b]y

doing nothing, I think we put our own moral credibility as a nation at risk." (Senate of Canada, 2007, pp. 172-173)

With a rights-based Children's Advocate in place, why is it so critical to adopt a "Children and Youth First" philosophy in Saskatchewan? Throughout our Office's advocacy, investigation (primarily child death and critical injury), research and public education work, we have found the safety, protection and well-being of children are often compromised. Following an investigation into the care provided by Oyate, a safe house for sexually exploited children, we noted in our Oyate systematic issues report that the lack of a "child first" approach within government services to children was not unique to Oyate, but that we had repeatedly observed this phenomenon—and its harmful and sometimes lethal effects—through our child death and critical injury investigations:

> The CAO has reported on a number of incidents in its Child Death Reviews whereby the current family-centred philosophy, with an insufficient child focus, has had devastating and life limiting effects on children. In the view of the Children's Advocate, the loss of life of one child is too many—but we have seen too many deaths and critical injuries that reflect this harmful philosophy of reducing children to the status of 'family chattels' to be fought over.
>
> In its investigation into the Oyate Safe House, the CAO found a similar pattern of repeated return to abusive and harmful family environments that contributed to the current lifestyle of many of the children interviewed, leaving them with a view of hopelessness and despair.
>
> Often, decisions regarding the child are made in isolation, without the child or his/her input, with an underlying philosophy that values family reunification and cultural considerations over the needs, protection and well-being of the child in question. Unfortunately, the ultimate price is most often paid by the child. If the behaviour of the family, and therefore the living environment, has not changed, the cycle simply continues and becomes inter-generational in nature. (Saskatchewan Children's Advocate Office, 2006a, p. 35)

CHILDREN'S CASE STUDIES: EXEMPLIFYING THE NEED FOR ESTABLISHING A "CHILDREN AND YOUTH FIRST" VISION

Over the years, the CAO has been witness to many examples of good case practice; however, we have also been witness to the confusion and poor practice that can occur when a "Children and Youth First" philosophy is not entrenched in legislation, policy and practice. The UN *CRC* is rarely referred to in legislation and policy (Howe & Covell, 2007), leaving practitioners unclear or confused about who the primary client is. As rights holders, children are entitled to protection services that put them and their best interests at the centre of the child welfare involvement. The following stories are those of actual children and illustrate how lack of focus on the child or youth as the primary client or lack of respect for the child's rights can have tragic outcomes. While the stories are real, the names have been changed to protect the children's right to confidentiality.[7]

Tyler, age 2

Tyler is a two-year-old boy who was beaten so badly by his father that he is now paralyzed on one side of his body. During the Children's Advocate Office's investigation into the services provided to Tyler and his family prior to his injuries, it was found that, over time, Tyler was severely malnourished; his parents continually exposed him and his siblings to known sexual offenders; the children exhibited symptoms of sexual abuse; the health of the children was compromised by the condition of the home (human excrement smeared in no less than fifty places, rotting food, molding clothes and excessive garbage found throughout the home); the children were often locked in the basement; abuse in the form of slapping and hitting was used on the children, including the infants; the parents had inappropriate age expectations of the children; and the parents refused support to learn new ways of parenting. Such a litany of abuse and neglect of children is shocking. However, equally shocking is the more than 40 documented referrals to the Department of Community Resources[8] over a 13-year time period. Despite Tyler's siblings being ap-

---

7   One exception is Karen Rose Quill, where the family provided consent to use her full name in a child death review conducted by the CAO.

8   The child welfare agency responsible for child protection in Saskatchewan has

prehended for brief periods of time, Tyler himself was never in care prior to his critical injury, and it was only after his injury that the remaining siblings were brought into care.

Following our investigation, we concluded that the Department of Community Resources did not sufficiently consider the severe and extensive child protection history with all adults involved, including the large number of referrals over the 13-year period during which Tyler and his siblings remained at risk. The frequency, nature and severity of the protection concerns, both reported to the Department of Community Resources and identified by the caseworker, in concert with the failure of the family to demonstrate any positive change, offer ample evidence that Tyler and his siblings were left in a high-risk living situation. The Department failed to protect these children from contact with perpetrators with long and substantiated histories of sexual abuse. Further, the Department of Community Resources was aware that the children were not receiving medical care, and yet did not intervene. The Department of Community Resources did not adhere to a child-centred philosophy in this case, nor did they apply sound principles of permanency planning. This was a family-centred approach at all costs. It is the opinion of the Children's Advocate Office that the critical injury to Tyler was preventable, had the Department of Community Resources provided Tyler with the child-centred protection services to which he was entitled. (Saskatchewan Children's Advocate Office, 2008). As Ron Ensom, co-author of the Joint Statement on Physical Punishment of Children and Youth, notes: "There is no benefit to a family that receives preservation services that permit repeated harm to a child" (Ensom, August 16, 2007).

Dylan and Brandon, ages 5 and 7

A CAO Child Death Investigation into the deaths of two siblings, Dylan (5) and Brandon (7), found casework that was solely focused on family reunification in spite of the parents' continued drinking and non-compliance with case planning. This was one of those families that could be easily written off as "only" neglectful and not abusive. Issues of neglect are at times minimized as simply being a product of poverty, when

---

gone through many name changes over the years. At the time of the writing of these investigations the name was Department of Community Resources. It is now known as the Ministry of Social Services.

compared to other child welfare issues. In reality, neglect can occur in any home, irrespective of income, and the outcomes can be just as damaging and tragic as abuse. It is for this reason that this investigation is being shared.

Dylan and Brandon were apprehended on four occasions in a five-year period due to their mother's severe addictions. There were serious neglect concerns, including abandonment in three of the four apprehensions, and an accidental house fire set by the mother in the fourth apprehension. At the time of the first apprehension, the boys were placed with their maternal grandmother briefly, in accordance with the family-centred policy prescribed by the Department of Community Resources until the grandmother refused to take care of them, due to their mother's disclosure that the grandmother's common-law partner had sexually abused her.

Although the two boys were never beaten, their basic needs were not met; they were often at risk due to abandonment, as well as at physical risk due to their mother's frequent intoxication. The mother was provided with a plethora of services related to her addictions and inadequate parenting. She was hosted in the foster home to improve her parenting and was provided with multiple hours of parent aide support, as well as in-patient and community addictions counselling. In spite of the mother's failure to maintain addictions treatment or sobriety, or follow through on any of the parenting supports, the child welfare authorities returned Dylan and Brandon to her. Prior to and shortly after their return, there were reports of continued alcohol abuse and abandonment by their mother. The boys had been returned to the same neglectful environment they had been removed from, in spite of alerts from concerned adults that it was still not a safe home. Very shortly after their return, as the adults were sleeping after drinking all night, the children started a house fire while trying to cook. Although the boys alerted the adults who escaped the blaze, the adults failed to bring the children with them when they fled. A neighbour, seeing the fire, was able to go back into the home and rescue the boy's sister, but was unable to find Brandon and Dylan. The lack of a clear child-centered plan, which in this case resulted in the return of these children to a home without identifiable change, placed them at further risk. The outcome was tragic. (Saskatchewan Children's Advocate Office, 2008).

Karen Rose Quill, age 20 months

In 1998, the CAO released a report on the death of Karen Rose Quill, a 20-month-old toddler who died while in foster care. Our Office concluded that Karen's death was preventable, and that management at all levels exhibited a tolerance for non-compliance with established policy and procedures with regard to Karen's placement and follow-up in an overcrowded foster home. Karen and her sibling increased the number of children to seven in the foster home where they were placed and where Karen died. The investigation into Karen's death clearly documented that the foster care system was under stress in 1998.

Unfortunately, our more recent advocacy and investigative work documented that the situation has not improved, and, in fact, for some children it has gotten worse. It has been reported to the CAO, and acknowledged in our discussions with the Department of Community Resources, that on some occasions there have been up to 21 children in one foster home. It has also been reported, and confirmed by the Department, that there are many homes that are regularly operating in non-compliance with policy. According to policy, the approved number of children who can be in a foster home is four, depending on the assessed capacity of the foster home and the needs of the children (Department of Community Resources, 2001).

It is hard to conceive how a child who is being removed from his or her family home and has specific needs relating to being removed from the family, who may have been abused or neglected, and/or may have a developmental delay or medical condition, would have his or her needs met when placed in a foster home that has up to 21 children or youth. Research findings continue to point to the fact that young people in state care lack meaningful participation in decisions affecting them and face early and abrupt emancipation from care and poor educational outcomes (Blackstock, Brown, & Bennett, 2007; National Youth In Care Network, 2004).

Discussion of Children's Case Studies

These three case examples and the current information about foster home overcrowding (Saskatchewan Children's Advocate Office, 2009) might otherwise be construed as isolated cases and not reflective of the good work that is being done by child welfare system generally. However, our Office has concluded, as a result of our cumulative advocacy and investigative experience, that the absence of a sustained focus on child-centred permanency planning has been a chronic problem in Saskatchewan's child welfare system.

There is no one simple answer when it comes to the rights, best interests and care of children who have experienced abuse and neglect. This is not to say that removal of children from their biological homes is the only answer; foster care has its obvious limitations as well. What is needed is individualized case planning for each child that meets the needs of the child from a rights-based perspective with a "Children and Youth First" direction. As Landgren (2005) pointed out, "A human rights approach to programming suggests that a wider range of interventions must be considered, based on keeping *all* children safe from harm" (p. 222). This means having access to all options and resources on the permanency planning continuum. For too long "children had to be hurt before they could be helped" (Kufeldt, Simard, Thomas, & Vachon, 2005, p. 305) in the child welfare system. We must be more creative with clinically sound, best interests, rights-based options for children. It is not enough to do the minimum, given that the *Convention* provides that "in all actions concerning children ... the best interests of the child shall be the primary consideration" (United Nations, 1989).

CHILD RIGHTS-BASED CHILD WELFARE PRACTICE

As mentioned earlier, it is time to embrace the final evolution of child rights, recognizing children as rights holders in child welfare services. It is our belief that if child welfare workers were conversant with the United Nations *Convention on the Rights of the Child*, they would be better equipped to bridge the chasm between protection and rights, thereby concurrently protecting children and youth and elevating children and youth's rights. In this context, it is important to note that

> Child protection workers are often the unsung heroes when a child is protected from harm or goes on to enjoy a happy and secure life as a result of judicious worker intervention. They should be admired for the importance of the work that they do and for the passion and commitment they exhibit on behalf of our most vulnerable citizens. (Bernstein, 2006, p. 14)

The protection of children and youth can only be strengthened by rights, as children move beyond victims who require a minimum protective service to persons entitled to protection and recovery services according to their best interests, with full participation. The preamble of the UN *CRC* states clearly "that the child, for the full and harmonious development of his or her personality, should grow up in a family environment, in an atmosphere of happiness, love and understanding" (United Nations, 1989, p. 1). This moves the State Parties' obligation far beyond the minimum level of protection services, which provide for survival, to an expectation of a higher best interests philosophy. "A broad definition of *child welfare* would encompass the general well-being of all children and the promotion of optimal child development" (Saskatchewan Social Services, October, 2000, p. 1). Similar to the *Convention* preamble, this definition goes beyond the limitation of protection for survival and speaks to optimal child development. Children and youth are clearly entitled to this, and with the *Convention* securely in their tool box of resources, child welfare workers will be better able to facilitate this.

All *Convention* articles are relevant to *all* children, but specific articles are particularly relevant to the core of child welfare work and the rights of the children involved in those systems. In order to fulfill this obligation, child welfare practice needs to be informed, at a minimum, by articles 1, 2, 3, 6, 9, 12, 19, 20, and 39. With this frame of reference in mind, we have developed the practice points below which, if carried out by child welfare workers, should bring a rights-based focus into their day-to-day child welfare practice. These practice points, as child welfare workers will recognize, are consistent with clinically sound and good casework practice:

1. Every human being under the age of 18 years is a child or youth and is entitled to basic human rights, as well as the special rights afforded by the United Nations *Convention on the Rights of the Child*. From the most vulnerable infant, who is unable to ask for what he/she needs to the most articulate adolescent at the age of 17, all are entitled to special child rights due to their developmental vulnerability. Child welfare systems need to be able to respond to children and youth of with age appropriate resources. (Article 1)

2. While there are many competing interests when child welfare issues arise, it is the child's or young person's best interests that

must be the priority when working with families. The children and youth are the reason why child welfare services are involved—their best interests are paramount. (Article 3)

3. Some children and youth do not survive until adulthood due to neglect and abuse. Child welfare services are obligated to protect children and youth from all forms of physical or mental violence, injury or abuse, neglect or negligent treatment, maltreatment or exploitation, including sexual abuse, while in the care of the parent(s), legal guardian(s) or any other person who has the care of the child. (Articles 6 & 19)

4. All children are entitled to rights-based child welfare services regardless of their race, colour, sex, language, religion, political or other opinion, national, ethnic or social origin, property, birth or other status. Child welfare services should be provided without discrimination, regardless of whether the child lives in the far north, a rural or urban area. These services must be provided with cultural competence, recognizing the distinctive cultures of minorities, with special recognition being afforded to the unique circumstances of Indigenous children. (Articles 2 & 30)

5. Children and youth have an uncharted course of their entire lives ahead of them and have the right to develop to their full potential. Explore their abilities, desires and hopes. Help them make these a reality and all of society will benefit. (Article 6)

6. Safe and healthy families make for happy and healthy children and youth. The United Nations *Convention on the Rights of the Child* states that children and youth are entitled to be with their parents unless it is contrary to their best interests. Every effort and resource should be accessed to make the familial home a safe and nurturing environment for the child or youth. These homes hold history, culture and identity. If a child can safely stay with family and flourish, this is the best place for him/her. However, some families do not have the capacity to care for their children, and, in such circumstances, safe and caring alternatives must be sought. (Article 9)

7. The child or youth is the primary client. Take the time to build a relationship, so that he/she will trust you and feel comfortable sharing vital information with you. Include him/her authentically in case conferences. Children being protected and served by

the child welfare system have a right to participate in discussions about them. This is their life; they have opinions and information that are vital to case management decisions. Children and youth are the experts when it comes to their own lives. (Article 12)

8. Alternative care must be supported, accountable, and monitored to ensure that the child is fully able to develop in his/her new home. This includes emergency homes, foster homes, group homes, extended family placements arranged by the child welfare agency, and persons of sufficient interest (POSI). Visit the children regularly and make sure you have time with them alone, so they can speak with you openly about their concerns. If you do hear concerns about a resource, investigate it fully. Moving a child typically means he/she requires additional resources, whether it is support to the home, counseling, new school books, or a set of winter clothing to get through the season. Moving is traumatic enough; children and youth are entitled to the necessities to make the alternative placement successful. (Article 20)

9. It is the responsibility of the child welfare system to provide appropriate services for children to heal from the abuse and neglect they have experienced. Recovery and reintegration of a child or youth is to be managed in a respectful manner. Think about what these children need in terms of support services to be successful. Many of them have suffered so acutely from previous abuse, neglect and placement changes that there may be a need for a number of services. They are entitled to all resources that will make their lives a little easier. (Article 39)

With an understanding of these particular UN *CRC* articles and how they can be applied to child welfare practice on the ground, child welfare workers will be much better prepared to address permanency planning from a rights-based perspective. Historically, permanency planning alternatives consisted of the biological family or closed adoptions. Permanency planning has evolved beyond these parameters with options such as kinship care, customary care, persons of sufficient interest, guardianship care, custom adoption, open adoption, and subsidized or assisted adoption. This more expansive permanency continuum needs to be further explored in this province to provide consistency, and offer permanence for children (Farris-Manning & Zandstra, 2007).

Children are entitled to permanency planning through detailed case work on an individualized basis throughout their exposure to the child welfare system, and must be considered the primary client in any planning. As Judge Thomas Gove wrote in his British Columbia "Report of the Gove Inquiry into Child Protection":

> The province needs to be clear that the child is the paramount client of the child welfare system. It needs to reflect this 'child-centredness' in legislation, training, policies, case supervision, case practice and advocacy. Doing so will demand that child welfare organizations act with undivided loyalty to the child, making choices based on what is best for the child. Such decisions might include assisting parents and other caregivers, when such assistance fosters the child's safety and well-being. Sometimes, it will mean removing the child. (Gove, 1995, pp. 245-246)

We *all* have an obligation to be child rights advocates to support these, the most vulnerable citizens—our children. It is imperative that children and youth have as many advocates as possible, be they natural family, community or statutory advocates. In this regard, we would encourage everyone—whether a parent, family member, teacher, caregiver, or professional—to become effective child rights advocates for children and youth and to find practical ways to help them on a day-to-day basis.

With this backdrop in mind, it is our Office's view that the current family-centred child welfare policy and legislation, combined with inconsistent child welfare practice, and an uneven application of relevant policy to *all* children, often converge in a manner that impedes the placing of "Children and Youth First" in the province of Saskatchewan.

"CHILDREN AND YOUTH FIRST" PRINCIPLES

We next turn to the question as to why it is important to advance a "Children and Youth First" vision in Saskatchewan. Although we see many examples of committed casework by individual service providers, in our daily work we do not see strong evidence that government legislation, policy, programming, or practice with respect to children and youth are being consistently developed in keeping with: 1) the principles of the United Nations *Convention on the Rights of the Child*; 2) a "Children and

Youth First" service philosophy; and 3) an inclusive consultation process with children and youth.

A report released by the Standing Senate Committee on Human Rights, entitled *Children: The Silenced Citizens* (Senate of Canada, 2007), supports our contention that the principles of the UN *CRC* have largely been ignored, both in Saskatchewan and throughout Canada. The Report concludes that Canada is failing to demonstrate respect for the rights of its children and is ignoring the promises it made when it signed the UN *CRC*.

The UN Committee's investigations have firmly led us to the conclusion that the UN *CRC* is not solidly embedded in Canadian law, in policy, or in the national psyche. Canadians are too often unaware of the rights enshrined in the *Convention*, while governments and courts use it only as a strongly worded guiding principle with which they attempt to ensure that laws conform, rather than treating it as an instrument necessitating concrete enforcement. No body is in charge of ensuring that the *Convention* is effectively implemented in Canada, and the political will is still lacking. (Senate of Canada, 2007, p. 193)

The Senate Committee Report makes the point that, while the vision of the UN *CRC* "properly puts children at the centre, in the context of their family, their community and their culture" (p. 28), there is nonetheless a "gulf between the rights rhetoric and the realities of children's lives" (p. 224) in Canada. In particular, the Senate Committee observed that "[c]hildren's voices rarely inform government decisions, yet they are one of the groups most affected by government action or inaction. Children are not merely underrepresented; they are almost not represented at all" (p. 27). The responsibility to address this situation appears to lie with all governments, including that of Saskatchewan—the Committee Report recognized that "all levels of government across Canada have a responsibility, and the capacity, to protect children's rights" (p. 50) and to implement the UN *CRC* within their respective jurisdictions.

Our Office's aggregate experience—in the areas of advocacy, public education, and child death and critical injury investigations—has demonstrated that, as a society responsible for the well-being and best interests of all children, we require a paradigm shift in attitude, policy, practice and legislation. To do a better job of addressing the needs of children, especially to place the interests of "Children and Youth First" in Saskatchewan, our Office felt it was necessary to develop a set of principles to firmly establish a "Children and Youth First" direction. As part of the process of developing these principles, we sought both internal and external feedback and used external focus groups with youth. This enabled us to continually refine and improve upon earlier drafts of our principles. These "Children and Youth First" principles, then, represent our Office's best efforts to simplify and highlight the most critical and relevant provisions in the *Convention*, based upon our observations and experience, and to make them explicitly applicable to all Saskatchewan children. They are as follows:

1. That all children and youth in Saskatchewan are entitled to those rights defined by the United Nations *Convention on the Rights of the Child*.[9]

2. That all children and youth in Saskatchewan are entitled to participate and be heard before any decision affecting them is made.[10]

---

9   United Nations, *Convention on the Rights of the Child*. (1989: Geneva). This is one of the beliefs listed in the Saskatchewan's Action Plan for Children, Policy Framework, (1995). See also Rae, J., *Indigenous Children: Rights and Reality: A Report on Indigenous Children and the U.N. Convention on the Rights of the Child*, (UN Sub-Group on Indigenous Children and Youth), University of Toronto: 2006, at p. 7, where it is stated that "the concept of 'children's rights' in the UN CRC resonates deeply with many Indigenous peoples today as comparable to, or at least compatible with, their own concepts of human dignity and childhood." The *Convention* is legally binding at the international level, and governments must take their obligations seriously to implement it in domestic practice, policy and legislation. In the absence of a clear conflict with domestic legislation, the United Nations *Convention on the Rights of the Child* should be used as a contextual tool for statutory interpretation. For instance, in *Baker v. Canada*, [1999] 2 S.C.R. 817 and *Winnipeg Child and Family Services v. K. L. W.*, [2000] 2 S.C.R. 519, the Supreme Court of Canada applied the presumption that an interpretation favoured by the *Convention* should be followed in domestic law. See also: Yoles, V., *The UNCRC: A Practical Guide for its Use in Canadian Courts* (Toronto: UNICEF Canada, 1998).

10   This principle is consistent with Article 12(1) of the United Nations *Convention on the Rights of the Child*, which provides that "States Parties shall assure to the child who is capable of forming his or her own views the right to express those views freely in all matters affecting the child, the views of the child being given due weight in accordance with the age and maturity of the child." The African expression "Say Nothing about Me Without Me" has been adopted by the Saskatchewan Children's Advocate Office and embodies this principle.

3. That all children and youth in Saskatchewan are entitled to have their 'best interests' given paramount consideration in any action or decision involving them.[11]

4. That all children and youth in Saskatchewan are entitled to an equal standard of care, protection and services.[12]

5. That all children and youth in Saskatchewan are entitled to the highest standard of health and education possible in order to reach their fullest potential.[13]

6. That all children and youth in Saskatchewan are entitled to safety and protection from all forms of physical, emotional and sexual harm, while in the care of parents, governments, legal guardians or any person.[14]

7. That all children and youth in Saskatchewan are entitled to be

---

11 This principle is consistent with Article 3(1) of the United Nations *Convention on the Rights of the Child*, which states that "In all actions concerning children, whether undertaken by public or private social welfare institutions, courts of law, administrative authorities or legislative bodies, the best interests of the child shall be a primary consideration." See also Saskatchewan's Action Plan for Children, Policy Framework, refinement of one of the Principles listed. The 'best interests' of the child should take precedence over any jurisdictional or political considerations: *supra*, note 4, Statement of Jordan's Principle.

12 This principle is consistent with Article 2(1) of the United Nations *Convention on the Rights of the Child*, which provides that "States Parties shall respect and ensure the rights set forth in the present Convention to each child within their jurisdiction without discrimination of any kind, irrespective of the child's or his or her parent's or legal guardian's race, colour, sex, language, religion, political or other opinion, national, ethnic or social origin, property, disability, birth or other status." This means that the minimum child protection bar under provincial child protection legislation is a constant and does not shift between different groups of children.

13 This principle is consistent with Articles 24-29 of the United Nations *Convention on the Rights of the Child*. .

14 This principle is consistent with Article 19 of the United Nations Convention on the Rights of the Child, which provides that "States Parties shall take all appropriate legislative, administrative, social and educational measures to protect the child from all forms of physical or mental violence, injury or abuse, neglect, or negligent treatment, maltreatment or exploitation, including sexual abuse, while in the care of parent(s), legal guardian(s) or any other person who has the care of the child."

treated as the primary client, and at the centre, of all child serving systems.[15]

8. That all children and youth in Saskatchewan are entitled to have consideration given to the importance of their unique life history and spiritual traditions and practices, in accordance with their stated views and preferences.[16]

---

15   This principle is consistent with Article 3(1) of the United Nations Convention on the Rights of the Child, supra, note 9. See Gove, Thomas (Judge), British Columbia Report of the Gove Inquiry into Child Protection, Volume 2, (Matthew's Legacy), (Ministry of Social Services, 1995) at pp. 245, 246, where he states that "the Province needs to be clear that the child is the paramount client of the child welfare system" and emphasizes the importance of "child-centredness" and placing the child "at the heart of" the child welfare system. See also Hatton, Mary Jane (Madam Justice), Report of the Panel of Experts on Child Protection (Toronto: Ontario Ministry of Community and Social Services, 1998), where it was determined that the pendulum had swung too far in favour of parental rights, with the necessary child-focus being sacrificed in the process. See further, Bernstein, M., Regehr, C., and Kanani, K., Liability for child welfare workers: Weighing the risks, in Bala, N., et al. (Eds.), *Canadian Child Welfare Law: Children, Families and the State*, 2nd ed. (Toronto: Thompson Education Publishing, Inc., 2004) at p. 405, where reference is made to the finding of the Ontario Coroner's Jury, in the Jordan Heikamp Inquest, that the child protection worker's focus in the case "was primarily on the mother and not on the child" and to the jury's recommendation that "it should be made clear to all Child Protection Workers and their Child Protection Supervisors that their client is the child in need of protection, not the parent or the family." This will mean that in the event of a conflict between the best interests of a child and the interests of other family members, it is the best interests of the child that are paramount.

16   This principle is consistent with Article 30 of the United Nations *Convention on the Rights of the Child*, which provides that "In those states in which ethnic, religious or linguistic minorities or persons of indigenous origin exist, a child belonging to such a minority or who is indigenous shall not be denied the right, in community with other members of his or her group, to enjoy his or her own culture, to profess and practice his or her own religion, or to use his or her own language." See *supra*, note 1, especially *Oyate Beyond 'at Risk' Systemic Issues Report*. See also: Draft United Nations *Declaration on the Rights of Indigenous Peoples*, Resolution 1994/45, (approved by the United Nations Human Rights Council, June 2006, but not yet passed by the General Assembly), Preamble, where it is stated, among other things, that "Recognizing the urgent need to respect and promote the rights and characteristics of indigenous peoples ... which derive from their cultures, spiritual traditions, histories and philosophies."

Our Office has developed these "Children and Youth First" principles to define our core beliefs in relation to the care and services that ought to be provided to Saskatchewan children and youth. This is important in order to avoid definitional ambiguity, since our Office often finds itself in conflict with government's interpretation of putting the needs of "Children and Youth First." In addition, we have to be able to put what we mean to the test as an accountability measure not only for the provincial government, but also for our own Office.

A CALL TO ACTION

Our Office has determined that there is a need for the provincial government to develop a revitalized "Children and Youth First" action plan. As a result, we have used our "Children and Youth First" vision and principles to engage government leadership and departments responsible for child-serving systems in a positive process of advancing and establishing a transformative action plan for children and youth. We have proposed four components to government, which are, in our view, foundational to a renewed action plan for children and youth. These are as follows:

1. A well-articulated and integrated vision that places the needs and interests of children and youth first.
2. The inclusion of references to both 'children' and 'youth' in action plan, vision statement and core principles. (A key component fundamental to a new action plan will be the need to expand the 'child' focus to include and identify 'youth,' so that the action plan is guided by a more inclusive "Children and Youth First" direction.)
3. The endorsement of all eight "Children and Youth First" principles that will anchor this new "Children and Youth First" vision.
4. A commitment to incorporate the "Children and Youth First" principles into existing and future government policy, practice, programming and legislation. (A commitment to incorporate the principles could generate the development of an enhanced and integrated 'child and youth-centred' permanency child welfare continuum, with expanded and more flexible options that are inclusive of aboriginal culture and spiritual traditions).

The challenge to implement the *Convention* has taken on significant weight in the context of the recent Supreme Court of Canada decision of *Syl Apps Secure Treatment Centre v. B. D.* (hereafter, *Syl Apps v. B. D.*), where that Court unanimously ruled on July 27, 2007, that government ministries and child welfare agencies have the right to intervene in the lives of families, without fear of being sued by parents or other family members, in order to protect vulnerable children who are at risk of harm and to promote their best interests. In particular, Madam Justice Abella, speaking for the entire Court, concluded that:

> [I]f a corresponding duty is also imposed with respect to the parents, service providers will be torn between the child's interests on the one hand, and parental expectations which may be unrealistic, unreasonable or unrealizable on the other. This tension creates the potential for a chilling effect on social workers, who may hesitate to act in pursuit of the child's best interests for fear that their approach, could attract criticism—and litigation— from the family. They should not have to weigh what is best for the child on the scale with what would make the family happiest, finding themselves choosing between aggressive protection of the child and a lawsuit from the family. (*Syl Apps v. B. D.*, 2007, para. 50)

The outcome of this decision acknowledges the vital role of families as being "the core social unit" (*Syl Apps v. B. D.*, 2007, para. 1) of primary care for a child, but also affirms that the rights of the family are subordinate to the "state's overriding duty to ensure that children are protected" (*Syl Apps v. B. D.*, 2007, para. 2).

This Supreme Court of Canada judgment has particular relevance for Saskatchewan, where the current child welfare system is grounded in family-centred legislation, policy, programming and practice. The direct impact on children is that the family-centred approach, in combination with inconsistent child welfare practice and an uneven application of relevant policy to all children, has compromised child safety, protection and well-being. Adding to the danger that children already face is the system-generated confusion exhibited, at times, by child welfare authorities about whether the primary client is the child or the family.

The Court's decision has clearly articulated that the 'child' and not the 'family' is the client to whom the duty of care is owed, and whose best interests are to be served at all times. The ruling is also consistent with two of our Office's previous public statements: first, that all government levels, provincial, federal and First Nations, cannot place other agendas—be they jurisdictional, political, or financial—ahead of the needs and best interests of children; and second, that while recognizing the importance of family, culture and community, such governmental entities cannot place family and blood ties ahead of the safety, protection and well-being of children.

Within a First Nations context, the Court's decision is consistent with Jordan's Principle, contained in a 2005 First Nations Child and Family Caring Society of Canada report, which asserts in memory of a five-year-old Manitoba First Nations child named Jordan Anderson, that the interests of children should always come first, ahead of inter-jurisdictional and funding disputes:

> In keeping with the United Nations *Convention on the Rights of the Child*, we recommend that a child first principle be adopted in the resolution of inter-governmental jurisdictional disputes. Under this procedure, the government (provincial or federal) that first receives a request to pay for services for a Status Indian child, where that service is available to other children, will pay for the service without delay or disruption. The paying party then has the option to refer the matter to a jurisdictional dispute resolution table. In this way the rights of the child come first whilst allowing for the resolution of jurisdictional issues. (First Nations Child & Family Caring Society of Canada, 2005, p. 107)

The pronouncement of the Supreme Court of Canada performs a positive service in acknowledging that "child protection work is difficult, painful and complex" (*Syl Apps v. B.D.*, 2007, para. 64) and in clarifying for child welfare authorities both the ambit and central focus of their statutory obligations. It also goes a great distance in establishing the need for a "Children and Youth First" commitment. Indeed, it recognizes that "it is not the family's satisfaction in the long-term to which the [child welfare legislation] gives primacy; it is the child's best interests" (*Syl Apps v. B.D.*, 2007, para. 43).

Accordingly, the Supreme Court of Canada judgment has provided the foundation and created the opportunity for our provincial government to implement a "Children and Youth First" vision relative to all programs and services provided to children. It is clearly time for a paradigm shift in attitude, legislation, policy and practice.

CONCLUSION: MOVING FROM "PAPER RIGHTS" TO "LIVED RIGHTS"

In conclusion, and to return to the theme of the Prairie Child Welfare Consortium Symposium, we wish to emphasize that, while it has been an extremely positive, enlightening and collaborative process to create and promote the "Children and Youth First" principles, what we are asking for is *action*—an action plan by our government that commits to a course of action by all government sectors to incorporate these principles into legislation, policy, programming and practice, so that we can achieve positive outcomes for children and youth. This action plan needs to be implemented with fairness, vigor and passion. It is not sufficient for these principles to be reduced to simple platitudes or reflect only "future good intentions"—they must, instead, be given a sense of urgency and be translated into "passionate action." Our children and youth deserve no less from all of us.

As a special tribute to National Child Day in 2007, when the UN *CRC* reached its majority, we must, as a province and community, pledge a stronger commitment to this new second generation of children with rights under the *Convention*. We must all seek opportunities to make a tangible difference in their lives and to ensure that they will be able to practically access and exercise their rights. In this way, we will go a great distance towards transforming these "paper rights" into actual "lived rights."

POSTSCRIPT

On February 25, 2009, in response to our Office's Special Report, entitled *A Breach of Trust: An Investigation Into Foster Home Overcrowding in the Saskatoon Service Centre*, where our Office profiled the serious plight of children residing in overcrowded foster homes, the provincial government announced an Action Plan which set out, for the very first time, the following commitment:

> ... The Government of Saskatchewan has adopted the "Children and Youth First" Principles as formulated by the Children's Advocate (see www.saskcao.ca/documents/cao-principlesweb.pdf). These Principles will act as a guide in examining policy and legislation and in developing and implementing both policy and legislative changes.

> ... The Government of Saskatchewan is committed to putting children and youth first, and to ensuring a better life for these vulnerable members of society (Ministry of Social Services, 2009).

In a subsequent letter, Premier Brad Wall provided the following supplementary statement:

> Our government is committed to providing children within our province, and specifically those within the care of the Ministry of Social Services, with the security and opportunities they rightfully deserve. The well-being of Saskatchewan children and youth is paramount to this government, and as a result, we were pleased to adopt the "Children and Youth First" Principles (Wall, 2009).

After close to two years of persistent advocacy by our Office, it was gratifying to see the provincial government's enlightened and progressive step towards elevating awareness of the rights, interests and well-being of children and youth in our province.

By adopting the "Children and Youth First" Principles, Saskatchewan has distinguished itself by addressing its obligations, after having endorsed the United Nations *Convention on the Rights of the Child*. Our Office is extremely pleased by this development and looks forward to working with all child-serving ministries, in the coming months and years, with a view to incorporating these Principles into legislation, policy and practice.

It is hoped that our experience can serve as an enduring teaching moment and that these Principles can act as a template to be applied and/or adapted in other jurisdictions.

REFERENCES

Bernstein, M. (2004). The decision of the Supreme Court of Canada upholding the constitutionality of Section 43 of the Criminal Code of Canada: What this decision means to the child welfare sector. *Ontario Association of Children's Aid Societies Journal, 48* (2), 2-14.

Bernstein, M. (2006). The challenge of professionalizing child protection work and retaining the title of social worker. *Canada's Children,* Fall 2006, (p42-46).

Bernstein, M., St. Onge, M., & Schury, R. (2006). *Saskatchewan children's right to participate and be heard in child welfare proceedings.* Paper submitted by the Saskatchewan Children's Advocate Office to the United Nations Committee on the Rights of the Child General Day of Discussion, Group 1, The child's right to be heard in judicial and administrative proceedings. Retrieved May 6, 2008, from http://www.saskcao.ca/documents/Saskatchewan%20Children's%20Right%20to%20Participate%20and%20be%20Heard%20in%20Child%20Welfare%20Proceedings.pdf

Blackstock, C., Brown, I., & Bennett, M. (2007). Reconciliation: Rebuilding the Canadian child welfare system to better serve Aboriginal children and youth. In I. Brown, F. Chase, D. Fuchs, J. Lafrance, S. McKay, & S. Prokop-Thomas (Eds.), *Putting a human face on child welfare: Voices from the prairies* (pp. 59-87). Toronto, ON: Centre of Excellence for Child Welfare and Prairie Child Welfare Consortium.

Canadian Heritage. (1989). *Convention on The Rights of The Child.* Canadian Heritage Booklet, Canada. Hull, Quebec: Human Rights Program, Department of Canadian Heritage

Committee on the Rights of the Child. (2002). *General comment: The role of independent national human rights institutions in the promotion and protection of the rights of the child.* Retrieved May 9, 2008, from http://www.unhchr.ch/tbs/doc.nsf/(symbol)/CRC.GC.2002.2.En?OpenDocument

Committee on the Rights of the Child. (October 2003). *Concluding observations: Canada.* Retrieved May 9, 2008, from http://www1.umn.edu/humanrts/crc/canada1.htm

Department of Community Resources. (2001). Family and Youth Division, Children's Services Policy and Procedure Manual, Chapter 4, Section 4, Subsection 7, pp. 47-51.

Ensom, R. (August 16, 2007). Written personal communication to Marvin Bernstein, Saskatchewan Children's Advocate.

Farris-Manning, C., & Zandstra, M. (2007). Children in care in Canada: A summary of current issues and trends with recommendations for future research. In Child Welfare League of Canada, *The welfare of Canadian children: It's our business: A collection of resource papers for a healthy future for Canadian children and families* (pp. 54-72). Retrieved May 9, 2008, from http://www.cwlc.ca/files/file/policy/Welfare%20of%20Canadian%20Children%202007.pdf

First Nations Child & Family Caring Society of Canada. (2005), *WEN: DE: We are coming to the light of day.* Retrieved February 23, 2008, from http://www.fncfcs.com/docs/WendeReport.pdf

Gove, Justice T. (1995). *Matthew's story: Report of the Gove inquiry into child protection.* Victoria, BC: British Columbia Ministry of Social Services, Vol. 2.

Hammarberg, T., (2007). The rights of the child – much more than charity. In J. Conners, J. Zermatten & A. Panayotidis (Eds.), *18 Candles: The Convention on the Rights of the Child reaches the age of majority* (pp. 113-119). Institut international de droits de l'enfant. Retrieved May 6, 2008, from http://www.ohchr.org/Documents/Publications/crc18.pdf

Howe, R. B., & Covell, K. (Eds.) (2007). *A question of commitment: Children's rights in Canada.* Waterloo, ON: Studies in Childhood and Family in Canada.

Kufeldt, K., Simard, M., Thomas, P., & Vachon, J. (2005). A grass roots approach to influencing child welfare policy. *Child and Family Social Work, 10,* 305-314.

Landgren, K. (2005). The protective environment: Development support for child protection. *Human Rights Quarterly, 27*(1), 214-248.

Leblanc, L. J. (1996). Reservations to the Convention on the Rights of the Child: A macroscopic view of state practice. *The International Journal of Children's Rights, 4,* 357-381.

Legislative Assembly of Saskatchewan. (December 11, 1991). Hansard's Transcript, per former Justice Minister, Bob Mitchell. Regina, Saskatchewan

Legislative Assembly of Saskatchewan. (1994). *Saskatchewan action plan fact sheet.* Regina, Saskatchewan: Author.

Legislative Assembly of Saskatchewan. (June 2001). *Special committee to prevent the abuse and exploitation of children through the sex trade final report* (2nd Session of the 24th Legislature). Regina, Saskatchewan: Author.

Ministry of Social Services. (February 25, 2009). News Release. *Putting children first: Province takes action on child welfare.* www.gov.sk.ca/news.

National Youth in Care Network. (2004). *Speak the truth in a million voices. It is silence that kills: Stories for change.* Ottawa, ON: National Youth in care Network.

OHCHR (Office of the United Nations High Commissioner for Human Rights). (1996). *General guidelines for periodic reports: 20/11/1996 CRC/C/58. (Basic reference document).* Retrieved July 21, 2008, from http://www.unhchr.ch/tbs/doc.nsf/(Symbol)/CRC.C.58.En?Opendocument

Pinheiro, P. (June 3, 2005). Statement by the independent expert to the North American regional consultation for *The United Nations Secretary-General's study on violence against children.* Retrieved May 6, 2008, from http://www.violencestudy.org/r25.

Saskatchewan Children's Advocate Office, (September 2006a). *Beyond 'at risk' children systemic issues report regarding sexually exploited children and Oyate safe house*, Saskatoon, Author. Retrieved May 10, 2008, from http://www.saskcao.ca/documents/Oyate%20Investigative%20Report.pdf

Saskatchewan Children's Advocate Office, (September 2006b). *"Child First:" The right focus*. Brief to the standing senate committee on human rights: Canada's international obligations to the rights and freedoms of Children, September 19, 2006, Saskatoon, Author. Retrieved May 8, 2008, from http://www.saskcao.ca/documents/Child%20First%20--%20The%20Right%20Focus%20(Submission%20to%20the%20Standing%20Senate%20Committee).pdf

Saskatchewan Children's Advocate Office. (June 2008). *Children's advocate office 2007 annual report. Children and youth first: The right action*. Saskatoon, SK: Author.

Saskatchewan Children's Advocate Office. (February 2009). *A breach of trust: An investigation into foster home overcrowding in the Saskatoon Service Centre*, Saskatoon, SK: Author. www.saskcao.ca.

Saskatchewan Social Services. (October 2000). *Child welfare in Saskatchewan.*

Senate of Canada, Standing Senate Committee on Human Rights. (2007). *Children: The silent citizens. Effective implementation of Canada's international obligations with respect to the rights of children: Final Report of the Standing Committee on Human Rights. Ottawa, ON, April 2007.* Retrieved May 9, 2008, from http://www.parl.gc.ca/39/1/parlbus/commbus/senate/com-e/huma-e/rep-e/rep10apr07-e.

Syl Apps Secure Treatment Centre v. B.D., 2007 SCC 38, [2007] S.C.J. No. 38.

Turpel-Lafond, M. E. (2007). Who listens to children? *The Verdict, 113,* 46-47.

UNICEF. (2005). *Convention on the Rights of the Child*. Retrieved February 1, 2005, from http://www.unhchr.ch/html/menu3/b/k2crc.htm

UNICEF. (1999). "Forward" in *A Human Rights conceptual framework for UNICEF*. Retrieved May 8, 2008, from http://www.unicef-irc.org/cgi-bin/unicef/Lunga.sql?ProductID=2

UNICEF Canada. (2005). *Violence against children regional consultation North America: United Nations secretary-general's study on violence against children*. Retrieved July 21, 2008, from http://www.violencestudy.org/a94

United Nations. (1989). *United Nations Convention on the Rights of the Child*. New York: United Nations.

Verhellen, E. (1996). *The Convention on the Rights of the Child*. In E. Verhellen (Ed.), *Understanding children's rights: Collected papers presented at the first International Interdisciplinary Course on Children's Rights* (pp. 27-43). Ghent, Belgium: University of Ghent.

Wall, B. (March 17, 2009). Written correspondence from the Premier of Saskatchewan to Marvin Bernstein, Saskatchewan Children's Advocate.

CHAPTER 3

From Longing to Belonging: Attachment Theory, Connectedness, and Indigenous Children in Canada

Jeannine Carriere and Cathy Richardson

> A drop of longing says as much about the human spirit as
> a grand gesture of love or defiance.
>
> —*Allan Wade, 2006*

INTRODUCTION

Many indigenous activists remember the life and death of Richard Cardinal as one tragic example of the systemic neglect and mishandling of indigenous children in a child welfare system (Trocmé, Knoke, & Blackstock, 2004; Obomsawin, 1986; Carriere, 2007, 2005; Sinclair, 2007). By the age of nine, after being placed in over 28 different living situations, Richard had given up his longing for love, for family, and for dignity. He ended his life, writing, "I just can't take it anymore" (Obomsawin, 1986).

SUGGESTED CITATION: Carriere, J., & Richardson, C. (2009). From longing to belonging: Attachment theory, connectedness, and indigenous children in Canada. In S. McKay, D. Fuchs, & I. Brown (Eds.), *Passion for action in child and family services: Voices from the prairies* (pp. 49-67). Regina, SK: Canadian Plains Research Center.

Given the gross and glaring ways that Richard's needs went unmet, it is easy to lose sight of the doubtless more subtle longings of his heart. Did anyone hear his longing? Or see it on his face or in his acts of living? And say to him, in word or deed, "I get it"? We have been greatly moved by Richard's life and death because of our personal locations. Richard was connected to Fort Chipewyan, the maternal village of Cathy Richardson, and Jeannine Carriere was involved in the investigation of his tragic circumstances after his passing.

Sadly, the situation since Richard Cardinal's death has not improved dramatically for indigenous children who become involved with child welfare services. While indigenous peoples comprise only 3.8 percent of the total population of Canada (Government of Canada, 2006), their children represent between 40 percent and 60 percent of the children who have been removed from their families and made wards of the state—in spite of already being "wards," according to the Indian Act, if they are status First Nation, as described in *Gathering Strength*, the Report of the Royal Commission on Aboriginal Peoples (Government of Canada, 1996). While some improvements have been made, the child welfare community continues to face serious problems with service delivery. Farris-Manning and Zandstra (cited in Trocmé, Knoke, & Blackstock, 2004) write:

> While Cardinal's death drew attention to the significant over-representation of Aboriginal children in state care, twenty years later the problem has become far more serious, with Aboriginal children representing approximately 40% of the 76,000 children and youth placed in out of home care in Canada. (p. 1)

In the region of British Columbia where the authors currently reside, this figure is as high as 50 percent in some jurisdictions, despite the fact that First Nation, Métis, and Inuit people constitute only 8 percent of the larger population in British Columbia (Government of British Columbia, March 2008). Blackstock (2008) describes these statistics within a context of poverty, stating that over 60 percent of cases of child welfare involvement for Aboriginal children are due to neglect that is directly related to poverty (p. 9).

Sinclair (2007) states that the situation for indigenous families is graver now than it was in the 1960s: "Child welfare interventions that began in the 1950s, referred to in retrospect as the Sixties Scoop, were the tip of the emerging iceberg of what is now the institution of Aboriginal child welfare" (p. 68). Lauri Gilchrist of Lakehead University notes that, given current child welfare statistics, the "Sixties Scoop" has merely evolved into the "Millennium Scoop" and Aboriginal social workers, recruited into the ranks of social services and operating under the umbrella of Indian Child and Family services, are now the ones doing the "scooping" (cited in Sinclair, 2007, p. 67).

In recent years, due to the influence of research conducted by Fraser Mustard (McCain & Mustard, 1999, 2002), who describes the importance of the first year and crucial aspects of mother/child bonding, attachment theory has been influential in child welfare decision-making. While the idea of a secure mother/child attachment and reliable patterns of nurturing and loving care has much to offer families and human service practitioners in terms of promoting healthy beginnings for children and mothers, the inappropriate application of this theory to child welfare decision-making with indigenous families in Canada is problematic. Arlene Hache, an activist for indigenous child welfare justice in the Northwest Territories, reports that Mustard's research regarding the importance of the first year has been used by judges to influence court cases wherein indigenous children are removed from their parents without their families being given the opportunity to demonstrate appropriate, safe care of their children. Hache notes: "The Mustard report lays the foundation for birth apprehensions in the Territories that almost exclusively targeted Aboriginal women (personal communication, Yellowknife, March 2008). Bennett (2007) reminds us that "very little research exists on Aboriginal mothers' experiences with child welfare" (p. 89), and Crichlow (2002) suggests that Canada's child welfare system "is one that reflects white dominant mainstream ideas and ideals and it has historically been used on Aboriginal peoples in ways that conflict and are inconsistent with Aboriginal people's values and family traditions" (p. 88). Crichlow cites Madame Justice Wilson, who stated in *Racine v. Woods* that "when the test to be met is the best interests of the child, the significance of cultural background and heritage as opposed to bonding abates over time. The closer the bond that develops with the prospective adoptive parents, the less important the racial element becomes" (in Crichlow, 2002, p. 94). Crichlow states that, currently, decisions to support the importance of

culture "are still the exception and not the norm and are usually dependent on the facts of the case" (p. 94). Gonzales-Mena (2001) cautions
us that when "early childhood professionals resolve differences about
best practices with parents in ways that discount diversity and impose
the dominant culture, they tread on issues of equity and social justice"
(p. 368).

Examining aspects of validity, cross-cultural application, indigenous
and non-indigenous worldview, and issues of human rights, the authors
of this chapter consider the implications of using attachment theory in
indigenous child welfare practice. It is the perspective of the authors
that it is crucial for the well-being of indigenous children, families, and
communities to preserve the culture and identity of indigenous children
and that practices that encourage extended family care and community
connection are more relevant in working with indigenous children and
families.

Terminology

Just as the word 'human' or 'mankind' is said to be an overarching term
including women, if women are indeed present, the usage of 'mother'
in this chapter includes the father where fathers are present. The term
'indigenous' is used in place of 'Aboriginal,' largely because it is less imposed than terms used in the Indian Act. The term includes First Nation,
Métis, and Inuit peoples as recognized in the Canadian Constitution.

CULTURALLY RELEVANT APPLICATIONS
OF ATTACHMENT THEORY

To date, little research has been conducted that reviews cases where attachment theory was used to justify the removal of children from their
families. In this absence, we can consider Carriere (2007, 2005) on attachment and connection issues with indigenous children who have been
adopted. In an article based on her Ph.D. dissertation, Carriere describes
the importance of connectedness in adoption. The term *connectedness*
is defined as a feeling of belonging, of being an important and integral
part of the world. Carriere states that an adoptee's sense of disconnection stems from an intrinsic sense that the environment in which he/
she has developed has been altered through adoption. Adoption has
created a different environment than initially intended by creation. In

turn, this intrinsic sense causes a spiritual dissonance that has an impact on health, which is connected to issues of loss. This spiritual dissonance can explain why an adoptee retains a permeating sense of loss despite a relatively nurturing adoptive home environment or a fairly positive and healthy lifestyle (p. 189). Several researchers have focused on aspects of connectedness and adoption (Borders, Penny, & Portnoy, 2000; Boss, 1999; Brodzinsky & Schechter, 1990; Hendry & Reid, 2000; Lee, Lee, & Draper, 2001). In examining connectedness specifically, Borders, Penny, and Portnoy (2000) found that more adoptees than a comparison group were "insecure and fearful avoidant" (p. 416); they concluded that "adult adoptees have meaningful stories to tell, and these stories could greatly inform clinicians, educators, and policymakers, as well as adoptive and birth parents" (p. 416). Brodzinsky and Schechter (1990) also explore the issue of connectedness from a psychological perspective. They state that "with the psychological need to separate, pushed by the biological changes of adolescence, the dissonances and differences for the adoptee are highlighted and eventually create, in our view, a driven need to experience human connectedness" (p. 85). This view is supported by Hendry and Reid (2000), who found that connectedness or "belonging to a community of others" (p. 706) acted as a deterrent, in adolescent adoptees, for high-risk indicators such as poor body image, a high degree of emotional stress, poly-drug use, school absenteeism, or risk of injury or pregnancy. Lee, Lee, and Draper (2001) discovered similar findings when examining the relationship between psychological well-being and connectedness. They found that "people with low connectedness often experience loneliness, anxiety, jealousy, anger, depression, low self-esteem, and a host of other negative emotions" (2001, p. 311). These studies reveal that high-risk behaviours are associated with a lack of connectedness to community. Connectedness to family has also been explored (March, 1995; Resnick, Harris, & Blum, 1993; Slap, Goodman, & Huang, 2001). Resnick, Harris, and Blum (1993) describe family connectedness as one of the most powerful protective factors in the well-being of adolescents (p. 380). Moreover, Slap, Goodman, and Huang (2001) propose that family connectedness can reduce the risk of suicide among adolescent adoptees (p. 2). March (1995) describes the act of searching as intimate, since it acknowledges and activates the part of self denied to adoptees through non-disclosure, thus bringing this hidden aspect into the light.

This feeling of awakening helps the individual to feel more whole and connected to the rest of the world: "By gaining access to their genealogical and genetic background, searching adoptees neutralize their sense of feeling different through adoption" (March, 1995, p. 74). In other words, the act of searching for family brings to life the adoptee's sense of connectedness and an expanded sense of possibility. Molloy (2002) supports this view by describing a follow-up study with adult adoptees. He proposes that connectedness is a sense of continuity which is completed only by a sense of a beginning and an ending (p. 177).

Boss (1999) addresses health and connectedness through her work with immigrant children. She writes that when "the psychological family is not in accord with the physically present family," a state of ambiguity is created, which Boss refers to as "ambiguous loss" (pp. 3-4). This sense of loss results in frozen grief, which may result in characteristics such as depression, anxiety and/or somatic illnesses, backaches, headaches, and stomach ailments (p. 10). Boss concludes that often when people are separated from their family of origin, the family that exists in their minds is more important than the one they live with.

Boss's conclusion supports Rillera's (1987) assertion that adoptees feel connected to people they do not even know. They go through motions of life with "a cellular consciousness of the experience" (p. 39), similar to the 'blood memory' described by Anderson (2000) and Atkinson (2002), who describe cellular memory and collective consciousness as ways of knowing that connect us to our ancestors (Rillera, p. 87). Explored in a spiritual context, this call of the ancestors enhances the feeling that one needs to search for a missing piece in one's life.

Although Wolin and Wolin (1993) propose that children can rise above disconnection from family and endear themselves to others, Brodzinsky and Schechter (1990) point out that this may be a case of attachment, but not assimilation. For Brodzinsky and Schechter, attachment is an emotional bond to the adoptive family, while assimilation is a state of integrating the adoptive family's characteristics and worldview. In other words, children may appear to be well-adjusted and integrated into a family, but they may have a deep internal drive to detach and seek a reason for being, or, as one adoptee in Brodzinsky and Schechter's study explains, "to know I wasn't hatched" (1990, p. 85). This drive to belong points to the importance for adopted children to experience a sense of balance in their lives through attachment and integration, as well as to the need for adoption policies that encourage these experiences.

The role of kinship and connectedness for First Nation adoptees

From a Western worldview, kinship has been studied and described by cultural anthropologists who have focused on patterns of behaviour, language, and cultural norms. However, two critical questions must be considered: "What is kinship from an indigenous perspective?" and "How can the importance of kinship inform decision-making for indigenous children?" Red Horse, Martinez, Day, Day, Poupart, and Scharnberg (2000) state that family preservation is linked fundamentally to tribal sovereignty and that history and tradition are important components of kinship, which is necessary to the survival of American Indian families. Other indigenous scholars concur (Littlebear, 2000; Youngblood Henderson, 2000; Yeo, 2003). Littlebear (2000) describes kinship as a "spider-web of relations" (p. 79); extended families are interconnected circles based on wholeness with the strength of providing balance. They include social and religious functions, and, "from the moment of birth, children are the objects of love and kindness from a large circle of relatives and friends" (Littlebear, 2000, p. 81). Within this worldview, kinship extends beyond human relationships to include kinship with the natural world. This ecological view of kinship categorizes social obligations such as reciprocity in relationship with plants and animals. Youngblood Henderson (2000) states that within this kinship system "plants, animals, and humans are related, and each is both a producer and a consumer with respect to the other, in an endless cycle" (p. 257). Furthermore, Youngblood Henderson states that this order of kinship "implies a distinct form of responsibilities or rights" and includes the obligation "to provide childhood experiences of collective support and attention combined with self-discipline and responsibilities to create a personality that is cooperative and independent, self-restrained yet individualistic, attuned to the feelings of others but non-intrusive" (2000, p. 260). This sacred order of the universe implies that, as human beings, we have kinship relationships that transcend the Western notion of the nuclear family.

Similarly, anthropological research suggests a kinship hypothesis in which the social roots of adoption are designed to strengthen ties rather than to sever them. De Aguayo (1995) notes that anthropologists have "found that all societies have terms to address each other, particularly kin" (p. 9) and that kin roles dictate how persons interact with each other. In such traditional societies, "adoption links close families even more closely" (p. 9). This finding demonstrates differing perspectives on adoption in Western and tribal societies. Worldview in a non-Western sense is formulated by experiencing an ecosystem (Bandura, 2003; Bevis, 1985). Based on this assumption, one could argue that the role of kinship connections for indigenous children in state care is to provide balance in their lives by providing them with cultural and ancestral knowledge. Janet Gonzales-Mena (2001) views these issues from a social justice perspective and states that "intact identities of children, not of the dominant culture, is both a goal and an issue of equity and social justice. Identity development of some children can be compromised in cross cultural care if they are immersed in the dominant culture. Culturally sensitive care is a preventative strategy for early childhood professionals to use in order to keep these children rooted in their culture and attached to their families" (p. 368). Bunting (2004), a legal researcher, examined a number of child placement decisions that concerned Aboriginal childrens' cultural background in the context of 'best interests.' She begins her article by stating that "there are no simple presumptions or tests that can capture the complexity and fluidity of children's heritage as well as their families and communities" (p. 140). Her research of legal cases and statutes is concluded with these remarks:

> First the importance of Aboriginal community or collectivist claims in individual cases should be given greater weight. Preserving connections between children and survival can be at risk after years of removal of children from Aboriginal homes. Cultural connections can also be important for children as witnessed by the poor track record for individual Aboriginal children severed from their heritage. (p. 163)

Carriere (1997) addresses the role of community in kinship care. In her interviews with kinship care providers from two First Nation communities, one participant stated that "seeing the community getting healthier" was an important aspect of kinship care, "as opposed to the children being raised 'out there' in non-Aboriginal foster homes" (Carriere, 1997, p. 50). Clearly, if the child protection industry cannot contribute to increasing the health and development of communities, then children will continue to be removed from their families and communities, and the legacy of the Sixties Scoop will never end. Kluger, Alexander, and Curtis (2001) indicate that more children in Canada are living in kinship care arrangements in response to high child welfare caseloads. However, Barbell and Freundlich (2001) warn that kinship care may be restrictive, in that caregivers hesitate to adopt "for fear of undermining existing familial relationships and due to strong cultural resistance to the termination of parents' rights" (p. 22). Walmsley (2005) states that the support for kinship care is part of family-oriented practice and that the representation of this practice is found among Aboriginal and non-Aboriginal practitioners; however, "it appears more frequently among practitioners in reserve communities and small towns, where the practitioner and family members have an ongoing relationship characterized by credibility and trust" (p. 130).

To foster a sense of balance, social workers must assist children to know their family and history. Through this process, children may then go on to recognize their place and responsibility in the larger universe, gained through cultural teachings. Importantly, this goal implies that retaining kinship ties is part of overall community health and strength. Chandler and Lalonde (1998) have explored cultural continuity as a preventative factor in the risk of youth suicide and propose that "suicide is a manifestation of failed attempts at sustaining a sense of personal and self-continuity (p. 16). Yeo (2003) contributes to this concept, stating that "the Aboriginal sense of self arises as a consequence of kinship bonds and communal life" (p. 294). As discussed earlier, kinship implies the importance of connectedness to relationships broader than those of the immediate family. Ross (1996) suggests that healing from unhealthy relationships begins with the realization "that life is a relationship and that acting individualistic in defiance of that reality will only lead everyone downhill" (p. 137). Ross implies that the more we realize that connection to others is a natural and healthy dynamic in our lives, the more whole we become. Connectedness may be described as a form of attachment that implies a broader grounding in a person's total environment than does attachment to one or two central figures. For these reasons connectedness may be a more appropriate term and framework for assessment than attachment in working with indigenous children and families.

Suggestions for practice

To make indigenous child welfare decisions without regard to historical and current social injustices such as the marginalization of indigenous women, the degradation of indigenous cultures, and the misappropriation and imposition of Euro-Western worldviews and practices onto indigenous peoples is to further these injustices.

The following suggestions are offered to assist child welfare workers to consider in culturally sensitive ways how children and their caregivers are being supported in their tasks of becoming attached and connected with each other in the parenting process. It is hoped that these suggestions will be used not only proactively but also as a means to respond constructively to difficulties by developing and strengthening the connectedness of those involved in the invaluable role of nurturing indigenous children's lives and cultures.

From attachment to connection: Dignity across the lifespan

As human beings, we long for the fulfillment of our needs. The basic needs of safety and security exist across the lifespan and take different forms according to age and where we are in the life cycle. The language of dignity may be a more culturally appropriate way of talking about connection between children and caregivers. The following descriptions of the need for human dignity at various life stages may provide workers with a guide to support safety and well-being in families. Richardson (2008) designed a diagram entitled "Dignity Across the Lifespan" as part of an indigenous human development curriculum. Richardson (2005) wrote about dignity and decolonisation in the process of family group conferencing with indigenous families. Richardson and Wade (2008) wrote about the importance of attending to human dignity in a paper entitled *Working with Safety: Response-based approaches to violence in child welfare*. This microanalysis of dignity came from teachings from former political prisoners and residential school survivors who identified humiliation as one of the worst indignities of violence. Many families who receive child welfare services experience this intervention as an affront to their dignity and a reminder of other humiliating professional interactions. As we have discussed, affronts to human dignity tend to interfere with well-intentioned child welfare interventions, and the energy diverted from parents in dealing with authorities may sabotage their chances of demonstrating what they are doing well. The fact that many child welfare interventions are involuntary means that the importance of dignity cannot be overlooked in the process.

At each stage of life, caregivers such as mothers and fathers need to be accorded dignity so that they can accord the same dignity to their infants and children. Although many parents do offer their children safe and secure relationships despite not having that same dignity extended to them, energy can be diverted away from parenting in times of negative social situations, creating challenges for parents. When parents talk about the challenges imposed by the outside world, they are sometimes seen as complaining, ranting or not taking responsibility for their part in it (for example, they receive a negative social response). This is particularly so for people who are socially marginalized and must deal with affronts to their dignity and autonomy on a daily basis. In parenting, dignity is accorded to children by attending to their daily and longer term needs, relative to the particular stage of development. As philosopher Vartan Gregoria (in Derrida, 1988) reminds us: "Dignity is not negotiable." Without dignity, people experience what can be called a "social wound," which may or may not be addressed or restored later in life. Treatment such as neglect, dismissal, humiliation, or abuse constitutes a social wounding, while care, attention, love, and respect (positive social responses) assist people of all ages in filling their being with a sense of worth. This self-worth serves a protective function and creates a feeling of holistic well-being that may then be carried into various life encounters. The preservation of human dignity became one of the main focuses of Richardson and Wade's work in relation to assisting people to recover from violence (2008).

In infancy, the dignity of the young one is met by responding, in culturally appropriate ways, to calls for love through the offering of physical contact, food, familiarity of voices and scents, cleanliness, and a safe family and community environment. Inuit mental health worker Edward Allan (personal communication, Vancouver, BC, March 2008) reports that Inuit children often identify family as being more important than food. Children have explained to him that if you have family, you are more likely to have food. Ideally, the mother/child dyad needs to be supported by the father and by extended family and community. The mother may need support for breastfeeding, for spending extended periods of time with the infant, and for taking time away from work. She may need financial and other support to provide nurturance in the form of food and drink, as well as emotional kindness. Mothering can be undermined in varying degrees by a lack of security, such as violence, humiliation, and psychological abuse.

At this stage in the life cycle, fathers may need to be supported in the role of protector, provider, and nurturer of the mother and the child. This support may take the form of flexible employment, support to be away from work for longer periods of time, and emotional support during a time of transition in the spousal relationship. For indigenous fathers, this may mean that society must address the extremely high rates of unemployment on reserves and the obstacles to hunting and food-gathering that exist in Canada. The expansion of the family may mean a change of routine and relationship for all family members.

Older children engage in exploration of their world, and they need safety and support, and trust that the caregiver will still be there when they return from their explorations. Children need the security of extended family, community, and culture to ensure a sense of belonging and to feel a part of the larger group. Children declare their need for dignity by responding intensely to being humiliated or mocked by others. During this stage, the mother's dignity can be supported when she is reminded that she is doing a good job, and when she is given time to rest and keep herself healthy, with good food and loving kindness from those around her. The dignity of the father is supported by being acknowledged for his role in supporting the mother and child, and by experiencing success and esteem in the outer world, as well as in the home. He can be assisted by Elders and other family members who share a perspective about raising children and becoming a parent in a long line of tradition in the family. For both the mother and father, learning about the histories of raising children in accordance with familial and cultural ways may support their unique situation, even more than learning through popular books and television. Of course, the dignity of the parents may be preserved at times by resisting unsolicited advice and doing things in a way that suit the unique child and the parents' own values and preferences.

In adolescence, a sense of safety and security is needed while teens test the limits of their parents' care. While an adolescent asserts her independence and seeks to consolidate her identity, we see the importance of cultural teachers and Elders in reminding her of the good way to live. The teen can experience indignity when asked (often repeatedly) to perform certain tasks—like cleaning her room—that have been assigned by others. Creating space for adolescents to choose, as much as possible, the ways in which they will contribute to the well-being of the family and household, along with parents both accepting their need for independence and holding the teen within safe parameters and value-based expectations for social interaction, may enhance the teen's dignity. Many indigenous adolescents are already parents and learn about culture and appropriate ways of being alongside their children, ideally with the guidance of Elders and teachers. The dignity of the whole family may be at stake when it faces discrimination, lack of employment, or various forms of humiliation in the social world and when forced to receive service, particularly from outside the community. Today, dealing with the workplace, educational institutions, or government bureaucracies often involves forms of power abuse that result in humiliation for individuals and that harm their personal dignity.

As adolescents move into the realm of young adulthood, and then beyond into mature adults, their dignity is enhanced by their sense of accomplishment and respect in the outer world. Many indigenous adults suffer due to the violence and even torture inflicted upon them in state-sponsored institutions and programs. Supporting healing in the community, in ways that proactively restore dignity and prepare adults for roles of leadership and community governance, simultaneously strengthens their capacity to function as role models for community members and as caregivers to children. Kim Anderson, an indigenous woman on a journey back to a cultural community, describes how the Elders were crucial in welcoming her home. She writes:

> The thing that I found most helpful was the way I saw elders look at me. Many seemed to look right through the barriers, the politics, the boundaries and the status debates. Reflected in their eyes, I began to see myself as a granddaughter, a member and a relation. (Anderson, 2000, p. 29)

Many Elders are the keepers of traditional knowledge and hold the important task of teaching, raising their grandchildren and supporting young parents. Yet Elders, too, need dignity, safety, and security to live out their traditional ways of being. Dignity includes having the freedom to extend caring to others, which is what Elders have often done in their communities.

Today, dignity is not always accorded to people in our society, and this lack of dignified treatment is often misread as intrapsychic dysfunction or pathology through the lens of professionals. Realistically, we see that Canadian society is rampant with discrimination against indigenous people and minority groups, and with violence against women and children. An appropriate social analysis must include issues of class, race and gender within the historical context of colonialism and imperialism. To understand the community devastation of indigenous peoples, it is important to become familiar with the Indian Act and how this legislation continues to undermine First Nation, Métis, and Inuit families in Canada. When families are humiliated and destabilized, in both mundane and large-scale ways, they have less freedom or "room to move" in terms of dedicating their energy to their children while being called upon to address social concerns. Many anti-oppression theorists tell us that "whenever people are treated badly, they resist in some way" (Brown, 1991; Scott, 1990; Wade, 1997). Dignity is the central concern in finding ways to preserve family safety and integrity while seeking one's own (and collective) liberation against violence and oppression.

One tool of intervention for families may be the connection to cultural tradition—but tradition as a living rather than a static entity. Laguna writer Leslie Marmon Silko (cited in Anderson, 2000) reminds us that tradition includes "making do with whatever [is] available" and "adaptation for survival" (p. 35). For service providers and those engaged in assessing families, it is crucial to use tools that seek to discover what is right with people, rather than what is wrong, and that consider the social context and how disrupted dignity skews the results of assessment. The BC Office of the Provincial Advisor for Aboriginal Infant Development Programs offers the following advice for practitioners:

> The AIDP office recommends either assessment with the knowledge neither is culturally specific or relevant. Aboriginal children, especially those living in traditional communities, start disadvantaged by many of the developmental assessments used in the ECD field. It is felt by many Aboriginal professionals and parents that the assessment tools do not show accurately what the children *do know*. (Office of the Provincial Advisor for Aboriginal Infant Development Programs, 2008, p. 3)

CONCLUSION

The longing for connection and home brings suffering to many indigenous children, as it did to Richard Cardinal. Like many indigenous children in Canada, Richard lived on "foreign ground" (Kroetsch, 1995, p. 395). The connection that he sought, sadly, remained a longing of the heart, until he could no longer bear its absence.

A better understanding is needed of how the connection between child welfare interventions and human dignity relate to positive outcomes for everyone concerned. More research is needed involving a microanalysis of child welfare court documents and psychological assessments to better understand how indigenous families are construed through the deficit lens of Western psychology, and how these constructions are influencing child welfare decisions. Walmsley (2005) reviewed child protection literature and policy and interviewed child protection workers. He concludes that his research demonstrates that "child protection practitioners with a social work education make little use of scientific knowledge in practice; rather, experience—whether professional, personal, familial or communal—appears most influential in practice decision making. Although experience is arguably a powerful influence in life, little is known about how it intersects with ideas, theories, or facts in the course of a social work education" (pp. 136-7).

The research conducted by and reviewed by the authors suggests that by supporting connectedness and cultural identity for indigenous children and families, service providers may help turn longing into belonging. This spiritual transformation will inevitably help indigenous children to deal with racism, ethnocentrism, and the many social challenges they will meet growing up on the foreign ground of Canadian soil. It is our hope that future social responses to the Richard Cardinals and the mothers of Richard Cardinals in the Canadian child welfare system will actively encourage a sense of dignity and belonging.

ACKNOWLEDGEMENTS

The authors extend gratitude to Richard Cardinal for what he is teaching us about ourselves and our profession. Also, a warm thanks to Sarah Flynn and Leslie Prpich for their multifaceted assistance and to Allan Wade for ongoing inspiration and encouragement to look at both the micro as well as the macro aspects of colonization and the helping professions.

REFERENCES

Anderson, K. (2000). *A recognition of being: Reconstructing Native womanhood*. Toronto, ON: Sumach Press.

Atkinson, J. (2002). *Trauma trials, recreating song lines: The transgenerational effects of trauma in Indigenous Australia*. Melbourne: Spinifex Press.

Bandura, A. (2003). On the psychosocial impact and mechanisms of spiritual modeling. *International Journal for the Psychology of Religion, 13*, 167-173.

Barbell, K., Freundlich, K. M. (2001). *Foster Care Today*. Washington: Casey Family Programs.

Bennett, M. (2007). Aboriginal mothers' involvement with child protection and family court systems: Examining alternative court processes. *Canada's Children* (Winter), 88-93.

Bevis, W. (1985). Native American novels: Honing. In B. Swann & A. Krupat (Eds.), *Recovering the word: Essays on Native American literature* (pp. 580-620). Berkeley, CA: University of California Press.

Blackstock, C. (2008). *The breath of life: When everything matters in child welfare*. Paper presented to University of Victoria Aboriginal Child Welfare Research Symposium, February 15, Victoria, BC.

Borders, D. I., Penny, J. M., & Portnoy, F. (2000). Adult adoptees and their friends: Current functioning and psychosocial well-being. *Family Relations, 49*(4), 407–418.

Boss, P. (1999). *Ambiguous loss: Learning to live with grief*. Cambridge, MA: Harvard University Press.

Brodzinsky, D. M., & Schechter, M. D. (1990). *The psychology of adoption*. New York: Oxford University Press.

Brown, L. M. (1991). Telling a girl's life: Self-authorization as a form of resistance. In C. Gilligan, A. G. Rogers, & D. O. Tolman (Eds.), *Women, girls, and psychotherapy: Reframing resistance* (pp. 71–86). New York: Haworth Press.

Bunting, A. (2004). Complicating Culture in Child Placements Decisions. *Canadian J. Women and the Law, 16*, 137-164.

Carrière, J. (1997). Kinship care: A community alternative to foster care. *Native Social Work Journal*. Sudbury, ON: Laurentien University.

Carriere, J. (2005). Connectedness and health for First Nations adoptees. *Paediatrics & Child Health, 10*(9), 545–548.

Carriere, J. (2007). Promising practice for maintaining identities in First Nations adoption. *First Peoples Child and Family Review, 3*(1), 46–64.

Chandler, M., & Lalonde, C. (1998). Cultural continuity as a hedge against suicide in Canada's First Nations. Transcultural Psychiatry, 35(2), 191-219.

Crichlow, W. (2002). Western colonization as disease: Native adoption and cultural genocide. Canadian Social Work, 5(1), 88-107.

De Aguayo, A. (1995). Background paper on customary adoption. RCAP Notes. Ottawa, ON: Royal Commission on Aboriginal Peoples Report.

Derrida, J. (1988). Limited, inc. Evanston, IL: University of Illinois Press.

Gonzales-Mena, J. (2001). Cross-Cultural Infant Care and Issues of Equity and Social Justice. In. Contemporary Issues in Early Childhood. Vol. 2. No. 3. 368-371.

Government of British Columbia. (2008, March). Statistics on Aboriginal children in care. Victoria, BC: Ministry of Children and Family Development.

Government of Canada. (2006). Statistics Canada: Aboriginal Peoples in Canada in 2006: Inuit, Metis and First Nations, 2006 Census. Catalogue no. 97-558.XIE. retrieved October 13, 2008.

Government of Canada. (1996). Gathering strength. Report of the Royal Commission on Aboriginal Peoples (Vol. 3). Ottawa, ON: Author.

Hendry, L. B., & Reid, M. (2000). Social relationships and health: The meaning of social connectedness and how it relates to health concerns for rural Scottish adolescents. Journal of Adolescence, 23, 705–719.

Kluger, M. P., Alexander, G., & Curtis, P. A. (2001). What works in child welfare. Washington: Child Welfare League of America.

Kroetsch, R. (1995). Unhiding the hidden. In B. Ashcroft, G. Griffiths, & H. Tiffin (Eds.). The post-colonial studies reader (pp. 394-396). New York: Routledge.

Lee, R., Lee, S., & Draper, M. (2001). Social connectedness, dysfunctional interpersonal behaviors, and psychological distress: Testing a mediator model. Journal of Counseling Psychology, 48(3), 310–318.

Littlebear, L. (2000). Jagged worldviews colliding. In M. Battiste (Ed.), Reclaiming Indigenous voice and vision (p. 77). Vancouver, BC: UBC Press.

March, K. (1995). The stranger who bore me: Adoptee-birth mother relationships. Toronto, ON: University of Toronto Press.

McCain, M. N., & Mustard, J. F. (1999). The early years study: Reversing the real brain drain. Toronto, ON: Children's Secretariat.

McCain, M. N., & Mustard, J. F. (2002). The early years study. Three years later. From early childhood development to human development: Enabling communities. Toronto, ON: Founders' Network.

Molloy, V. (2002). Identity, past and present in an historical child-care setting. *Psychological Practice, 8*(2), 163–178.

Obomsawin, A. (Director). (1986). *Richard Cardinal: Cry from the diary of a Métis child* [Film]. Ottawa, ON: National Film Board of Canada.

Office of the Provincial Advisor for Aboriginal Infant Development Programs. (2008). *Newsletter*. Victoria, BC: BC Association of Aboriginal Friendship Centres.

Red Horse, J., Martinez, C., Day, P. A., Day, D., Poupart, J., & Scharnberg, D. (2000). *Family preservation: Concepts in American Indian communities*. Portland, OR: National Indian Child Welfare Association.

Resnick, M. D., Harris, L. J., & Blum, R. W. (1993). The impact of caring and connectedness on adolescent health and well-being. *Paediatric Child Health, 29*(Suppl. 1), S3–S9.

Richardson, C. (2008). *Indigenous Parenting as Healing*. For the Temiskaming Native Women's Support Group, Ontario.

Richardson, C. (2005). Steps to dignity and decolonization: Family group conferencing in Aboriginal communities. Restorative Directions, March.

Richardson, C., & Wade, A. (2008). Taking Resistance Seriously: A Response-Based Approach to Social Work in Cases of Violence against Indigenous Women. In S. Strega and J. Carrière (Eds.), *Walking this path together*. Winnipeg: Fernwood Press.

Rillera, M. J. (1987). *Adoption Encounter: Hurt, Transition and Healing*. Huntington Beach: Triadoption Library.

Ross, R. (1996). *Return to the teachings*. Toronto, ON: Penguin.

Scott, J. (1990). *Domination and the arts of resistance: Hidden transcripts*. New Haven, CT: Yale University Press.

Sinclair, R. (2007). Identities lost and found: Lessons from the sixties scoop. *First Peoples Child and Family Review, 3*(1), 65–82.

Slap, G., Goodman, E., & Huang, B. (2001). Adoption as a risk factor for attempted suicide during adolescence. *Pediatrics, 108*(2), 1–8.

Trocmé, N., Knoke, D., & Blackstock, C. (2004). Pathways to the over representation of Aboriginal children in Canada's child welfare system. *Social Services Review*, December, 578–599.

Wade, A. (1997). Small acts of living: Everyday resistance to violence and other forms of oppression. *Journal of Contemporary Family Therapy, 19*, 23–40.

Wade, A. (2000). Resistance to interpersonal violence: Implications for the practice of therapy. Unpublished doctoral dissertation, University of Victoria, Victoria, BC.

Walmsley, C. (2005). *Protecting Aboriginal Children*. Vancouver: UBC Press.

Wolin, S. J., & Wolin, S. (1993). *Bound and determined: Growing up resilient in a troubled family*. New York: Villard Press.

Yeo, S. S. (2003). Bonding and attachment of Australian Aboriginal children. *Child Abuse Review, 12*, 292–304.

Youngblood Henderson, J. S. (2000). Postcolonial ghost dancing: Diagnosing European colonialism. In M. Battiste (Ed.), *Reclaiming Indigenous voice and vision* (pp. 57–76). Vancouver, BC: UBC Press.

CHAPTER 4

Jumping through Hoops: A Manitoba Study Examining Experiences and Reflections of Aboriginal Mothers Involved with Child Welfare in Manitoba

Marlyn Bennett

INTRODUCTION

In 2005 Ka Ni Kanichihk, an urban-based Aboriginal organization in Winnipeg, launched a study focusing on the experience and the dispro-portionate representation of Aboriginal women involved in the child protection system in Manitoba and consequently the role of the justice system in their lives and that of their children. Ka Ni Kanichihk, along with several community organizations and institutions, initiated a co-alition of stakeholders to oversee the project and to explore the nature of Aboriginal mothers' experiences in child protection cases before the courts in Manitoba. It was necessary to understand the nature of Aborigi-nal mother's experiences before we could actually begin to understand

SUGGESTED CITATION: Bennett, M. (2009). Jumping through hoops: A Manitoba study examining experiences and reflections of Aboriginal mothers involved with child welfare in Manitoba. In S. McKay, D. Fuchs, & I. Brown (Eds.), *Passion for action in child and family services: Voices from the prairies* (pp. 69-98). Regina, SK: Canadian Plains Research Center.

and implement alternative dispute resolutions processes and how to prevent Aboriginal mothers from experiencing adversarial interaction with
the child welfare and legal systems.

This paper briefly describes Aboriginal mothers' experiences with
child welfare workers, the child welfare system, legal representatives
and Aboriginal mothers' understanding of alternative dispute resolutions. The findings draw from in-depth recorded interviews and talking
circles conducted with 32 Aboriginal mothers[1] during the time between
March and June, 2007. The voices, perspectives, emotions and child
welfare experience of Aboriginal mothers are the heart and soul of this
research, and only the findings and themes extrapolated from these interviews and talking circles held with Aboriginal mothers are addressed
in this chapter. In addition, this paper highlights solutions and recommendations identified by the mothers involved in this study about how
child welfare and family court systems can begin improving relations
and working better with and for Aboriginal mothers and their children.

OBJECTIVES

The research initiative was designed to specifically address a gap in
knowledge for Ka Ni Kanichihk around the process and outcomes of Aboriginal women's experiences with Aboriginal and non-Aboriginal child
welfare agencies on- and off-reserve, as well as agencies situated in urban or rural localities. The study focused on four areas:

- Describing and analyzing the experiences of Métis, First Nations,
  Inuit and other Aboriginal women who are or have been involved
  in child welfare/protection cases before the courts in Manitoba.
- Examining the experience and understanding of service providers and other advocates working with Métis, First Nations, Inuit
  and other Aboriginal women involved in child welfare/protec-
  tion cases in the courts in Manitoba.
- Examining the experience of lawyers tasked with representing
  Métis, First Nations, Inuit and other Aboriginal women involved
  in child welfare/protection cases before the courts in Manitoba.

---

1   Many of the women who participated in this study also identified as being
    grandmothers. This paper reflects the voices and perspectives from both moth-
    ers and grandmothers. They have been collectively referred to as "mothers"
    throughout.

- Seeking ideas and suggested solutions to inform less adversarial and least intrusive approaches to dealing with child protection matters involving Métis, First Nations, Inuit and other Aboriginal women and children.

METHODOLOGY

This research took a phenomenological approach to understanding the lived experiences and perceptions about child welfare and legal systems experiences through the personal lens of Aboriginal mothers and grandmothers. Phenomenology is about the essential meanings individuals give to their experiences, as well as the social construction of group realities. To gather such data, in-depth interviews were undertaken with mothers who had directly experienced the phenomenon of interest; that is, they had a "lived experience" as opposed to second-hand experience (Patton, 2002). A variety of qualitative activities were utilized in collecting data for understanding Aboriginal mothers' experiences, including:

- A literature review (focusing on the following seven areas: the context of Aboriginal lives; child welfare and family court experiences of Aboriginal women in Canada; alternative forms of dispute resolutions in the child welfare context; mediation in child protection cases; family group conferencing and family group decision-making in child protection; access to legal counsel; and alternative response models);
- Creation of a survey-based personal information form (for statistical and background purposes);
- One-on-one interviews with Aboriginal mothers who have been at risk of having, or have had, their children apprehended because of child protection concerns;
- Facilitation of talking circles[2] with Aboriginal mothers about their child welfare and court experiences.

---

2   Since we wished to audio record the discussions that were held in the circle, we decided to conduct a talking circle instead of a traditional sharing circle which does not allow for recording. The talking circle is a way for Aboriginal people to share and/or solve problems. It is a very effective way to remove barriers and to allow people to express themselves with complete freedom and allows for recording unlike other types of sharing circles (see Mi'Kmaw Talking Circles at http://www.muiniskw.org/pgCulture2c.htm).

The research activities, in addition, centered on capturing Aboriginal mothers' ideas and solutions for change that could be implemented to create greater awareness about Aboriginal mothers' experiences with the child welfare and child protection matters before the courts.

Ethics

Various research instruments and consent forms were developed prior to collecting data. An ethical review was conducted through the Prairie Women's Health Centre of Excellence (PWHCE) in Manitoba. Three Aboriginal women (scholars with University affiliations), in addition to staff at PWHCE, assisted in conducting the ethical review and all provided written statements for strengthening the project. This feedback was incorporated into the data collection phase of the project.

Recruitment

Aboriginal mothers who had involvement with the child welfare system in Manitoba were recruited from Winnipeg and The Pas, Manitoba. Recruitment was done through an email strategy and by word of mouth, utilizing the networks of Ka Ni Kanichihk, the Steering Committee,[3] the Research Team, and the First Nations Child & Family Caring Society of Canada. In addition, posters about the project were distributed through various community organizations both in Winnipeg and The Pas, Manitoba. Members of the research team fielded random calls from interested Aboriginal women. The first 32 women who met the criteria for the study were then invited to participate in either an interview or talking circle. The criteria required that participants be Aboriginal (First Nations, Métis, Inuit and non-status Aboriginal) women, eighteen years of age or older. Participants had to have had direct experience of apprehension or had to have been at risk of having their children apprehended by either an Aboriginal / First Nations Child Welfare service agency and/or a non-Aboriginal Child Welfare service agency within the province of Manitoba. The women had the choice of participating in either a one-on-one interview or in a talking circle or both. The reason for having

---

3   The members of the steering committee were appointed by Ka Ni Kanichihk. The steering committee was comprised of individuals representing various organizations within the community who had a vested interest in the research conducted.

two different ways of collecting data was simply to get an individual and collective social understanding of Aboriginal mothers' phenomena in dealing with the child welfare and legal systems in Manitoba. The personal interviews and the talking circles were conducted between March and June in 2007. Members of the research team met mothers in their homes or the mothers met with the members of the research team at their offices or they met at neutral and safe locations within the community where the mother resided.

LIMITATIONS

We were not able to interview as many service providers and/or advocates as originally targeted in the work plan because of the attention on the child welfare system by the media during the later part of the summer and into the fall of 2007. During the data collection phase of this project the Government of Manitoba commissioned two external reviews into the child and family services system as a result of the tragic death of five-year-old Phoenix Sinclair in March 2006. Two subsequent reports were completed (Strengthen the Commitment Report, which focuses on case management practices across the system, and Honouring Their Spirits Report, which examined child deaths between 2003 and 2006[4]). Over 200 recommendations emerged for improving the child and family services system with an overarching theme of continued commitment to the Aboriginal Justice Inquiry-Child Welfare Initiative (AJI-CWI). The AJI-CWI represented a joint initiative among four parties: the Province of Manitoba; the Manitoba Métis Federation; the Assembly of Manitoba Chiefs; and the Manitoba Keewatinook Ininew Okimowin. The purpose of this joint initiative was to work together through a common process to develop and subsequently oversee the implementation of a plan to restructure the child welfare system in Manitoba. An essential feature of this restructuring was the expansion of off-reserve authority for First Nations and the establishment of a province-wide Métis mandate. Restructuring of the child welfare system was completed in 2005.[5]

---

4   Changes for Children, Strengthening the Commitment to Child Welfare (October 13, 2006), highlights the Manitoba government's response to these reviews in which they committed $42 million in new funding until the end of the 2008/09 to implement the recommendations from the two external reviews.

5   In November 2003, the Child and Family Services Authorities Act proclaimed

In addition to the two external reviews, the four provincial Child and Family Services Authorities immediately announced that they would be conducting their own reviews in which child protection workers within the province were asked to have contact with every child in care or receiving service from the child and family services system. This extraordinary measure was taken to assure families and the public that children receiving services from the system were known, accounted for and safe. It is therefore understandable and recognized that these events and activities may have had some impact on the participation and inclusion of frontline child welfare staff in this study.

Further, the subjective nature inherent in this research needs to be acknowledged. Finally, no claim to universal generalizability of the results can be made.

PROCEDURES

Interviews

A total of 32 women participated in this study. Twenty-five of the 32 mothers participated in interviews. The interview format included a) the establishment of rapport, b) sharing of narratives, and c) appropriate closure. During the engagement process with Aboriginal mothers, roles were clarified and issues of confidentiality and anonymity were reviewed. In order to encourage Aboriginal mothers/grandmothers' participation, the actual interview was open-ended, was minimally structured, and had no time limitations.

Individual interviews lasted anywhere from twenty minutes to one and one-half hours in duration. Interviews with the mothers were conducted by one of the three team members. Two talking circles were held

---

the establishment of four child and family service authorities in Manitoba (Northern, Southern, Métis and General Authorities) – all parties signatory to the Memoranda of Understanding under the Aboriginal Justice Inquiry-Child Welfare Initiative (AJI-CWI) agreed to this. These authorities are each responsible for the governance of their respective child and family service agencies. These authorities play a key role in coordinating child welfare services province-wide and are the governing bodies overseeing services, dispersing funds and ensuring that culturally appropriate standards and practices are delivered by their respective agencies and are consistent with the applicable Provincial Child and Family Services and Adoption Acts.

in Winnipeg, while one talking circle took place in The Pas, Manitoba. All interviews and talking circles were audio-taped and later transcribed verbatim. During the course of the interviews and talking circles, participants were asked to clarify and expand on issues that required further elaboration. When the participants appeared to become detached from the topic, they were gently re-directed. When researchers felt that the participants' experiences had been fully articulated, mothers were asked: Is there anything else that you would like to add that has not yet been addressed? Following the verbatim transcription, a copy of the transcript was shared with the mothers, who were then thanked and invited to reflect and elaborate further on their experiences.

Participants involved in the talking circles were encouraged to share their thoughts and perspectives but were asked to respect the privacy of other women participating in the circles. They were asked to keep everything they heard and learned from others in the circles confidential. Participants signed the consent form, agreeing to keep what they heard in the circles confidential. Copies of the transcript from the talking circles were shared with the participants, who then had an opportunity to provide feedback on the contents.

Stages of Data Analysis

Immediately after each interview, the audio tape was carefully listened to and reviewed, in an attempt to gain an awareness of the experiences described by the Aboriginal mothers. Each interview was then transcribed into a written protocol and read in its entirety several times. During final readings of the entire protocol, significant statements were extracted, paraphrased, and given meaning. Once transcribed, the interviews and talking circles conducted for this study yielded over 500 pages of rich narrative text.

After analysis of the research findings, several predominant themes emerged, along with interrelated subthemes. Collectively, the mothers' narratives about their experiences with the child welfare and legal profession revealed six predominant themes. These included:

- How Aboriginal mothers came into contact with child welfare;
- Understanding the background context of Aboriginal mothers' lives;
- Treatment by staff within the child welfare system (i.e., treatment by child welfare staff and supervisors, racism, visitation, etc.);

- The mothers' insight into their experiences (acknowledging their own mistakes, emotions, coping, etc.);
- Mothers' experiences with lawyers; and
- Mothers' knowledge of alternative dispute resolutions used in the child welfare context.

Due to space constraints this chapter doesn't address the full extent of the themes. The report which captures the full essence of these findings can be downloaded from the Caring Society website.[6]

We met many Aboriginal mothers and grandmothers who shared amazing stories about their experiences with both urban and rural Aboriginal and non-Aboriginal child welfare agencies in the province of Manitoba. The mothers often started out by sharing stories about how they first came into contact with the child welfare system within the province. For many of these mothers, involvement with the child welfare system first began when they were children or youth and then again when they grew into adulthood and had children of their own. The majority of the women we interviewed were 41-50 years old and were single mothers. Their stories reflect collective and common perceptions about how the child welfare system functions and operates against them because of their poverty and substance misuse. They all indicated needing assistance accessing services to support them in their roles as parents. As time was a factor the analysis of the data was conducted primarily by the main investigator, with assistance from the research team and advisory committee.

LITERATURE REVIEW[7]

Meager research exists about Aboriginal mothers' experiences with child welfare systems or the courts in relation to child protection issues in Canada. Seminal research first conducted on the issue of Aboriginal motherhood and the child welfare system was done by University of British Columbia law professor Marlee Kline. Kline laid the groundwork for understanding how the inter-sectionality of race, gender and

---

6   http://www.fncaringsociety.com/projects/docs/FCDP_Final_Report_Bennett_2008.pdf

7   A more extensive literature review can be found in the final report. Portions of this review were also published previously in the journal *Canada's Children* (Bennett, 2007).

class worked in relation to the application of child welfare laws in cases involving First Nations mothers. Kline challenged assumptions about what makes a "good mother," including the ideal of "motherly self-sacrifice" and the notion that all mothers belong to a nuclear family. Kline (1989) indicated that this ideology was an improper yardstick to use for Aboriginal mothers, particularly because Aboriginal families view the sacrifice of child-rearing as a shared one. In a thesis prepared for her Masters of Law degree, Kline (1990) clearly analyzed the centrality of the "best interests of the child" doctrine as applied in First Nations child welfare cases. The substance of Kline's thesis deduced that this doctrine is a major contributing factor in the destructive and assimilationist impacts of the child welfare system on First Nations children and families because the judicial decision-making has downplayed, if not completely negated, the relevance and importance of maintaining a child's First Nations identity and culture.

In another highly quoted article, Kline (1993) argued that dominant ideologies of motherhood are imposed on First Nations women in child welfare cases. First, Kline observed that the law created a conceptual framework within which First Nations women are blamed for the difficulties they experience in child-raising, which in turn obfuscates the roots of those difficulties in the history and current dynamics of colonialism and racial oppression. Secondly, Kline pointed out that "the ideology of motherhood operates to impose dominant culture values and practices in relation to child-raising in First Nations families, and conversely to devalue different values and practices of First Nations families. The combined effect of these two processes is to leave First Nations women particularly vulnerable to being constructed by courts as 'bad mothers' in child welfare proceedings, and consequently open to having their children taken away as a result" (p. 306). Kline's important research on the legal issues impacting Aboriginal motherhood and their encounters with the judicial system around issues of child welfare law were truly groundbreaking both in Canada and internationally.

The correlation of Aboriginal women and the child welfare systems is also the focus of research conducted by Patricia Monture-Angus, a Mohawk woman, lawyer and scholar. Monture-Angus (1989, 1995) has written exclusively about the way legislative bodies and courts have historically undervalued or ignored the cultural identity of First Nations children in child protection matters. This disregard for the "indigenous factor," along with the pressure to assimilate, places tremendous psychological burdens on First Nations children, families and communities. Monture-Angus argues that removing children from their homes and communities has resulted in the destruction of the traditional way of life within Native communities; in the process, cultures are being destroyed. Removing First Nations children from their homes and placing them in a foreign culture has been characterized by Monture-Angus as an act of genocide, an accusation that has been supported in subsequent judicial reports (see Kimmelman, 1985).

Two more current resources looking at the experiences of Aboriginal women involved with the child welfare system are based on research conducted in British Columbia. One is a study focused on the experiences of women involved with child welfare services conducted by the National Action Committee on the Status of Women in British Columbia (Kellington, 2002). A second companion document outlines findings from community forums held with Aboriginal women in British Columbia (MacDonald, 2002).

Aboriginal mothers were among the three particular communities of mothers at the heart of the National Action Committee on the Status of Women in British Columbia (NACBC) study which sought to understand the social factors that act as causal instigators to mothers' involvement with the child welfare system in BC. The study recognized that mothers came into contact with the child welfare system in one of three ways: (1) through a self-referral process; (2) on the basis of reports made by other people; or (3) through other government system referrals that might have come about as a result of their children needing medical care. Kellington (2002) observed that background factors must be acknowledged that may help to shed some light on the experiences that have shaped mothers' lives at the time of their interaction with the child welfare system. Some of these factors include women's past histories of abuse. Many of the women were survivors of childhood abuse, either physical, sexual or both. Some were still learning to deal with the ramifications of these experiences in their own lives at the time their children were involved with the child welfare system. Some of the mothers had themselves been in care as a child, and many had been exposed to various forms of abuse while they were in care as a child. This experience was especially noted by the Aboriginal and First Nations women who were conscious of the systemic devastation and destruction of their communities as a result of residential schools and a multitude of other historic oppressions (p. 15). One of the other mitigating background factors identified was that many of the women involved with child welfare were living in abusive relationships at the time child welfare came into their lives, a situation, they noted, that replicated the very relationships of power, control and authority they were attempting to leave behind in their abusive relationships.

Kellington's report on women's experiences with the BC child welfare system also provides insight into the negative and positive experiences of women involved with child welfare that transcend the racial, cultural and class barriers. Some of the ways that mothers coped with the stress of child welfare intervention in their lives were also identified. Kellington notes that one of the most important reasons for conducting this study was to find out what women wanted to see happen to improve their experiences with the child welfare system in BC. The recommendations suggested by the mothers who participated in this study include ideas on how to implement more comprehensive and broad-ranging preventative services that would be useful and would impact on mothers and children in a more positive way than what currently exists. Current punitive approaches in child welfare do little to produce healthy, productive societies, and punishing women is all too often what happens (Cull, 2006). This is not the most socially supportive response that should come from governments. Women indicated that services should be aimed directly at parents as a means of ensuring resources also reach their children. Another recommendation included instituting a "Mothers' Advocate Office" to assist mothers in particular with a stronger voice in articulating their needs and concerns at the policy-making and developmental levels when dealing with government. Their recommendations also reiterate that there needs to be better resources and protection to those responsible for raising children.

Kellington (2002) noted that very little literature exists in the form of studies, reports, or articles giving voice to the experiences and perspectives of mothers' interactions with the child welfare system. Furthermore that very little exists about how Aboriginal mothers' experience with the children welfare system differs from that experienced by non-Aboriginal mothers. Thus, a companion report to the NACBC study—the "Missing Voices Project"—was prepared by Kelly MacDonald later in the same year (2002) to fill this void. Forty-one Aboriginal women were encouraged to share their stories and experiences with respect to their involvement with the child welfare systems in BC (MacDonald, 2002). In some cases, women reported that it was unclear to them as to why their children had been removed (p. 25). Most of the removals were court-ordered and very few mothers were given the option of voluntarily placing their children in care while they dealt with their underlying issues.

Many of the Aboriginal mothers expressed that the manner in which their children were apprehended was traumatic. Mothers' perceptions were that the child abuse investigations were inadequate and missed important information. Many mothers expressed frustration with what they perceived as social worker's changing expectations or with the perceived lack of attention given by social workers to mothers' concerns. Mothers shared that they endured numerous changes with respect to the social workers assigned to their case, resulting in their children staying in care longer. This contributed to difficulties developing trust in the Ministry. Mothers noted that their social workers were young, making it difficult to relate to them. Racism and disrespect toward Aboriginal mothers were also evident in many of the stories related to MacDonald. One participant in particular shared that the "social worker I dealt with was condescending, rude, disrespectful of me in front of my children. She attacked my parenting she attacked everything about me in front of my children" (p. 31).

MacDonald documented that there were concerns with respect to the lawyers assigned to Aboriginal mothers involved with child welfare. Some Aboriginal mothers felt that they were inadequately represented, while others spoke highly of their legal representatives. Many mothers noted that their lawyer advised them to be agreeable with the child welfare plans and court orders presented to them in court; the assumption was that they would get their children back sooner. Their lawyer did not see merit in challenging court decisions. When MacDonald presented the mothers with a guide that was designed specifically to assist Aboriginal mothers with navigating the child welfare system in BC, many of the Aboriginal mothers were unaware of what their legal rights were (p. 32). Many mothers indicated that they were misled into believing their children would be in care only for a short period of time (3 months) when, in fact, the time turned out to be longer (6 months or more).

The forums conducted by MacDonald on Aboriginal experiences with the child welfare system provided many of the mothers with their first opportunity to voice concerns respecting the child welfare system in BC. Many of the mothers talked about the emotional repercussions from losing their children. These emotional repercussions centred on grief and loss and the guilt associated with the removal of their children. What was clear to MacDonald was that there was a need for Aboriginal mothers to have more opportunities to express and deal with as well as heal from the pain of losing their children through the child protection process. MacDonald, relying on the findings of another professional (Vera Fahlberg, M.D.), stated that mothers feel and experience the same level of psychological ramifications from removal as do children who are removed (p. 34).

As MacDonald (2002) noted in her research, alcohol abuse by the mother was the primary reason behind the apprehension of many of the Aboriginal mothers' children in BC. What is interesting to note is that many of the Aboriginal mothers who participated in MacDonald's forums felt that child welfare workers did not understand the dynamics of alcohol and drug addiction. One participant noted that "relapse is part of recovery" and research conducted by Callahan and colleagues (1994) found that "lack of training opportunities for workers, particularly in alcohol and drug misuse, was noted repeatedly as an organizational barrier to best practice" among social workers (p. 34). This was also identified by MacDonald as a serious void in the training of social workers by universities and the Ministry. Many of the women in MacDonald's study increased their alcohol intake as a result of the emotional pain they experienced when their children were apprehended. The emotional turmoil experienced by mothers who had children apprehended was further compounded by the prior experiences of mothers who themselves had been in care as a child.

In addition to the stories of pain shared by mothers in this study, concerns about the placement of their children in non-Aboriginal homes were expressed. Many of the mothers expressed concerns that they were not consulted with respect to the plans made for their children while in care. Those who were able to make arrangements to place their children with family members reported that it took an enormous amount of energy and effort to have their children placed with family. Sometimes the homes in which Aboriginal children were placed were arguably more harmful to them than their own homes (p. 40). The other issue that came to light through MacDonald's report was that many of the Aboriginal mothers involved in this study were unable to get any information about their children while in care and after children were returned.

As with the first study conducted by Kellington (2002), MacDonald posited that the stories and experiences articulated by Aboriginal mothers in relation to BC's child welfare system are important for increasing public awareness around issues of gender, race and class as contributing factors to Aboriginal women's involvement in the child welfare system. These stories are useful in understanding the disintegrative and powerless processes that colonization has inflicted particularly on Aboriginal mothers in BC but also in other child welfare jurisdictions across Canada. The stories the mothers shared can be utilized as a tool to begin the process of awareness and understanding. Moreover, MacDonald states that it is important to be able to provide a forum for Aboriginal women to contextualize and understand their life experiences within the context of colonization as perpetrated through the child welfare system. MacDonald's elucidation of stories on child welfare experiences and questions on how to move forward helped Aboriginal women in moving beyond the pain of colonization and remembering trauma inflicted by the child welfare system. The recommendations directed specifically at social workers by the Aboriginal mothers in MacDonald's study include a need for more:

- Cross-cultural, sensitivity, and anti-racism training for social workers;
- Specific training on alcohol and drug addiction;
- Sensitivity training on the stresses of parenting and poverty;
- Training on how to empower and engage Aboriginal mothers in determining and designing their own "expectations";
- Discussion and explanations by social workers as to mother's legal rights;
- Support to ensure that grief, loss and counselling is provided to Aboriginal mothers upon removal of their children;
- Aboriginal social workers to be recruited and retained by the BC Ministry responsible for child welfare.

The review of the literature in this area provides a beginning framework for understanding the extent and complexity of Aboriginal mothers' experiences with the child welfare and court systems within Canada today.

RESULTS/FINDINGS

The following section of the paper is organized so that the voices and the perspectives of the Aboriginal mothers in this study take center stage. It is important to note that researchers did not validate the views presented by the women but simply accepted them in their own words. Italicized text is used to present quotes drawn from comments made by the 32 mothers during their interviews and talking circles. The quotes have been lightly edited for grammar. Great care has been taken to ensure that this editing does not change the content nor does it alter the intent of the original comments made by the mothers who participated in the study. The purpose of laying out the data in this way is to ensure that readers get a sense of some of what the mothers in this study had to say about their experiences. In doing so, the perspective of the researcher has been minimized, while the individual and collective voices of the mothers associated with this study have been amplified. This narrative approach obligates readers to hear and listen to the voices and perspectives of Aboriginal mothers. This chapter reflects upon select comments drawn from three of the six themes identified in the final report: 1) experiences with the child welfare system, 2) experiences with lawyers, and 3) knowledge of alternative dispute resolution mechanism used in the child welfare context.

Experiences with the Child Welfare System

Fear of Child Welfare

Mothers expressed great fears around child welfare intervention. Mothers indicated they were afraid to get help from child and family services. Mothers stated they were afraid to seek out treatment for fear that their children would be apprehended if they sought out this needed assistance as reflected in the following comment:

> I was even scared to go for treatment because I figured … if I'm gonna go for treatment then it means I got a problem and they're gonna find a reason to take my kids away and that's what happened, right. I … tried to do that anyway and then they wound up taking my kids away so … so either way, I just kinda … had this feeling that … I had to stop what I was doing but I didn't know

how and I didn't know where to go. I didn't know who
to trust cause I was alone.

Being Monitored

A few of the mothers' narratives speak of being subjected to drug and
alcohol testing by the child welfare agencies staff. One mother in particular stated that she was required to undergo random drug testing at least
three times a month by the child welfare agency involved with her family. Closely related to drug and alcohol testing was the feeling of being
watched by child welfare. Mothers felt strongly that being under scrutiny was an invasion of their privacy, as was noted by this mother:

> ... and they always managed to get me to that point because
> they knew I had company, they would get somebody to
> spy on my home, they knew people were coming in there,
> they had specific names. They had people watching my
> home and I'm going to try to make a court case saying
> that's invasion of my privacy and movement. A bunch
> of people that are watching my home that are watching
> what is going on, coming in and out of my house.

Triggering Mothers' Anger

Mothers in this study noted that it appeared to them that social workers
deliberately tried to make them angry, doing everything in their power
to trigger anger, as this mother reflected:

> They want to set you up. There are key words and there
> are key things they try to throw at you to make you fly off
> the handle. I'm not stupid, I know their game.

Visitation Arrangements

Mothers who participated in the interviews and talking circles unanimously conceded experiencing many problems and difficulties around
their visitation rights. Visits were inconsistent, held infrequently, and
were often too short. Mothers stated that visits were often supervised
and took place in the office of the child welfare agency they were dealing
with:

> I looked forward to the Saturday visitations I had with them for an hour. That was very hard, very hard. To see them crying because they had to leave me and it's not like I could walk to a park and be alone with them, I had to be supervised. I'm not an abusive mom … that I could not understand. What did they think I was going to do with my kids? It was awful.

Harm to Children while in Care

In addition to the pain and loss experienced by Aboriginal mothers when their children were removed, many mothers expressed fear and concern over the impact of the removal on their children. The most frequently cited worry that mothers brought to our attention was the possibility their children may have been or were sexually abused while in care:

> At one point my family had to intervene because my kids were in a foster home where it was a cult. There was sexual abuse going on, there was physical abuse going on, the foster mom actually got her licensed pulled … a lot of my son's and my daughter's psychological abuse and physical abuse stemmed from that particular foster home.

Mothers say the biggest impact on children as a result of being removed is the loss of the development of a deep relationship between mother and child, as this mother lamented:

> My 18-year-old son grew up in this child and welfare system. My son … has a lot of anger and abandonment issues …. But he always has a safe home to come home to. I still love him and I'll always be here … he has trust issues. He does come home but when he does come home, all he does is he showers, packs clothes and then he leaves. I have not had a relationship with my son and I blame the child welfare system for that.

Child Welfare Expectations and Programming

Many of the mothers shared with us that they attended numerous programs at the request of the child welfare worker and agency. There is a sense that there is no rhyme and reason to the types and/or number of programs that mothers are required to attend. For many of the mothers it seemed that they were over-programmed and the child welfare expectations seemed to change from month to month.

> I had to jump through hoops ... going through parenting programs ... I don't even know how many programs ... I went for treatment. ... I got so many certificates it's unreal.

Another mother explained she was exhausted from all the programming she had to attend:

> I've been through so much programs in the last three months. Sometimes I barely ate. I've even barely slept. I went from 8, 9 o'clock in the morning right to 9:30 at night. Sometimes all day long from 3 programs a day. Then I get up and have to go to another one. But I did it! I'm glad I did it. And I told [my worker] I'm just so programmed out.

Jumping through Hoops

Mothers reported feeling that they had to jump through hoops and play the game to satisfy child welfare, whether that meant taking more programming or just, it seemed, to satisfy the whim of social workers to prove they were doing what needed to be done to get their children returned or to ensure visits with children currently in care. This was a comment made so often by the mothers we interviewed that it became the central title of the final report and is reflected in the following comments made by some of the mothers in this study:

> You're a person who's trying to live your life and then you're going to try and jump through hoops ... this jumping through hoops business was getting me mad.

> He wanted me to jump through hoops and I didn't like ... You have to try and prove to them that you're trying to get them back and you're trying to do everything they want you to do. In order to do that you've got to ... I felt like I was always kissing their ass ....

> I have never, ever once had a good experience with Child and Family, never with anything. If the kids are taken it takes so much to even try to get to see them and put it this way ... you've got to jump through hoops to even try and get a visit with your kids.

> It's just one frustration after another. It's like you have to jump through hoops ... they don't tell you exactly what it is that they want....

Experiences with Lawyers

In our conversations with mothers, the issue of rights or lack of knowledge around their rights as parents was a predominant theme in their narratives. In addition, mothers also expressed views, opinions, and feelings about the positive and negatives experiences they had in dealing with the lawyers that represented them in child protection cases. Mothers' discussions also touched upon the court experience and their knowledge or lack of knowledge about alternative resolutions to child welfare matters.

Lack of Awareness Regarding Rights

Mothers stated that when their children were first apprehended by child and family services they did not know where to turn for help and assistance. They were not sure how to obtain a lawyer or where to get Legal Aid assistance, and the child welfare social workers they came into contact with were unhelpful in providing information that mothers needed to help themselves understand what to do next. They did not know what their rights were:

> I didn't know any of my rights. I didn't know I could've hired a lawyer. I could have had support services come in .... CFS didn't sit down and say, "look we can give you a support worker; we can suggest this program and that program to you." None of that was done. It was just "okay, here's a court date, come for your kids."

Aboriginal mothers made many comments about the quality of services provided by the Legal Aid lawyers who represented them in child protection matters before the courts. The comments about their lawyers were both positive and negative. However, evaluation of the quality of legal services received was for the most part primarily negative. Many mothers indicated that their lawyers did not appear to represent them. Many said their lawyers counseled them to agree with the decisions made by the child welfare agency. For many, it appeared that the lawyers worked for child welfare agencies and that many of the decisions were made in consultation with the child welfare agencies rather than with the mothers they represented, as these mothers adamantly shared:

> I don't know who told me … they said [the lawyer] works for Child and Family Services … wouldn't that be a conflict of interest for her to take my case against them because she works for them? All she was trying to do was make me sign papers to do whatever they wanted. I knew deep down inside no I'm not doing it I don't feel right about it.

In addition to the confusing terminology used the court room, mothers indicated that they did not feel their lawyers did enough to defend or represent them in court:

> My lawyer was just doing whatever … it's not fair because if the social worker's allowed to talk to them, why can't you defend yourself and then have them already swaying the judge because they are so educated they know exactly what to say. Meanwhile, half of those words you don't even understand you're supposed to be up there trying to get your lawyer to defend yourself and you don't even know half the words that they're saying. When I sat there the first time … why the hell isn't my lawyer saying anything? What's going on here? It's just the one thing that the judge hears and that's it. Your lawyer's not defending you because she's working for them … it's a no-win situation.

In many instances, mothers indicated that they had minimal amount of time with their lawyers prior to the courtroom experiences and many felt their lawyers were essentially strangers who did not provide them with the sort of strength, comfort and friendship they needed under the circumstances:

> I wasn't looking for sympathy, but there was never … not even … a friendship thing with my lawyer … it was just more business.

The majority of mothers interviewed for this study were in agreement that family law courts are not an appropriate environment to oversee child protection issues involving Aboriginal families. The common response from the mothers in this study was that court was a very intimidating experience where many felt harshly judged. The mother's intimidations were connected to difficulties understanding the terminology and language used within the courtroom. Their collective perceptions center around the belief that the decisions made by judges within the court setting are racist, biased and one-sided in favour of the child welfare agency's interpretation of the situation. Judgment came not only from judges and child welfare staff but also their own lawyers.

Lack of Courtroom Supports and Advocates

Mothers expressed concerns about not being allowed to bring supportive people into the courtroom with them to face the judge, lawyers, child welfare staff and numerous other courtroom personnel and/or witnesses. The inequity of the situation was reflected by this mother in this way:

> The advocate … wasn't allowed in the courtroom. Well … what I said was, "oh, you guys are allowed all your people but I'm not allowed to have mine?" I think it is important for these women to have someone there with them because they become emotional … you've got these people bashing you, your character and your parenting. No you need someone there! They need to change that definitely. You should be allowed whoever you want in court with you and maybe you're not allowed 10 people, or 5 people, but at least 2 peoples should be allowed, or 3 even, your lawyer and 2 other people.

Knowledge of Alternative Dispute Resolution Mechanism Used in the Child Welfare Context

None of the mothers interviewed for this study were aware of the various alternative dispute resolutions (i.e., mediation or family group conferencing) that could be utilized in the child welfare context. Mothers admitted to not being knowledgeable about any mediation approaches that might have been helpful to them in dealing with the negativity they encountered when interacting with child welfare staff. Very few of the Aboriginal mothers had ever heard of the Family Group Conferencing model or understood how it worked. Furthermore, Aboriginal mothers reported that child welfare staff and lawyers rarely offered suggestions to alleviate the tension that is inherent throughout the child welfare experience. The only alternative was really no alternative, as this mother noted:

> I don't know any alternatives other than going to court and trying to fight and saying no, I want my kid back and that's the only thing I know … I know a little bit about restorative justice because you know I was part of stuff like for a number of years before. But there's nothing. I don't know if there is … what there is … for someone in my situation. I felt like I was literally in 10 foot, 20 ft brick wall all the way around me and I couldn't get out and that's a really horrible suffocating feeling you know, when you know there's no way out. You've got to … the only way is their way and … they're the law, they're the justice system.

Regardless of the time children spend in care, mothers are very optimistic that they will resume a relationship with their children when they come of age. Despite their circumstances the mothers we spoke to were optimistic; they prayed and continue to work on themselves to become strong for that day, as this mother poignantly shared:

> It hurts but I know one day my children are going to be 18 and if they turn 18 and they decide to come home, I want to be mentally and physically ready for my children. And I want to be healthy for my children. So I know I have a lot of healing and work to do on myself.

MOTHERS' RECOMMENDATIONS AND SOLUTIONS FOR CHANGE

This study gave Aboriginal mothers an opportunity to voice their perspectives about their experiences and to suggest simple changes and solutions for helping mothers understand the child welfare system. The following recommendations were formulated from a combination of the responses provided by the mothers during the talking circles and interviews, augmented by the researchers' observations and analyses of the findings. There are seven recommendations in all:

1. **Development of an Aboriginal Mothers' Advocates Office/ Institute:** This would involve the development of a formal organization to assist Aboriginal mothers navigate all aspects and complexities of the child welfare system within the province of Manitoba.

2. **Establishment of a Training Program for the Aboriginal Mothers' Advocates**: The Aboriginal Mothers' Advocates Office would, in addition to other purposes, be responsible for training Aboriginal mothers to become advocates for the proposed Aboriginal Mothers' Advocates Office. It was suggested by the mothers in this study that advocates be mothers who have intimate knowledge and experience dealing with the child welfare and legal systems.

3. **Development of a Manual on Understanding the Child Welfare and Legal Systems:** Development of a manual outlining what Aboriginal mothers can expect in terms of the child welfare/court processes. including: 1) time lines; 2) user-friendly terms and definitions; 3) information on the legal process; 4) information on how to access and instruct legal counsel; and 5) information on access to programs and treatment resources for Aboriginal mothers involved with the child welfare system.

4. **Development of Mothers' Support Groups:** The mothers in this study identified the need to develop more support groups across the province for Aboriginal mothers/grandmothers involved with the child welfare system. These support groups would meet monthly and act as an information and support forum for women to meet and learn from other women who've had similar experiences.

5. **Courtroom Advocates:** Mothers in this study suggested that in addition to their lawyers and the Aboriginal Mothers' Advocates, close family, friends and other supporters should be allowed into courtrooms.

6. **Development of a Website:** The website would include information about the Aboriginal Mothers' Advocates Office, courtroom advocates, training opportunities, calendar of activities for the support groups and a listing the resources, programs and treatment options available to Aboriginal mothers involved with child welfare within the province of Manitoba. A listing and link to the contact information of lawyers who specialize in child welfare matters should also be included.

7. **Development of an Anthology of Aboriginal Mothers/Grandmothers' Stories and Experiences:** There are very few resources that celebrate what it means to be an Aboriginal mother and grandmother. The last recommendation would see the creation of a book that focuses on providing Aboriginal mothers and grandmothers with a chance to share stories that reflect on the challenges, strengths and the resilience of Aboriginal women and mothering.

The economic and logistical feasibility of moving these recommendations forward are yet to be explored. Aboriginal mothers should be involved in exploring, developing and implementing these recommendations and Elders must also be involved at every stage of developing these recommendations.

DISCUSSION

The recommendations arising from this research may seem to advocate "tinkering" with the system instead of making fundamental change. This may in part be due to the lack of knowledge by Aboriginal mothers (and many service personnel working in the child welfare system) about alternative dispute resolution mechanisms available. It may also be due to the fact that Aboriginal women lack the power to ensure profound changes to these systems. In addition to the recommendations arising from interviews and talking circles with Aboriginal mothers and grandmothers, there is an urgent need to move the child welfare and legal systems toward utilization of alternative strategies when working with Aboriginal families. Family Group Conferencing, for instance, is an approach that is more conducive to Aboriginal families, but legislative and financial support is needed for implementing and practicing this approach with families. Fundamental changes to the child welfare system are needed, but these can happen only when room is made for collaborative dialogue with those who have the power and courage to change system structures that continue to oppress.

More and more Aboriginal children are coming into care, and it appears these numbers are not decreasing. As portrayed by this research, the length of time that Aboriginal children remain in substitute care is an issue. Intentionally or unintentionally, child welfare intervention frequently leads to long-term placement of children in care. This can have the effect of keeping some natural parents from ever developing lasting and meaningful relationships with their own children. Indeed many mothers alluded to this fact when they shared that they often don't know their children when they turn 18 and return home from substitute care. In many cases the mother/child relationship is irreparable and whatever bond once was there is, in some cases, irretrievable. This is akin to what occurred to Aboriginal children when they returned home from residential schools (Bennett, Blackstock & De La Ronde, 2005). In this sense, the child welfare system can be said to perpetuate, through substitute care, the assimilation agenda of the federal Indian Act of the past century.

More tragically, the outcomes for children and youth who experience substitute care, including non-Aboriginal children, have not been positive. There is a growing interest in research on the importance of recognizing long-term impacts as well as measuring outcomes for children/youth that have been in long-term care in Canadian child welfare systems (Trocmé, Nutter, MacLaurin & Fallon, 1999). A large percentage of homeless "street kids" have been products of the child welfare system (Serge, Eberle, Goldberg, Sullivan, & Dudding, 2002). These young people have experienced multiple placements, mistreatment and sexual abuse which has led many youth, upon aging out of the child welfare system, to experience exploitation by the sex trade (Kingsley & Mark, 2000) and/or involvement in criminal activities leading them into youth offender institutions and later into adult corrections institutions (Trevethan, Auger, Moore & Sinclair, 2001). Former Aboriginal youth in care are generally characterized as more likely to: be undereducated; be unemployed or underemployed; if employed, experience lower earnings with many living below the poverty line; become parents younger; experience homelessness; live in unstable housing arrangements; become incarcerated or involved in the criminal justice system; be dependent on social

assistance; have mental health issues; and be at a higher risk for substance abuse (Tweddle, 2007; Reid, 2007). Even upon returning to their
families and communities, former children who have experienced substitute care have difficulty and often are not capable of becoming functional
members of their communities (Sasaki, 1994).

When youth leave the child welfare system unprepared for independence and without ongoing support, the indirect costs are felt in other
government departments such as healthcare, education, justice and social services (Social Planning Council of Winnipeg, 2007). If these are the
outcomes that Aboriginal children face as a result of being in care, how
is it that any child is better off in substitute care than remaining at home
with their mothers? This is a difficult question and there are no easy answers. Aboriginal experts and Elders have noted that healing does not
happen alone or in isolation from family and community (Aboriginal
Corrections Policy Unit, 1997). The mothers in this study indicated that
they need to be with their children in order to heal. They can't heal without them. The current parenting programs mothers are required to take
are ineffective insofar as the system does not allow mothers the opportunity to exercise what they have learned if children do not return home to
benefit from their mother's attempts to improve their parenting. It is near
impossible for mothers to use and practice the new parental knowledge
gained in these instances. In effect, mothers are denied and deprived of
learning (or improving upon) their new-found parenting skills. Healing
takes time and the child welfare system and its bureaucracy needs to recognize that current legislation, policies and practices impede, rather than
enhance, the healing needed among the Aboriginal families they come
into contact with.

Aboriginal families coming into contact with the child welfare system
differ from non-Aboriginal families for historical and cultural reasons.
For these reasons, it is essential that child welfare intervention policies
and practices take into account the injustice and trauma that Canada
has inflicted on Aboriginal peoples in the past. From this perspective,
the imperative of Aboriginal women's right to be successful as mothers
and grandmothers must be emphasized. The breakdown of connections
between children and their mothers erodes the bonds of love and cultural responsibility that mothers have with respect to their children and
to the prolongation of Aboriginal nations. The profound importance of

Aboriginal women's roles as mothers is once again being diminished, just as it was during the residential school era. Being an Aboriginal mother involves navigating parenthood under the pervasive, critical glare of the state (Cull, 2006). Moreover, Aboriginal mothers encountering the child welfare system today are held responsible for their own healing in the context of monumental harms from the colonial and assimilative policies of the past. These historical harms continue to impact on successive generations of Aboriginal families that come into contact with the child welfare and family court systems in Canada. In this way, current child welfare practices too often contribute to intergenerational traumas that have been forced upon and experienced by Aboriginal families since early contact with Europeans. There is an urgent need for a new response system that seeks to ensure the safety of children and also ensures that balance in the family is restored as quickly and painlessly as possible in times of crisis. The need for healing for both children and their families as a result of their experience with the child welfare system is paramount, but, to date, little attention has been paid to this aspect.

The voices of these mothers and the narratives about their experiences with the child welfare system within Manitoba confirm what MacDonald (2002) noted in her own report that Aboriginal mothers' voices have been missing for far too long from the literature and the book shelves of our child welfare authorities and higher learning institutions – these preliminary findings confirm MacDonald's earlier findings and contribute to evidentiary research in Manitoba that can help child welfare administrators, policy makers, front-line staff and funders assess and tailor their services towards developing more conscientious services that will engage Aboriginal mothers, children and families in a more participatory manner that ensures cultural appropriateness and more respectful human responses. Federal and provincial governments need to ensure that Aboriginal people and their organizations are given adequate resources for this work.

CONCLUSION

The importance and sacredness of mothers as life-givers has been lost to our cultures, and through the process of evolution, subjugation and marginalization the importance and sacredness of Aboriginal motherhood has been diminished. It is time that we honour our mothers again to help them get back to understanding, feeling and experiencing the true beauty and sacredness of their roles and contributions to humanity, the world and to their children despite their human frailties. It is the right and just thing to do. And, yes, there are times that children must be protected, but mothers also need to be protected and supported so that they learn over the course of their lives how to protect and keep safe the children they brought into this world. More importantly, we need to ensure that fathers understand the importance of their role and participation in the lives of the children they helped create and bring into this world. Aboriginal mothers should not have to shoulder the responsibility of raising children and dealing with the child welfare system alone, as they currently are left to do. The burden of dealing with child welfare must be shared, and it is hoped that governments will recognize that only when Aboriginal mothers, fathers, families and communities are given adequate resources for health, education, housing, respite and supports will we see healthier and safer Aboriginal children. Nurtured Aboriginal children, after all, eventually grow into adulthood to be nurturing, conscientious parents themselves. We must ensure that the sacredness and profound importance of motherhood is continually transmitted from generation to generation to ensure healthy, intact generations to come.

REFERENCES

Aboriginal Corrections Policy Unit. (1997). The Four Circles of Hollow Water. Ottawa: ON: Aboriginal Peoples Collection, Solicitor General Canada. Retrieved from http://ww2.ps-sp.gc.ca/publications/abor_corrections/199703_e.pdf

Bennett, M. (2007). Aboriginal mothers' involvement with child protection and family court systems: Examining alternative court processes. *Canada's Children, 13*(1), (Winter), 88-93. Available at http://www.cwlc.ca/files/file/Canada's%20Children/CC%20Spring%202007.pdf

Bennett, M., Blackstock, C., & De La Ronde, R. (2005). *A Literature Review and Annotated Bibliography on Aspects of Aboriginal Child Welfare in Canada* (2nd Ed.). Winnipeg, MB: The First Nations Research Site of the Centre of Excellence for Child Welfare and the First Nations Child & Family Caring Society of Canada. Available online at http://www.fncaringsociety.com/docs/AboriginalCWLitReview_2ndEd.pdf

Callahan, M., Lumb, C., & Wharf, B. (1994). *Strengthening families by empowering women.* Victoria, BC: Ministry of Social Services.

Cull, R. (2006). Aboriginal mothering under the state's gaze. In D. M. Lavell-Harvard, & J. Corbiere Lavell (Eds.), *Until our hearts are on the ground: Aboriginal mothering, oppression, resistance and rebirth* (pp. 141-156). Toronto, ON: Demeter Press.

Kellington, S. (2002). *Missing Voices: Mothers at risk for or experiencing apprehension in the child welfare system in BC.* Vancouver: National Action Committee on the Status of Women.

Kimmelman, E. (1985). No Quiet Place: Manitoba Review on Indian and Métis Adoptions and Placements, Final Report to the Hon. Muriel Smith, Minister of Community Services. Winnipeg MB: Manitoba Community Services.

Kingsley, C., & Mark, M. (2000). *Sacred Lives: Canadian Aboriginal Children and Youth Speak Out About Sexual Exploitation.* Ottawa: Save the Children Canada.

Kline, M. (1989). Child welfare law, "Best Interests of the Child" ideology, and First Nations." *Osgoode Hall Law Journal, 30*(2), 375-425.

Kline, M. (1990). Child welfare law, ideology and the First Nations. Thesis (LL.M.)-- York University.

Kline, M. (1993). Complicating the ideology of motherhood: Child welfare law and First Nation women. *Queen's Law Journal, 18,* 306-342.

MacDonald, K. A. (2002). *Missing Voices: Aboriginal Mothers Who Have Been at Risk of or Who Have Had Their Children Removed from Their Care.* Vancouver, BC: NAC-BC.

Monture-Angus, P. (1989). A vicious circle: Child welfare and the First Nations. *Canadian Journal of Women & the Law, 3,* 1-17.

Monture-Angus, P. (1995). Organizing against oppression: Aboriginal women and the Canadian state for First Nation women. In P. Monture-Angus (Ed.), *Thunder in my soul: A Mohawk woman speaks* (pp. 169-188). Halifax: Fernwood Publishing.

Patton, M. Q. (2002). *Qualitative Research & Evaluation Methods.* London: Sage Publications.

Reid, C. (2007). The transition from state care to adulthood: International examples of best practices. *New Directions for Youth Development, 113* (Spring), 33-49.

Sasaki, L. (1994). The Contribution of the Child Welfare System to the Deterioration of Aboriginal Culture and the Need for Aboriginal Control. *Aboriginal Women's Law Journal, 1*(1): 54-69. Retrieved from: http://www.nwac-hq.org/en/documents/AboriginalWomensLawJournal.pdf.

Serge, L., Eberle, M., Goldberg, M., Sullivan, S., & Dudding, P. (2002). Pilot Study: The Child Welfare System and Homelessness among Canadian Youth. Ottawa, ON: National Secretariat on Homelessness. Retrieved from http://www.cecw-cepb.ca/files/file/en/HomelessnessAndCW.pdf.

Social Planning Council of Winnipeg. (2007). Ready or not, here I come: Youth "aging out" of the child welfare system. In Poverty Barometer, January 2007. Winnipeg, MB: The author.

Trocmé, N., Nutter, B., MacLaurin, B., & Fallon, B. (1999). Child Welfare Outcomes Indicator Matrix, October 1999. Bell Canada Child Welfare Research Unit, Faculty of Social Work, University of Toronto, and Ontario Association of Children's Aid Societies' Web site: http://www.oacas.org/resources/casstats.htm.

Trevethan, S. Auger, S., Moore, J-P., & Sinclair, J. (September 2001). The effect of family disruption on Aboriginal and non-Aboriginal inmates. Ottawa, ON: Correctional Service Canada, the Assembly of First Nations, the Department of Justice Canada, the Department of Indian Affairs and Northern Development, Native Counselling Services of Alberta and the Aboriginal Healing Foundation. Retrieved from: http://www.csc-scc.gc.ca/text/rsrch/reports/r113/r113_e.pdf.

Tweddle, A. (2007). Youth Leaving Care: How do they fare? *New Directions for Youth Development, 113* (Spring), 15-31.

CHAPTER 5

Rehearsing with Reality: Exploring Health Issues with Aboriginal Youth through Drama

Linda Goulet, Jo-Ann Episkenew, Warren Linds and Karen Arnason

INTRODUCTION

This chapter describes an innovative approach to engaging Aboriginal youth using theatre workshops to address issues affecting their health, such as peer pressure, addictions, suicide, gangs, and lack of self-esteem. The project emerged from a partnership between the health educator for the File Hills Qu'Appelle Tribal Council (FHQTC) in Saskatchewan and a group of researchers, two from the First Nations University of Canada and one from Concordia University. FHQTC has a history of developing proactive and innovative programming designed to address problems identified by the communities it represents, including those facing First Nations youth. The university partners had used Augusto Boal's (1979) concepts of Theatre of the Oppressed and Forum Theatre to facilitate workshops for urban youth. We could see that the issues of oppression and identity of the urban youth were similar to those issues identified as

SUGGESTED CITATION: Goulet, L., Episkenew, J., Linds, W., & Arnason, K. (2009). Rehearsing with reality: Exploring health issues with Aboriginal youth through drama. In S. McKay, D. Fuchs, & I. Brown (Eds.), *Passion for action in child and family services: Voices from the prairies* (pp. 99-118). Regina, SK: Canadian Plains Research Center.

problematic by the First Nations youth, so we decided to adapt Boal's theories and practice to design workshops for the youth in the FHQTC area. These workshops would comprise a component of a research project that would examine the efficacy of theatre for helping youth examine the decision-making processes that affect their health.

Our challenge was to apply approaches that would engage youth participation in the project. Throughout the workshops that ensued, the youth drew our attention to their significant health concerns. Because youth identified peer pressure as the main issue affecting their decisions, it became the issue around which we focused the research.

In this chapter we will describe the methods that we employed in both our youth workshops and our research project and will share our findings. We anticipate that our theatre techniques will provide child and family service practitioners and policy makers working with Aboriginal youth an innovative means of health education to prevent youth, and their subsequent children, from becoming involved in the child welfare system.

RESEARCH

We began our research with the assumption that "Forum Theatre" (Boal, 1979; Diamond, 1997) workshop processes would give voice to Aboriginal youth so that they could play a vital role in identifying and examining the socio-cultural issues that have a marked effect on their health and that of their community. We shared a belief that engaging youth in an examination of the factors that affect their decision-making is of utmost importance in the development of optimum health. Past experience working with youth and Forum Theatre has clearly demonstrated that the workshop process creates an environment that is both challenging and supportive. Linds and Goulet (2008) note that theatre can give participants experiences to denormalize current behaviours and the confidence needed to try out or "rehearse" new behaviours. Conrad (2005) made the same observation in her work with "risk-taking" youth. Catterall (2007) found positive change in pro-social behaviours as a result of engaging in a drama process and Beare and Belliveau (2007) found drama and theatre processes contributed to "positive youth development" (Kaczmarek and Riva, 1996; Breinbauer and Maddaleno, 2005). We hypothesized, then, that the kind of environment that Forum Theatre workshops create would foster growth in the Aboriginal youth participants by supporting them in a process whereby they could critically examine themselves and their communities. Ultimately, we hoped that the youth would become health researchers, albeit informal, and health advocates in their communities.

Our research project, *Developing Healthy Decision-Making with Aboriginal Youth through Drama*, used Forum Theatre workshops to help Aboriginal youth in the FHQTC area critically examine the choices they make that affect their health and to utilize the power of theatre to explore other choices and their potential consequences. Forum Theatre workshops include storytelling and improvisation exercises. Participants collectively develop scenes that enable them to enhance their understanding of their own lives by representing the world they live in and imagining the world they hope for. Through this imaginative process, youth discover positive, creative solutions to problems they face and identify the obstacles that get in the way of their dealing with critical personal and societal issues. In this way, the workshop straddles the line between fiction (theatricalizing lived experience) and reality (the lives of the participants), a "pooling of knowledge, tactics, and experience ... a rehearsal for reality" (Jackson, in Boal, 1992, p. xxi).

BACKGROUND

The legacy of colonization

Smith (1999), a Maori scholar who analyzed colonization from an Indigenous perspective, identified colonization as the process that facilitated the economic, political and cultural expansion of European power and control by subjugating Indigenous populations. Paul (1993), Wesley-Esquimaux and Smolewski (2004), and Archibald (2006) described the ensuing devastation and documented the complex system of European colonization in Canada that used, among other things, trade and military power, combined with the ideology of Eurocentrism and racism, to secure the resources of the Aboriginal peoples of Canada. Indigenous peoples' resistance to colonization took many forms, including armed struggle, political movements for self-determination (Adams, 1989; Paul, 1993), court challenges (Smith, 1999), and the creation of narratives that asserted their identity and their own peoples' histories (Said, 1993; Nelson, 2001).

Colonization affected, and continues to affect, Aboriginal people economically, politically, emotionally, and spiritually. The loss of land and territory, and the depletion of resources such as buffalo and fish, wiped out the economic base of Aboriginal societies, causing poverty, death, and trauma (Adams, 1989; Paul, 1993; Wesley-Esquimaux and Smolewski, 2004; Archibald, 2006). First Nations and Métis communities have started to rebuild an economic base, but Aboriginal peoples for the most part remain impoverished, "the poorest of the poor" (Bear Nicholas, 2001, p. 20; Richards, 2008), often without adequate access to the resources needed for present-day economic development or to support adequate social programs. In addition, Aboriginal peoples' decision-making processes were suppressed during colonization, often by military force (Adams, 1989; Archibald, 2006), and their political systems were replaced with a European model of governance (Paul, 1993; Archibald, 2006). Most decision-making took place outside the community, and authority was externally imposed. Today, Aboriginal people struggle to regain their democratic rights through the development of self-determination, but it is a slow process because many communities' capacities were decimated through colonial practices (Wesley-Esquimaux and Smolewski, 2004; Brant Castellano et al., 2008).

It is a testament to the strength of Aboriginal peoples that they survived the onslaught of colonization, but survival was not without its toll. Colonization impacted Aboriginal people's perceptions of personal and cultural worth and the view of their own capabilities and those of their people (Acoose, 1995; Miller, 1996). The turmoil caused by cultural denigration is enacted in personal and social problems of the community and is handed down by parents to the next generation (Kelly, 2008; Silver and Mallett, 2002). Duran and Duran (1995) write that, since the beginning of colonization, the Aboriginal people experienced a "soul wound" that has continued through generations of Aboriginal people who face the continual pressure to acculturate into settler society, the same society that created the genocidal policies and oppressive bureaucratic actions that have caused such harm. They argue that "[a]cculturation stress is a continuing factor in the perpetuation of anxiety, depression, and other symptomatology that is associated with PTSD [post-traumatic stress disorder]" (p. 32). The "other symptomatology" includes violence, rarely against the settlers, but rather against oneself or against other Aboriginal people, and includes addiction as a form of self-medication to ease the pain of the soul wound and the despair that violence and powerlessness causes.

Duran and Duran list a host of scholarly articles that hypothesize why Indigenous people suffer disproportionate rates of alcoholism. The list includes "poverty, poor housing, relative ill-health, academic failures, cultural conflict with majority society, and racism" (p. 95). They go on to argue that government policies lie at the root of these problems. Today, multiple generations of indigenous people live with intergenerational post-traumatic stress disorder, which are the direct result of colonial policies all focused at dealing with the "Indian problem." Mitchell and Maracle (2005) argue that diagnosing Aboriginal people with a "disorder" pathologizes the victims and that "post-traumatic stress response" is a more appropriate term.

Wesley-Esquimaux and Smolewski (2004) draw on the work of Maria Yellow Horse Brave Heart (1999) who developed the concepts of "historic trauma and historical trauma response." Historic trauma response (HTR), they explain, affects the descendents of people who have suffered genocide. The descendents "not only identify with the past, but also emotionally re-experience it in the present" (p. 55). Wesley-Esquimaux and Smolewski (2004) contend that PTSR is only one component of HTR, which can comprise many social and psychological conditions, all of which affect not only individuals but their communities and which continue through the generations.

Involvement in the child welfare system is another legacy of colonialism. Citing the 1998 Canadian Incidence Study on Reported Child Abuse and Neglect, Blackstock (2008) points out that Aboriginal children "were drastically overrepresented in the child welfare system at every point of intervention *despite the fact that they were not overly represented for reports of sexual abuse, physical abuse, emotional abuse, and exposure to domestic violence*" (pp. 166-7, emphasis in the original). Because Aboriginal people are more likely to be poor, to live in substandard housing, and to abuse substances to self-medicate from hopelessness and despair, they are more likely to come under the gaze of child welfare authorities.

The health concerns of the FHQTC suggest that their communities continue to be deeply affected by colonialism through HTR. Wesley-Esquimaux and Smolewski argue that the "goal of any healing process is a recovery of awareness, a reawakening to the senses, a re-owning of one's life experience and a recovery of people's enhanced abilities to trust this experience" (p. 78). Yellow Horse Brave Heart (1999) advocates storytelling as a means of healing from HTR. Drama can provide youth, who may be reticent to articulate their individual stories, with a safe, collaborative means to express the stories of the collective. In this way, they are able to begin the healing process.

The potential of drama

Applied theatre involves activities that are used with an explicit intent to translate, adapt, and transform theatre processes to work with, upon, between and against the social environment or community in which they are used. Through theatrical means we draw on participants' experiences to engage in the discussion of issues important to participants. Therefore, "[i]t is an unfinished act that generates its power within the process of the meeting of what are often highly different zones of practice" (Thompson, 2003, pp. 199-200).

There is a body of evidence that examines why and how Aboriginal communities have embraced applied theatre in their efforts to heal from the effects of historical trauma. Episkenew (2009) observes that the inherently communal nature of theatre makes it a particularly attractive genre for Aboriginal communities to use when grappling with the social problems that are a result of historical trauma. Seidlitz (1994) explains that theatre is a medium that fits comfortably within Aboriginal traditions, cultures, and ways of expression. Both Favel Starr (1997) and Manossa (2001) argue that contemporary indigenous theatre is not merely an adaptation or appropriation of European theatrical tradition but rather a form of expression that easily fits within Aboriginal traditions because it is rooted in traditional Aboriginal performance arts. Contemporary Aboriginal people have recognized that transformative element of theatre and have applied it to examine and heal individuals and communities from the social problems that are the result of unresolved grief and trauma. Taylor (2003) contends that applied theatre functions as a catalyst for healing because "it helps people reflect more critically on the kind of society in which they live" (p. 1). To that end, applied theatre regularly forms an important component of the many healing conferences that take place throughout the Aboriginal community.

Healing can enable the development of strong identification with one's community. Phinney and Kohatsu (1997) cite several research studies that show that adjustments among ethnocultural adolescents is associated with "positive attitudes and interactions with members of their own group, of other groups, and of the larger society" (p. 438). This combination comes from those who have actively developed their own identity as a member of a community so that they "have reached a secure, integrated understanding of themselves" (p. 438) as members of their particular community. An Australian study (Mulligan et al., 2006) of the ways community-based arts and cultural projects can enhance community well-being in isolated and marginalized communities indicates that they can help generate and sustain a different form of meaning at a time when communities are challenged and disrupted. Theatre appears to have significant power when applied in the areas of educational and community development. Taylor (2003) writes of theatre's potential as "an applied theatre form in which individuals connect with and support one another and where opportunities are provided for groups to voice who they are and what they aspire to become" (p. xviii). Thompson (2003) adds that such programs "can be a vital part of the way that people engage in their communities, reflect on issues and debate change. They can be central to different groups' experiences of making and remaking their lives" (p. 16).

Several studies have found that theatre processes contribute to socialization, self-confidence and self-esteem. Snow, D'Amico and Tanguay (2003) showed that putting on a theatre performance enables experiences of healthy functioning and healthy relationships, creating "enhanced psychological well-being" (p. 81). In an analysis of several youth arts programs, Clawson and Coolbaugh (2001) found that there was increased self-esteem among participants and an increased sense of accomplishment and pride. The arts programs taught self-respect, resistance to peer pressure, and self-efficacy. Most importantly, theatre processes enabled youth to work in a team environment specifically to experience "the importance of taking responsibility for their actions" (p. 9). Saitzyk and Poorman (1994), working with African-American and Native American girls, found that theatre as an intervention process helped participants share in the emotions being expressed by other group members through "mutual empathy" (p. 5) whereby group members attend to cognitive and affective cues and respond to the perspectives of others.

The workshop process

Our particular approach used Forum Theatre workshops as the foundation of our research. Such workshops explore the inter-related aspects of becoming aware of our bodies, enabling us to use our bodies to create a vocabulary of expression, and creating short plays through verbal and non-verbal language in order to come up with alternative ways to approach situations we have been exploring. We conducted these workshops with Aboriginal youth in grades 7 to 11 and supportive school personnel in two First Nation communities in the FHQTC area. During the workshops youth participated in a series of theatre exercises that address mental and social health issues. The workshops used different drama techniques to enable youth to look into moments of critical decision-making in their lives. Youth shared stories of their experiences to identify common concerns. They then transformed the stories into images (static human sculptures) and developed short plays based on the images. The plays examined issues that participants identified as most important to them and their community.

Risks are inherent in discussing what we want to de-normalize, and health and decision-making are risky subjects, partly because youth are not often asked to express the reality of their social choices in school (Freire, 1993, Vibert et al., 2002, Kumashiro, 2007), and partly because the issues are a complex interweaving of power, identity, attitudes, behaviours, and institutional and cultural structures (Riecken et al., 2006). Nicholson (2002) asserts that drama education involves the "enactment of trust" (p. 84). Accepting and taking risks in drama often makes people vulnerable. Trust is both an attitude and a process through which people allow themselves to enter situations of risk. Trust is performed and is "dependent on context, continually negotiated and re-negotiated according to the specific context and circumstances" (p. 88), enabling participants to share their lived experiences.

We began each workshop with a circle led by an elder from the community. Then we introduced ourselves and the project. We asked the youth to share something about themselves. In an effort to establish a sense of equity and to ease the youth into the day, we asked questions that we thought would be non-threatening, for example, "What is your favourite music?" Most students responded with only a few words. Yet, although youth were reluctant to participate in discussions, they were enthusiastic about participating in theatre games in which they could move around the space.

Following the circle, we asked youth to participate in trust, group building, and theatre games. Development of trust was enabled by blind games, where participants were encouraged to close their eyes and move around the room. These games encourage youth to pay attention to senses of which we are not normally conscious. The games were structured to develop from simple to more complex. Participating in games helped youth express their ideas and feelings. The games also helped to develop group cohesion and to encourage trust among the participants. They also brought together youth who do not normally associate with one another, either in school or out in the community. Although youth embraced the games, distractions and waning energy were often issues we had to address. Consequently, as facilitators, we often needed to employ energizing or concentration games to re-engage the participants.

Michael Rohd (1998), who has adapted Forum Theatre to his work with communities in the United States, conceives warm-up games as activities that "get a group of people playing together in a safe space, energize that space, and create a sense of comfort in the collective doing of specific and structured activities …. It's all about creating moments where participation is impossible to resist, moving forward into the process you have set up, and having fun along the way" (p. 4).

These games were not separate from the process: they built a sense of common purpose, with a goal of not only "creating links in the working group, building group awareness and trust" (Diamond, 2007, p. 91), but also unlocking issues the group is investigating. On several occasions in our workshops, for example, a name game helped, as we all began playing with our names, adding an adjective with the same initial letter as our first names, and then including a motion to describe ourselves. For example, one of the authors identified himself as "Wonderful Warren" while dramatically opening his arms. Everyone then repeated the name with adjective and the motion, causing much laughter among the participants and a subsequent lowering of barriers.

Storytelling through image

Renk (1993) writes that "drama teachers have inadvertently found a method of communicating that is much better adapted to the human process of understanding and orientating than the abstract and denotative teaching prevalent in schools" (p. 198). Wright (2000) asserts that drama has two interrelated aspects—embodied experience and reflective explanation of experience. In this process, drama becomes an alternative space where potential becomes possibility.

Stories are central to the learning process, as they mediate between self and others. In Forum Theatre workshops, youth begin to represent their world by sharing such stories non-verbally through snapshots of their experiences. As participants recall an incident or experience they have had, they create a series of body shapes or "image" to represent that experience. Imaging enables the participant to fill the body shapes with feelings and thoughts that come from the interplay between the physical shape and experience. Thoughts and words initially emerge from the individual's awareness of the static body in the image and the world around the image. Images can be activated into motion, movements that arise out of the interplaying of the physical shapes of bodies and their interpretation in words and action.

As participants create different sets of images, they develop the capacity to give expression to experience. Not only does this emphasize the traditional aphorism of "show us, not tell us," it also leads those looking to be able to interpret the images according to their own experiences. A key to understanding this process is the concept of *metaxis* (Boal, 1995), which is "the state of belonging completely and simultaneously to two different autonomous worlds: the image of reality and the reality of the image" (p. 43). In this way, the participants' stories of their experiences become a concrete form that can be interpreted and manipulated in many ways. The participants work in the world of the image to modify the story that the image tells. Boal claims that "if the artist is able to create an autonomous world of images in his own reality, and to enact his liberation in the reality of these images, they will then extrapolate into his own life all that he has accomplished in fiction" (p. 44).

Image as narrative is introduced through "Complete the Image" (Boal, 1992, p. 130), which is first done by two people shaking hands in a frozen image in front of the whole group. Anyone who has an idea can tap one of the pair shaking hands and replace them in a new body shape in relation to the other, adding a new element, creating a different image, a new story. After a few images in pairs, more characters are added to one of the images until there are six or seven people who are making a story out of the original paired image. We emphasize that one image can be interpreted in many ways, from many perspectives. When it seems the group has understood the method, we begin again. This time we ask the group to think of a particular theme such as "life in school" while completing the image. We then ask the group to interpret the image. For example, we ask questions about who the people are in the image story, who has more power than others, and how this power is represented. Having such an image frozen in time, we can view it from different angles and perspectives. Often the image can become a catalyst to look at relationships within the group. Often we ask people standing outside the image to stand behind the person in the image that best represents their own experience and we talk about that, either in the whole group or in smaller groups, where each "character" sits down with people who resonated with their situation in the image.

Participants were asked to use their bodies to create frozen images that portrayed ideas or events which occurred in their lives. Although many participants communicated ideas more clearly with physical images rather than by verbalizing to the group or by writing in journals, they still found this a challenge. After participants became comfortable and competent creating images, we drew their focus to the health issue that they felt they and their communities faced. Youth were asked to identify and prioritize health issues facing the youth in their community. The participants shared stories of their lived experiences, which formed the foundation of short interactive plays. Youth were also asked to reflect on their learning by writing in journals, by creating a mural, and, in the follow-up workshop, through images. Youth were most engaged in creating a cooperative group mural in response to pictures taken of their participation in games and images. During one-day follow-up workshops, youth engaged in similar workshop processes and activities to help them reflect upon what they had learned from the project.

FINDINGS

The theatre processes we used clearly engaged the youth by providing them with an opportunity for learning with fun and laughter, which contribute to healing and health. It is significant that one of the teachers remarked that she had never heard her students laugh in the way that they did during the games. At the same time, our view of how the youth participants might become health advocates and health researchers changed considerably. The complexity of the context in which Aboriginal youth decision-making takes place became evident, so we as researchers gained a greater understanding of the challenge of offering health education that would impact the lives of youth.

We also learned much about the participants' interpretation of their reality when we asked groups of youth to create short images to represent issues and plays to tell the story of their experiences of decision-making in their lives. The plays that they created dealt with stories of peer pressure, which was the issue that youth identified as being at the core of their decisions to engage in unhealthy or risky behaviours. We learned to differentiate peer pressure from bullying: there was no violence involved and, indeed, rather than being pressured by others, the youth often pressured themselves to engage in unhealthy or risky behaviours because they valued belonging to the group more than they valued their own well-being.

Youth performed their plays for the other participants in the workshops. As we examined each play to identify commonalities and differences, youth recognized that they were not alone in their experiences. Boal (1995) uses the term "analogical induction" (p. 45) to describe this recognition of self in the experience of others. This moment of "analogical induction" enables a distanced analysis of an experience; at the same time, it illustrates the commonalities shared by the youth, thereby forging bonds among them. After youth watched and commented on a play, we as facilitators would use an activation technique to further explore issues inherent in the play. Facilitation techniques included such things as asking characters to identify their motives for making the choices they were making, taking the play backward or forward in time to explore consequences or decisions leading to the experience, or asking audience members to intervene as a character to see if they could change the outcome. In this way, youth explored the interconnectedness of one story and alternatives to the actions, while thinking about their own stories. Doing so gave youth voice so that their issues led the program within the structure set by the adult leaders.

The images and the plays depicted the great strength of Aboriginal communities. When asked to portray what they liked about living on the reserve, the students all created images of close, personal, caring relationships. One image was of people walking together with arms on each other's shoulders. Other images represented the group's cohesiveness and close connections in similar ways. One image that was more complex had students standing on each other, creating a web of people that needed the whole group to physically support each other to sustain the structure. When other students saw it, they commented on how well it represented their reality. It became evident that students were immersed in strong, social systems with deep bonds among peers, family members, relatives, and community members.

We also learned that, while students felt connected and supported in their communities, these bonds also manifest in their lives as peer pressure. Peer pressure, as represented in the stories and images created by Aboriginal youth, was significantly different from bullying, in that peer pressure affects their decisions about participating in both healthy and unhealthy activities. When students were asked to identify and prioritize health issues affecting their lives, in fact, they saw peer pressure as the most powerful issue affecting their decision-making in terms of health; in doing so, they reflected the power of the strong social bonds in Aboriginal communities. However, while strong social bonds are a positive strength of Aboriginal communities, these social systems have been and continue to be affected by historical colonization and ongoing racism. Coping with colonization often brought activities that at first were alien to or imposed upon Aboriginal communities, which can, "after years of repetition, become an unquestioned part of daily life" (Benyon 2008), what Freire (1993) refers to as "limiting situations." Certain activities among the Aboriginal youth become normalized ways of socializing. Rather than the youth being forced (or bullied) into making unhealthy choices in most situations, they didn't see that they had a choice.

Their very real need to cope with historical trauma was evident in the students' images and plays: all involved alcohol and/or drug abuse that led to violence, risky behaviours or criminal activity. One skit represented friends smoking marijuana at a house and then going to the store. At the store, one of the youth is pressured by the others to steal some snacks. Several of the scenes showed parties where youth alcohol and drug abuse led to fighting. In one, a group of boys were drinking together, sharing alcohol bought by one of the boy's older relatives. When a person who was not from their reserve comes to the party and tries to help himself to their alcohol, a fight ensues. In another scene, a group of girls, who are celebrating a birthday, pressure a girl who doesn't drink to try drinking. The conversation leads to gossip about one of the girl's ex-boyfriends for whom she still has feelings. This leads to a fight and forces the girls present to choose sides. The next day, they have to face one another in school.

The youths' plays revealed a problematic norm in their social systems.

Drugs and alcohol profoundly affect their lives and relationships, and decisions that affect strong relationships are too often made under the influence of drugs and alcohol. Youth, then, must live with others who know of their actions done under the influence of drugs and alcohol. This can lead to shame and more self-denigration and more self-medicating using drugs and alcohol. As a consequence, the system becomes self-perpetuating.

When asked to represent how they feel about the health issues in their communities, students created images of their heads buried in their hands, heads bent down in sorrow, and fists against their heads. When asked to say one word to give verbal expression to that image, students expressed hopelessness, frustration, helplessness, and fear of the violence and drug and alcohol abuse that besets their community. The feeling of helplessness translates into action, or rather inaction, portrayed in the skits as a lack of agency and volition. In another skit, the students portrayed youth at a party where some were drinking heavily. One boy had a car, so he and another boy decided to go to town. Two girls accompanied them. The driver was quite drunk and tried to light a marijuana joint while driving. As a result, he got into an accident. When the girls were asked why they would ride with a person who was drunk and, maybe more importantly, why they would let their friend get into this dangerous situation, they responded that they hadn't thought about it. Both shrugged their shoulders and said, "I don't know. I'm just along for the ride."

While students portrayed negatives issues in their lives, we also asked them to represent positive activities as well. Participation in sports and cultural activities were seen as important to them. The love of sports was particularly evident in one school, where every break was spent in the gym shooting baskets or playing with the volleyball. Many of the students spoke of the strength they drew from attending community events such as powwows or ceremonies. Learning the cultural arts gave students pride, as was evident when we were asked by some students to observe them learning how to jig. At one workshop, students who were part of a drum group offered to close our session with a drum song. The transformation in those boys as they sat to play the drum was evident; they became strong young men, proud of their culture and their skill as powwow drummers and singers.

CONCLUSION

King, Boyce, and King (1999), in their survey of trends of health in Canadian youth, point out that "the mental health of young people and the degree to which they engage in health-risk behaviours are strongly associated with the relationships they have with their peers" (p. 103). Furthermore, most interventions that are targeted at individual risk behaviours have little success. Thus "an integrated and systematic approach that recognizes the role of home, the school, the peer group and the community is required" (p. 104).

Fostering relationships among partners who work with Aboriginal youth in the areas of the arts, health, and social services is one way we can create conditions to share findings, compare strategies, and learn from one another. This would enable partners to develop and disseminate effective teaching and learning principles and methods for using theatre's power with and for youth in Aboriginal communities. Fostering relationships among these community-based projects will lead to substantial exchange of knowledge, growth in capacity, and opportunities to disseminate findings as they affect policy and practice, first among partners; secondly, to a wider group committed to effective aboriginal youth development; and thirdly, to the Aboriginal youth involved.

Sharing their experiences in the workshops helped Aboriginal youth overcome isolation and opened a space for them to talk about the reality of their social lives where alcohol and drug abuse are too often present. One participant who had been reluctant to speak in the larger group shared her experience with one of the facilitators. She explained how children in her community were involved in the child welfare system and how her family cared for foster children whose families had been shattered by the parents' alcohol and drug usage. This participant wanted to make things better for her foster siblings, but the only solutions that she could envision were ones that involved changing the parents. She asked if we could help recruit "someone" to come to the reserve to "fix" the people with addictions. As a youth, and as a community member, she felt helpless.

Similarly, in debriefing with the group as a whole, another participant summed up the feelings of many of the participants (indicated by the nodding of heads of other youth), "What can we do? Everybody uses alcohol and drugs. That's just the way it is on the reserve." Although, in fact, not everyone on the reserve abuses drugs and alcohol, this statement reflects the youths' perspective of their community and particularly of their life choices at this particular time in their lives. This view was expressed at the end of our follow-up workshop, indicating that although our workshops had provided space for expression, long-term work was needed if youth were to overcome the sense of powerlessness they expressed.

Through the plays and the workshop, it became evident that the youth were embedded in peer, family, and community systems affected by colonialism and exhibiting historical trauma response. Their stories revealed their perceived lack of volition and agency in decision-making. The "characters" in their plays often participated in drug and alcohol use without too much thought or conscious choice because it was what they perceived as the norm—what "everyone" did for recreation and fun. Drinking and drug use were a big part of the life of their peer group. Often older siblings or family members were involved as well. At the same time, the youth identified healthy activities, too, for example, community strengths such as sports and cultural activities. The youth had strong social relationships that supported them. They had personal connections with others and close relationships that translate into peer pressure— peer pressure that affects decisions to participate in both healthy and unhealthy activities.

As the workshops progressed, we realized that although the workshops could start the process of youth becoming health advocates, such a role would require a longer time commitment on the part of the researchers/facilitators and participants alike. In the one-day follow-up workshop at one of the communities, the students were not motivated to participate. On reflection, we believe that youth were not so committed because they did not have a stake in the process. Although we hoped to do something with them in the future, we were unable to make definite plans. As a result, many participants did not clearly understand the purpose of the follow-up workshop, and their participation, therefore, lacked the enthusiasm that they had first exhibited.

Our research has shown that Aboriginal youth are embedded in community and family systems damaged by colonialism and, consequently, find it difficult to see themselves as agents of change. Lack of agency leads to loss of volition, and, for these youth, following the crowd can appear to be a better choice than living in isolation and frustration. Granted, all youth must learn to identify the aspects of their lives they have the power to change and those they do not. However, this is a particularly difficult lesson for Aboriginal youth whose families and communities are only beginning the long road to empowerment after being completely marginalized and disenfranchised by colonialism.

At the same time, our research has also shown that drama is one way to engage Aboriginal youth in the investigation of the health issues in their lives, and thereby prevent involvement in the child welfare system, because its form and process gives space for youth to voice their perspectives. MacKay (1996) writes, "I have long felt that we cannot speak of cures, but rather experiences of healthy functioning and healthy relationship which may become benchmarks in future development" (p. 166).

The drama process also demonstrated the need for ongoing, long-term innovative programming that supports Aboriginal youth decision-making if they are to make healthy choices in their lives. Accompanying the programming is the need for research to document effective health education practices and to determine how to work in collaborative partnership with Aboriginal youth to identify and create spaces in their lives where different choices, and, consequently, different realities, are possible.

REFERENCES

Acoose, J. (1995). *Iskwewak—kah ki yaw ni wahkomakanak: Neither Indian princesses nor easy squaws.* Toronto, ON: Women's Press.

Adams, H. (1989). *Prison of grass: Canada from a native point of view.* 1975. Revised and Updated. Saskatoon, SK: Fifth House.

Archibald, L. (2006). *Decolonizing and healing: Indigenous experiences in United States, New Zealand, Australia and Greenland.* Ottawa: Aboriginal Healing Foundation.

Bear Nicholas, A. (2001). Canada's colonial mission: The great white bird. In K. P. Binda (with S. Calliou) (Eds.), *Aboriginal education in Canada: A study in decolonization* (pp. 9-33). Mississauga, ON: Canadian Educators' Press.

Beare, D., & Belliveau, G. (2007). Theater for positive youth development: A development model for collaborative play-creating. *Applied theatre researcher, 8,* 1-16.

Beynon, J. (2008). *First Nations teachers: Identity and community, struggle and change.* Calgary, AB: Detselig.

Blackstock, C. (2008). Reconciliation means not saying sorry twice: Lessons from child welfare in Canada. In M. Brant Castellano, L. Archibald, and M. DeGagné (Eds.), *From Truth to reconciliation: Transforming the legacy of residential schools* (pp. 165-178). Ottawa, ON: Aboriginal Healing Foundation.

Boal, A. (1979). *Theatre of the oppressed*. Trans. C.A. McBride, M.L. McBride, & E. Fryer. London, UK: Pluto Press.

Boal, A. (1992). *Games for actors and non-actors*. Trans. A. Jackson. New York: Routledge.

Boal, A. (1995). *The rainbow of desire: The Boal method of theatre and therapy*. Trans. A. Jackson. New York: Routledge.

Brant Castellano, M., Archibald, L., & DeGagné, M. (2008). Introduction. In M. Brant Castellano, L. Archibald, & M. DeGagné (Eds.), *From truth to reconciliation: Transforming the legacy of residential schools* (pp. 1- 10). Ottawa, ON: Aboriginal Healing Foundation.

Breinbauer, C., & Maddaleno, M. (2005). *Youth: Choices and change. Promoting healthy behaviors in adolescents*. Scientific and Technical Publication No. 594, Washington, DC: Pan American Health Organization.

Catterall, J. S. (2007). Enhancing peer conflict resolution skills through drama: an experimental study. *Research in Drama Education, 12* (2), 163-178.

Clawson, H. J., & Coolbaugh, K. (2001). The YouthARTS Development Project. *Office of Juvenile Justice and Delinquency Prevention Juvenile Justice Bulletin* (May) 1-15.

Conrad, D. (2005). Rethinking "at-risk" in drama education: Beyond prescribed roles. *Research in Drama Education, 10*(1), 27-41.

Diamond, D. (2007). *Theatre for living: The art and science of community-based dialogue*. Victoria: Trafford Publishing.

Duran, E., & Duran, B. (1995). *Native American postcolonial psychology*. Albany: SUNY Press, 1995.

Episkenew, J. (2009). *Taking back our spirits: Indigenous literature, public policy, and healing*. Winnipeg: University of Manitoba Press.

Favel Starr, F. (1997). The artificial tree: Native performance culture research 1991-1996. *Canadian Theatre Review 90* (Spring), 83-85.

Freire, P. (1993). *Pedagogy of the oppressed*. New York: Continuum.

Kaczmarek, P. G., & Riva, M. T. (1996). Facilitating adolescent optimal development: Training considerations for counselling psychologists. *The counselling psychologist, 25*(3), 400-432.

Kelly, F. (2008). Confessions of a born again pagan. In M. Brant Castellano, J. Archibald, & M. DeGagne (Eds.), *From truth to reconciliation: Transforming the legacy of residential schools* (pp. 11 - 42). Ottawa: Aboriginal Healing Foundation.

King, A. J. C., Boyce, W. F., & King, M. A. (1999). *Trends in the health of Canadian youth*. Ottawa, ON: Health Canada.

Kumashiro, K. (2007). *Six lenses for anti-oppressive education: Partial stories, improbable conversations*. Bern, Switzerland: Peter Lang.

Linds, W., & Goulet, L. (2008). Performing praxis: Exploring anti-racism through drama. In S. Moore & R. Mitchell (Eds.), *Power, pedagogy and praxis: Social justice in the globalized classroom* (pp. 199 - 218). Amsterdam, Netherlands: Sense Publishers.

MacKay, B. (1996). Brief drama therapy and the collective creation. In A. Gersie (Ed.), *Dramatic approaches to brief therapy* (pp. 161-174). London: Jessica Kingsley.

Manossa, G. (2001). The beginning of Cree performance culture. In A. Ruffo (Ed.), *(Ad)dressing our words: Aboriginal perspectives on Aboriginal literatures* (pp. 169-180). Penticton, BC: Theytus.

Miller, J.R. (1996). *Shingwauk's vision: A history of native residential schools*. Toronto, ON: University of Toronto Press.

Mitchell, T., & Maracle, D. (2005). Healing the Generations: Post-traumatic stress and the health status of Aboriginal people in Canada. *Journal of Aboriginal Health, 2*(1), 14-23.

Mulligan, M., Humphery, K., James, P., Scanlon, C., Smith, P., & Welch, N. (2006). *Creating community: Celebrations, arts and wellbeing within and across local communities*. Melbourne, Australia: VicHealth and Globalism Institute (RMIT University).

Nelson, H. L. (2001). *Damaged Identities: Narrative Repair*. London, UK: Cornell UP.

Nicholson, H. (2002). Drama education and the politics of trust. *Research in drama education 7*(1), 81-93.

Paul, D. N. (1993). *We were not the savages: A Micmac perspective on the collision of European and Aboriginal civilization*. Halifax, NS: Nimbus.

Phinney, J. S., & Kohatsu, E. L. (1997). Ethnic and racial identity development and mental health. In J. Schulenberg, J.J. L. Maggs, & K. Hurrelmann (Eds.), *Health risks and developmental transitions during adolescence* (pp. 420-443). Cambridge, UK: Cambridge University Press.

Riecken, T., Scott, T., & Tanaka, M. (2006). Community and Culture as Foundations for Resilience: Participatory Health Research with First Nations Student Film Makers. Journal of Aboriginal Health, 3(1), 6-14.

Renk, H. E. (1993). The art form of drama and the new paradigm of constructivism. In E. Errington (Ed.), *Arts education: beliefs, practices and possibilities* (pp. 193-200). Geelong, Australia: Deakin University Press.

Richards, J. (2008). Closing the Aboriginal – Non-Aboriginal Education Gap: A S.I.P.P. Armchair Discussion. A presentation to the Saskatchewan Institute of Public Policy, Regina, SK, March 4, 2008.

Rohd, M. (1998). *Theatre for community, conflict and dialogue: The Hope is Vital training manual.* Portsmouth, NH: Heinemann.

Said, E. W. (1993). *Culture and imperialism.* New York: Alfred A. Knopf.

Saitzyk, A. R., & Poorman, M. (February, 1994). Transition to Adolescence Program: A program to empower early adolescent girls. Paper presented at the Biennial meeting of the Society for Research on Adolescence, San Diego, CA. ED 370062. http://eric.ed.gov/ERICDocs/data/ericdocs2sql/content_storage_01/0000019b/80/16/13/55.pdf

Seidlitz, L. S. (1994). Native theatre for the seventh generation: On the path to cultural healing. Unpublished Masters thesis, Dalhousie University, Halifax, NS.

Silver, J., & Mallett, K. (with Greene, J., & Freeman, S.). (2002). *Aboriginal education in Winnipeg inner city high schools.* Winnipeg Inner City Research Alliance. Winnipeg, MN: Canadian Centre for Policy Alternatives – Manitoba.

Smith, L. T. (1999). *Decolonizing methodologies: Research and indigenous peoples.* London, UK: Zed Press.

Snow, S., D'Amico, M., & Tanguay, D. (2003). Therapeutic theatre and well-being. *The arts in psychotherapy, 30*(2), 73–82.

Taylor, P. (2003). *Applied theatre: Creating transformative encounters in the community.* Portsmouth, UK: Heinemann.

Thompson, J. (2003). *Applied theatre: Bewilderment and beyond.* Berne: Peter Lang.

Vibert, A. B., Portelli, J. B., Shields, C., & LaRoque, C. (2002). Critical practice in elementary schools: Voice, community, and a curriculum of life. *Journal of educational change, 3*(2), 93-116.

Wesley-Esquimaux, C., & Smolewski, M. (2004). *Historic trauma and aboriginal healing.* Ottawa: Aboriginal Healing Foundation.

Wright, D. (2000). Drama Education: A self-organising system in pursuit of learning. *Research in drama education, 5*(1), 23-31.

Yellow Horse Brave Heart, M. (1999). Oyate Ptayela: Rebuilding the Lakota nation through addressing historical trauma among Lakota parents. *Journal of human behavior and social environment, 2*(1/2), 109-126.

CHAPTER 6

Making the Connection: Strategies for Working with High-risk Youth

Peter Smyth and Arlene Eaton-Erickson

INTRODUCTION

High-risk youth are "the disconnected." Sadly, they rarely have family they can rely on. They rarely have a healthy support network to help guide them. They typically have difficulty trusting adults and perceive they are on their own in this world. High-risk youth struggle to be stable and, when involved in the child welfare system, use a disproportionate amount of resources, especially placements, resulting in greater vulnerability (Wilson & Woods, 2006). In general, they are hard to engage, slow to change, test frequently, and challenge one's practice, ethics, and boundaries. These youth also teach you to become intensely self-aware and thoughtful and to profoundly understand that they are very unique and deserve to be treated as individuals. These are not "at-risk" youth; they are "high-risk" youth. They are not heading in a bad direction or on

SUGGESTED CITATION: Smyth, P., & Eaton-Erickson, A. (2009). Making the connection: Strategies for working with high-risk youth. In S. McKay, D. Fuchs, & I. Brown (Eds.), *Passion for action in child and family services: Voices from the prairies* (pp. 119-142). Regina, SK: Canadian Plains Research Center.

a path to self-destruction; they are there already. Despite this, all youth have strengths to build on and demonstrate resilience. A number of strategies offer direction and ideas to those who have a passion for working with high-risk youth. These strategies encourage a practice that strives to be anti-oppressive, flexible, responsive and harm-reducing. Such a practice is non-traditional and creative and, according to youth, a better way to meet their needs.

We have received feedback from a number of practitioners employed by child welfare jurisdictions from across Canada indicating that they, too, are struggling to meet the needs of this population (Smyth & Eaton-Erickson, 2007). Our own experience has shown us that these youth are often seen as defiant and manipulative when in "the system" and, consequently, have difficulty accessing appropriate services. Many youth have shared that they expect their relationship with their child welfare workers to be problematic. We have come to believe that all youth want connection, but attempting to connect with high-risk youth is a risk-filled journey that requires patience. Although they have learned that they cannot trust, deep down they are hoping someone will love them (Kagan, 2004). When we choose to share powerful experiences with these youth, they teach us much.

This chapter will focus on our experience and observations, the voices of the youth we have worked with, and the strategies we have used in working with high-risk youth within the Edmonton High Risk Youth Initiative. Many of the observations made have been formulated through our direct experiences working with these youth since 1998. At the time the project was initiated, little (if any) research had been done on high-risk youth (HRY) within the child welfare system. Since then, the work of Ungar (2002, 2004, 2005, 2006) has been a philosophical "fit" for the work that we have been engaged in, and we have included this to strengthen the theoretical framework from which we work.

In a unique move for government child welfare services, a harm-reduction philosophy was adopted for the Edmonton High-Risk Youth Initiative, which allows for a focus on both relationship-building and working in partnership with youth in developing services that will meet their needs. The High Risk Youth Unit (HRYU) officially started on November 1, 2005, and is a partnership between Edmonton and Area Child and Family Services, Region 6 (Alberta Children and Youth Services), other government departments and community agencies. The initiative uses a model that was designed in the Edmonton Region in 1999 (Smyth and Eaton-Erickson, 1999). While there are some risks inherent in a harm reduction approach, it is argued that these are fewer than in traditional intervention which appears adversarial to the youth.

HISTORICAL PERSPECTIVE

The concept of working specifically with high-risk youth within Children and Youth Services in Edmonton emerged in January 1999, when the authors wrote a report for the Edmonton and area Child and Family Services agency titled, "High Risk Teen Caseload" (Smyth and Eaton-Erickson, 1999). As child welfare workers with Alberta Children and Youth Services, we acknowledged that, "High-risk teens are difficult for child welfare workers to deal with as they are often AWOL, defiant, and persist in engaging in behaviours that could jeopardize their safety" (Smyth and Eaton-Erickson, 1999, p. 1). In the report several barriers to working effectively with these youth were identified: high caseload sizes which made it difficult to spend time with youth and develop relationships with them; little time (and education) coordinating with other agencies who worked with the same population group; the community's lack of trust in the child welfare system; casework being reactive instead of proactive; and the reluctance to meet youth where they were at. It was clearly acknowledged and articulated that the current way of working with high-risk youth was not effective, because:

- High-risk youth continue to AWOL frequently, often for months at a time.
- These teens continue to expose themselves to high-risk situations that they often cannot control (i.e., sexual exploitation, drugs).
- There is a feeling of helplessness when youth are AWOL; thus, few efforts are made to find the youth and connect with agencies who work with street youth.
- High-risk youth become a low priority, as they are difficult to connect with, and this is perceived as being defiant and being resistant to change.
- It is not uncommon for high-risk youth to tell workers that "the system" does not work for them, does not meet their needs, or is a "joke" because they can manipulate it so easily (Smyth and Eaton-Erickson, 1999, p. 3).

There was a need to do business differently when working with high-risk youth—to be available, to meet them, in colloquial terms, "where they were at", to develop significant relationships, to connect youth with appropriate services, and to connect with the community in a meaningful way. To accomplish this, the agency capped caseloads at 15 youth per child welfare worker, employed a full-time therapeutic youth worker, and adopted a strength-based, harm-reduction approach.

RATIONALE AND PHILOSOPHY

It is important to listen to the voices and stories of high-risk youth in both the development and the provision of services to them. When a child welfare worker is introduced to a youth and their response is, "I hate fucking social workers," followed by walking away with a look of disgust, inevitably the worker pauses to think about what has just transpired. The first thought is: "This is going to be a challenge." The second is: "How do I approach this situation without alienating the youth further?" After getting past thinking that this is "about me," thoughts turn to why this youth is so hostile to child welfare workers and Children and Youth Services.

In our research report *"The Word On The Street: How Youth View Services Aimed at Them"* (Smyth, Eaton-Erickson, Slessor & Pasma, 2005),[1] most youth who fit into the category of high-risk youth reported that they had had negative experiences with "the system" and believed it either did not help them or made their situation worse. These experiences included a lack of meaningful relationships with social workers and service providers, a lack of support during life transitions, and not feeling heard by the system. A common theme was that programs were being developed that better met the needs of the system, rather than the needs of those who were the intended recipients of the services. Youth expressed feeling constricted by rules and expectations. While they saw basic rules as important to avoid chaos, they did not think that they had any input

---

1   The report was completed by the High Risk Youth Task Force which was a subcommittee of the Edmonton and Area, Child and Family Services, Region 6, Group Care Sector. The Task Force was formed to examine issues around why a relatively low number of youth were using a high number of placement beds in group care yet there was little or no positive outcomes perceived among these youth. The Task Force, made up of Region 6 and agency staff, decided to hold a series of youth forums targeting areas in which higher-risk youth were known to hang out and access services on a more street-level basis.

into developing such rules, thus their relevance became suspect. They believed child welfare workers did not have time for them, did not hear them, and did not understand them. Most youth were not familiar with service plans, and therefore did not appear to feel connected to the helping process. The aforementioned made them suspicious of the system and generally, while they acknowledged that they needed help, they did not see Children and Youth Services as a viable provider of such assistance (Smyth et al., 2005).

Despite this, an overall theme of the report was one of opportunity and hope. As the youth spoke, it became clear that, if they perceived that they had a positive relationship with their child welfare worker, they appeared to view the whole system in a positive light. Conversely, if they believed that they had a negative relationship with their worker, they saw the whole system as negative (Smyth et al., 2005). This was also true for youths' relationships with service providers such as youth workers, family workers, and therapists. This illustrated to the authors that it is important for youth to have a positive connection and relationship, even if it is difficult for them. Secondly, if workers focused on building relationships with youth, not only would youth be open to this approach, they may also attain a level of buy-in that could initiate a process of healthy change. Relationship-building also demonstrates to youth a collaborative *working with* stance (Masten, 1994), rather than doing to or doing for (Wharf, 2002, 13), which youth have identified as a barrier to feeling connected to the system (Smyth et al., 2005). There have been many examples in our practice to show that when youth are told what to do, where to stay, and how to behave, especially before any kind of positive relationship has been developed, youth do not "buy in." This often results in a power struggle and youth are unable to access the services they need.

DEFINITIONS

Because a wide range of concepts are used in this chapter, it is important to provide a common set of definitions that will be used. There is some confusion that surrounds the issue of being "at risk" (Capuzzi & Gross, 2004), and for the purposes of the High-Risk Youth Initiative it is important to distinguish between youth at risk, and those youth who are "high risk." As well, much research has been done on resiliency (Bernard, 1991; Masten, 1994; Ungar, 2005; Werner, 1996), and these writers have developed strategies to build and strengthen resiliency. The work of Ungar (2002, 2004, 2005, 2006) has provided a philosophical and research base that has strengthened the work that the HRYU is doing. Definitions for *high-risk youth, harm reduction, resiliency, and "the system"* are included here to provide a framework and a rational for the strategies used to build relationships with and engage high-risk youth.

High-risk Youth

The following definition for "high-risk youth" was adopted for Region 6, Edmonton and Area Children and Youth Services, and acts as a guide when accepting youth into the HRYU. Besides the specified age range, which is 14–22 years, all youth in the unit fit into at least five of the following criteria:

- their use of drugs and/or alcohol seems to be interfering with their day-to-day functioning;
- the choices they are making may jeopardize their safety including where they are living and with whom they associate;
- they cannot identify a healthy adult in their lives outside of the professional community;
- there have been multiple placements, including Secure Services and/or Edmonton Youth Offenders Centre;
- there have been multiple file closures due to lack of follow-through by the youth;
- there has been multi-generational involvement with Children and Youth Services;
- they struggle with authority and have few, if any, people they can trust; and
- they struggle with mental health disorders and are living an unpredictable day-to-day existence (Smyth et al., 2005)

The definition of "high-risk youth" is to be distinguished from "hard-to-serve youth," which is a broader category under which "high-risk youth" falls.

Harm reduction

Harm reduction has been a principle in the development of the High Risk Youth Unit (Edmonton and Area Children and Youth Services, Region 6), encouraged through consultation with community partners, and as a result of experiences from the high-risk youth caseload (1999). As noted earlier, this philosophy has been used to build relationships with the youth and to involve them in the decision-making process. Adapted from the work of Richard Elovich and Michael Cowing (1993), this definition of harm reduction was incorporated into the report entitled *The Word On The Street: How Youth View Services Aimed at Them*:

> Harm reduction is defined as a set of strategies and tactics that encourage individuals to reduce the risk of harm to themselves and their communities by their various behaviours. Its major goal is to educate the person to become more conscious of the risks of their behaviour and provide them with the tools and resources with which they can reduce their risk. Some of the major principles include: a humanistic approach; does not deal solely with behaviours, but the whole person with complex needs; accepts that risk is a natural part of life; places risky behaviour on a continuum within the context of a person's life; looks at a person's relationship to the behaviour as defined by him/herself; accepts that behavioural change is often incremental, any positive change is seen as significant; interventions are not rigid but require creativity and innovation reflective of the person's life situation; builds on existing strengths and capacities; is helpful for communities most affected to be involved in creating safe places to get help by organizing harm reduction interventions and programs; and though commonly associated with drug use, harm reduction is applicable to any social welfare and/or public health issues. (Smyth et al., 2005)

Resiliency

The work of Michael Ungar expands on the traditional definition of resiliency as being solely *the capacity to overcome adversity*. Ungar suggests that resiliency is equally present in young people who have been labeled as dangerous, delinquent, deviant and/or disordered; that resilient youth take advantage of whatever opportunities and resources that are available—even those we consider negative or destructive; and that negative behaviours can be a pathway to hidden resilience … focused on the need to create powerful and influential identities for themselves (Ungar, 2005, p. 1). Ungar (2006, p. 3) talks about how adolescents "seek something special to say about themselves, something that will bring with its next revolution the hopes of *power* and *acceptance*." Ungar (2000, p. 5) adds that, in our haste to change our children's behaviour, practitioners overlook how these behaviours make sense to the children themselves, and how these may be their *search for health*. Building positive relationships with high-risk youth can help the practitioner avoid making the assumption that the youth's behaviours do not serve a meaningful purpose. Through talking intentionally with the youth, strategies can be developed to build on these strengths in a safe, non-destructive way. Ungar (2006, p. 7) describes this process as one that can help youth find substitutions for their behaviours—alternative behaviours that offer the same quality of experience as that achieved through his or her problem behaviours.

"The system"

"The system" is a term often used by youth, families, and the community, to refer to having involvement, or more formally having legal status (whether voluntary or non-voluntary) with Alberta Children and Youth Services (ACYS), and receiving services, whether provided through ACYS staff directly, staff employed through other government departments, and/or agencies contracted by the government to deliver a variety of services to children, youth (who may or may not be in care) and families. This definition was accepted and used by youth and facilitators for the study *Word on the Street* (Smyth et al., 2005).

STRATEGIES FOR WORKING WITH HIGH RISK YOUTH

Youth have spoken to us repeatedly about the importance of their relationships with their social workers and the impact these relationships have on the services that are offered to them (Smyth et al., 2005). Recognizing that the formation of these relationships is essential to youth, and in an effort to provide some feedback to practitioners who sought clarification into how to build these relationships, we developed a number of strategies that would articulate some values and principles that could assist in building relationships with youth. These strategies have been shared with youth, and their feedback has validated them for us. These strategies are not comprehensive, but serve to provide a guide to practitioners working with youth, whether in the child welfare system or the community.

Believe that youth are valued and are worth the effort

Believing that youth have value has to be the beginning. The soul-deep belief that youth *are* worth it—worth the acknowledgement that youth do fall through the cracks of a service system that does not adequately meet their needs, the courage to speak of these deficiencies and acknowledge *your* role in the creation or perpetration of them. One must have the willingness to think, and act, outside the box, the philosophical belief that youth are the experts respecting their own lives, the commitment to listen to what youth have to say, and the passion (and persistence) to do things differently. This can, and will, be accomplished only if there is a driving belief that youth are worth it.

Be available

Our research clearly indicates that effective work with youth is done in their time frame, not that of the worker. The caseworker's desire to talk, address the issues and move forward can only be accomplished if the groundwork of acknowledgement, trust and comfort has been established with the youth. The worker's skills of engaging with youth and asking the right "open-ended" questions will not succeed if a youth is not ready to engage. Being available is about being available both physically and emotionally when the youth is ready to participate.

Youth have identified that a barrier to this availability is the nine-to-five routine of many professionals. Youth have made it clear that their lives do not move into this schedule very easily or successfully. Given the lifestyles of high-risk youth, whose schedules are more nocturnal, morning appointments and programming are rarely successful. Youth often find themselves in crisis situations when service delivery systems are closed, and express the need for workers to be available during these times.

Being available emotionally is also important—to be intuitive about what a youth is feeling and thinking, and when they need support and services. When a youth is ready to engage, it is crucial to be attendant, to be responsive to the youth in the "here and now." In theory, this sounds simple, but experience has highlighted some practicalities to consider when with youth, for example: turning off cell phones or pagers, pulling over if driving, having crisis services available if necessary, etc. Emotionally, this can be challenging. At 4:00 p.m. on a Friday afternoon, after a long week of work, it is difficult to be "fully present" when a youth determines it is time to engage. Our research has shown that being self-aware is vital. Being able to communicate to the youth where you are situated on an emotional level allows the youth to gauge what is being said.

Our experience has shown that youth understand that child welfare workers do have lives beyond their jobs, and they will respect those boundaries. However, it is important for the youth to become knowledgeable about the availability of both formal and informal supports that exist in their communities. This wider support network allows youth to access help as needed, rather than only during standard work hours. Wharf (2002) argues that this type of "community social work and community organizing are neglected but potentially powerful strategies for improving child welfare" (p. 9).

Go the extra mile

Sometimes going the extra mile is as simple as finding out what a youth's favourite chocolate bar is and bringing it to them. Sometimes it is finding out about the music they like and learning about it. Sometimes it is a visit to a youth correctional centre on a weekend because a youth is profoundly lonely and sad. Some youth believe that they are not worth spending time with, others blame themselves for their situation, and still others feel they are not worthy of being loved. Thus, small things can carry a lot of meaning, despite an often-portrayed overt "I-don't-care-anymore" attitude.

Our experience has shown that going the extra mile also forces the youth to ask "why is this happening?" Sometimes their reaction to the worker's additional efforts is positive. But the reaction can be negative if the youth interprets the extra attention as having a hidden agenda, or as a form of manipulation by the child welfare worker. Youth's view of the world can be threatened by having a person show they care, but, over time, the youth can take comfort in the fact that someone cares about them. Having someone care about them is also something the youth cannot control, and while they can find this frustrating initially, it can become acceptable given that the youth do want connection.

Monica's Story:
Monica, 17, has recently come from out of town and is with another youth who has an open file with the HRYU. They stay at the same place, though Monica is not there by choice due to a probation order. Monica states that she

thinks social workers are a "fucking waste of time and they have never helped me anyway." She states that she liked one worker in the past but, as usual, she didn't stick around. She wants her independence and doesn't need a "loser social worker" telling her what to do. I tell her I have heard stories like this before and that it is unfortunate that she can't get the help she needs. I see her a few days later and ask how she is doing. She tells me her social worker is a "bitch" and doesn't want to talk to her. Staff say Monica is cranky at times but has been doing well keeping curfew, not using drugs, and helping around the home. I focus on these positive aspects, suggesting she could be getting closer to a supported independent living placement. She doubts this would happen and again generalizes about social workers being quite useless and not following through on what they say. She says that once she turns 18 she is "out of here," so I congratulate her on her goal and ask how I can help her achieve it. Later she tells me she needs some clothes, so I tell her I can call her worker and discuss it. Having been able to facilitate this, she is curious as to why I would help her even when I'm not her social worker. Monica agrees to meet for coffee so I can learn more about her situation and we can look at options around her moving into an independent living program. She acts tough and swears a lot, though not at me. She is honest, tries to get a reaction from some of her stories, and agrees she has a very difficult time trusting anybody, adding "why should I?" I agree and tell her that trust must be earned, but in the meantime, she has to work with the system, given that she is under a permanent status with the government. She is thankful for the opportunity to talk, and starts initiating calls with ideas about how she can get support.

Be self-aware

Self-awareness is a critical aspect of all social work practice. It is especially important when working with youth. Youth have a keen ability to detect

authenticity, truth and integrity in others–in fact, they grow up honing
these skills. High-risk youth have stated that this skill is essential in order
to survive on the streets—knowing who to trust, who not to trust, and
when you are being "played"—could mean the difference between life
and death (Alberta Child and Youth Services, 2007). Youth have reported
that they know whether their social worker cares about them or if they
are "just another caseload" (Alberta Child and Youth Services, 2007). We
have found that it is important to have congruency between beliefs and
actions when working with this population group. As a youth recently
stated, "My social worker is awkward around me; I don't think he really
likes me."

Youth present with a myriad of issues and experiences, and they report it is particularly important that they do not feel judged. When a
youth perceives that he or she is being judged, an internal barrier rises immediately and a "flight or fight" response typically occurs. Youths either
attempt to verbally (and/or physically) defend themselves from further
feelings of pain and rejection, or they will emotionally (and/or physically) retreat to escape the judgment. Either way, the youth disengages,
creating an imbalance that makes the helping relationship difficult.

It is critical that we are aware of who we are as people and professionals: our beliefs, values, judgments and power (Bishop, 2002). Each
of these will affect what we believe about ourselves, about youth, and
how the relationship between youth and ourselves will be perceived. For
example, a white, heterosexual woman would be situated in a stratum of
life that looks very different than where a two-spirited, aboriginal young
man would exist. Being aware of these differences, acknowledging the
power differential, and the diverse lived-realities of the two individuals
allows for the youth to remain the "expert" in his (or her) own life, and
enables the worker to become an ally with them in accessing relevant
and appropriate services (Bishop, 2002; Madsen, 2001). Both the youth
and the child welfare worker are aware of the differences, acknowledge
them, and can discuss the strengths and limitations that both bring to the
relationship.

Be consistent—"I will not give up"

Youth need the assurance that the adults involved in their lives are committed and will not give up on them before they will invest and engage
(Kagan, 2004; Levy & Orlans, 1998). Many youth on the High Risk Youth

Unit have had childhoods marked by inconsistency, abandonment and physical or emotional isolation. Many of these youth do not believe that child welfare workers will be there for the long haul, that it is only a matter of time before they will "give up" on them. Many behaviours and choices of the youth will test the child welfare worker in an attempt to have the worker prove that they are committed (Kagan, 2004, p. 187). The consistent message—"I will not give up on you"—backed by visible actions, demonstrates to the youth both the consistency and commitment they need to begin to invest in the helping relationship.

Jennifer's Story:

Jennifer would scream, saying she didn't want anybody to "fucking care about me." She demonstrated this through her actions by disappearing into the street life of hard drug use, crime, violence and prostitution. It was rare that she would seek out help, although she had a small number of workers involved in her life over the years. She grew up independent, looking after her mother, who was a chronic alcoholic and whose life was wrapped up in meeting her own needs. Her father detached himself from the situation, so Jennifer never knew him. Jennifer's life became one of being in and out of jail. She often said that she could beat drugs if she chose to. She presented as an adrenalin junkie whose need for excitement was almost matched by her need to get high. There were violent relationships, drug debts, and warrants to beat. Jennifer was in and out of locked treatment facilities and while intensely angry at losing her freedom, she could understand that her life was spinning out of control. She never expected to live to be 18. However, shortly after turning 18 she found herself in adult jail again. She was tough and smart and could handle her own. Three professionals who had known Jennifer for a number of years decided to visit her in jail. We could see Jennifer coming toward the visiting room with her head down. She came in and looked up and saw us. She burst into tears and threw herself into the arms of her former foster mother. Her hug was intense and long, and one followed for each of us. Since she had turned 18 and was in jail, she had expected that she would have been forgotten, and that people would have finally given up on her. She was shocked. She talked about her criminal life, that she was now pregnant, and how she needed to clean up her life. She readily agreed to accept help once she was released. She could articulate how she needed to keep some distance with her mother who had taught her to use needles and who maintained her dependency on Jennifer. Jennifer did give birth to a healthy baby and was, for the most part, able to control her addictions. While she has tried to "go straight," she still struggles. She continues to believe that she is not destined for anything better and has a lot of guilt for the things she has done over the years. It continues to be a challenge to convince her that she does deserve a better life, but there are flashes of optimism. She has finally accepted that we won't go away.

Remain committed during testing

Experience tells us that youth want connection; youth want positive relationships. However, if their past experiences have been negative, traumatic, or manipulative, they are not going to take the risk of form-ing a relationship with anybody without testing the waters first. This is simply part of working with high-risk youth. A majority of youth on the HRYU have had negative experiences with child welfare workers so are, rightfully, sceptical and suspicious. As such, they will push, swear, disappear, argue, challenge, occasionally threaten, sabotage, lie, say they don't care, threaten suicide, use drugs/alcohol, run away, and hide. The youth will expect the "power card" to be played: they expect to be told what to do and when to do it; they expect to hear that there will be con-sequences (perhaps file closure or residential treatment) if they don't do what they are told. They know how to read the script—they have been in such power struggles before and through practice are skilled. It is a sur-vival technique—they force the rejection before they get hurt again (Levy and Orlans, 1998; Kagan, 2004). Often childhood trauma has made them wary of adults, so they become skilled at a young age in keeping people at a distance. The more adults reading their script, the more reinforced the behaviour becomes. Youth have demonstrated that it is during this testing phase where they are often lost. If the youth's belief that adults do not help is reinforced, they will likely perceive that there will be little to gain from working together.

Child welfare workers/intake workers/investigators/assessors may label the youth as defiant and/or manipulative and conclude that they are not ready for services. Some youth come to believe that they are beyond help or that they are too insignificant for anyone to worry about them or care about them. Workers must pass the test and take seriously their threats about our safety and their own. The message conveyed must be that they are still important and that they can't push us away so easily.

Be intentional in your interactions

Relationships with youth should be intentional, significant and purpose-filled. Relationships should be based on shared power (Bishop, 2002) and a desire to learn and understand, and should have specific goals and outcomes. Our research has shown that, in general, youth can understand the extent of these relationships, the boundaries that exist and the roles and responsibilities of the worker. It is extremely important for youth to understand what they can expect from their social workers, as child welfare workers have specific provincial/territorial legislation under which they must work.

Don't make gaining trust the main goal

Kagan (2004), Neufeld and Mate (2004), and Levy and Orlans (1998), among others, outline the importance of gaining the trust of children and youth. Of course, if this happens, there are many benefits; however, our experience with youth indicates that this does not need to be the end goal. The child welfare worker sets out to support, advise, guide, help, and learn from the youth. If through this process a trusting relationship emerges, the connection will definitely be stronger. The concern when the push is to establish trust is that the helping process can very easily become the child welfare worker's agenda, rather than having the youth set the agenda for what makes sense to them.

Despite the efforts of the child welfare worker, it is possible that youth are still not able to see the relationship as one of mutual trust. Youth have reported to us that it is important to them to know that their worker will not hurt them emotionally, that they will be heard, that they will not be judged, and that they will not be rejected or abandoned. Youth demonstrate that it is at this level where there can be some "buy in," and work can be accomplished. An example of this are the youth who do not maintain regular contact with their workers, but will reach out to their workers for help when experiencing a crisis, acknowledging that they cannot manage everything on their own.

> ### Annie's Story:
> Annie, 15, had been through a number of foster homes, group homes, and family placements. In each case, she either left or the caregiver asked for her to be removed. She actively sabotaged placements and could articulate that she was not going to let anyone get close to her. Every significant person in her life had either abandoned her and/or abused her, sexually, physically, mentally and emotionally. At times Annie was the tough street kid, while at other times she was a little girl who wanted a mother to love her and cuddle her; what she wanted most she fought so hard to avoid. It took time and patience to get Annie to a point that she could see we were not trying to hurt her. One day, out of the blue, she left a voice message on my cell phone. She was trying to get words out through heartfelt sobbing and said her mother had asked how she was doing for the first time in her life. Her mother, who had serious health problems due to chronic drinking, could never be available for her daughter, but Annie could not get over this. Slowly, she started to reach out despite risking further hurt in life.

Create healthy confusion

Related to avoiding the scripts that youth set out for us is the strategy of creating healthy confusion for the youth. This entails challenging the youth's negative belief system (Levy and Orlans, 1998) and their dark view of the world. Our work with high-risk youth has demonstrated that such thinking can be challenged by doing things they don't expect, including being a safe, consistent, and genuine adult in their lives.

All of the youth in the HRYU have relationship, trust, and bonding issues. This does not mean that they are all youth with Reactive Attachment Disorder (RAD), though a number have been diagnosed with this, meaning their attachment process was disrupted before they reached the age of 36 months (Kagan, 2004; Levy and Orlans, 1998). While patterns of behaviour are identifiable for those who are diagnosed with RAD, attachment in general remains a core issue with all of the youth. By the time the youth have come to the HRYU, they have built thick walls around themselves to keep people at a distance and have developed sophisticated skills in reading people and avoiding any kind of emotional connection. Although this could be viewed as a dark and lonely place to be, youth say it can be a comfortable place for them because there is less fear of being rejected and hurt again.

Our work with this population has shown the effectiveness of challenging youth on their beliefs that they have to rely on themselves to get by in the world; that others will take advantage of them; that adults cannot be trusted to help; that people who say they care are not telling the truth; and that people do not understand them. The challenging should occur in a sensitive and respectful way (Levy and Orlans, 1998), as the tendency to push too hard results in the youth pushing back. In such cases we end up back in the power and control relationship, with the youth being labelled uncooperative and defiant, and with very little progress being made. Our experience has shown us that the youth will go at their own pace—one that is safe for them. If this safety is evident, then there is a better chance that they will allow their view of the world to be challenged.

Again, being respectful, thoughtful, and non-judgemental are basic but crucial professional stances. In general, people do not give up their belief systems easily, and when trust is not present, it can become more difficult. We have observed that when one is consistent and patient, it becomes possible for the youth to slowly allow you into their world. This process is important as it can encourage youth to take further risks by allowing others into their world, which builds their external support network.

Celebrate small successes (inspire hope)

When working with high-risk youth, it is essential to remain hopeful—to believe that youth are not "stuck," that change can occur, and that youth are strong and resilient. Working from a harm-reduction approach is about being aware of what the young person sees as important, and remaining focused on their individual definition of success. It is a philosophical shift to define success through the eyes of a youth, and not as the "expert" (Elovich & Cowing, 1993). It is important to celebrate the success, no matter how small, and maintain communication to assess that progress is being made in a way that makes sense to the youth. For example, when a youth returns from the streets, rather than punishing them, celebrate their return and use this as an opportunity for relationship-building and learning. These situations will present themselves daily, and workers have the opportunity to remain intentionally focused on "celebrating the small things" and inspiring some measure of hope in all situations.

Work from a strengths-based perspective

Discussion in the area of strength-based practice has increased; however, there continues to be emphasis on the deficit or "at-risk" paradigm (Hammond & Nuttgens, 2007), or the traditional medical/pathology paradigm (Blundo, 2001). Blundo (2001) notes, "We look for what is going wrong, symptoms, what might be failings, pathologies" (p. 297). He adds that changing to a "strengths/solution-focused perspective is a considerable challenge for social workers," especially given that students come "ready-made with a bias toward seeing problems and then trying to fix them by making suggestions to the client." We tend to use "problem-saturated" language (Madsen, 2001; Worden, 1999), which again, conforms to the expectation of disconnected youth who have heard such language most of their lives. Michael Ungar (2005) tells us that youth who receive the most attention in our communities are labelled into four categories: dangerous, delinquent, deviant, and disordered. However, he notes that resilience is equally present in these youth as they survive and take advantage of any available opportunities and resources—even those we consider negative or destructive.

And survive they do. High-risk youth have many skills that they use to get by and to create their identity. "Couch surfing" is a way to solve the problem of not having a placement. Pushing people away and "manipulating" is a way to avoid more rejection and hurt. Dropping out of school is a way to avoid feeling like a failure. Committing a crime and getting caught is a way to gain safety and structure when feeling out of control, or when wanting a feeling of power and status to be re-established. The key is to provide substitutes for the problem behaviour rather than trying to suppress the behaviours (Ungar, 2005), which is what youth would expect and is part of their scripts. When the substitutes we offer meet the needs of the youth for a powerful and socially acceptable identity, they are far more likely to take advantage of them. Once we understand what children/youth gain from "playing at being bad" we can offer substitute behaviours that reward them with the same power and control derived from the problem behaviour (Ungar, 2005).

Blundo (2001) claims that

> [t]raditional social work practice is disempowering as workers use technical skills such as confrontation, overcoming resistance, and managing the "manipulative" client while at the same time manipulating the relationship to enhance compliance with professional decisions .... In contrast, from a strengths perspective, the "manipulative" client is understood as using considerable skill and thought for a purpose that is meaningful to that person. It is resistance only when these actions are perceived by the worker as the client challenging what the worker wants to take place (p. 302).

Blundo (2001) challenges the worker-is-the-expert perspective, which he believes is the prevailing norm in social work, resulting in the worker feeling it is their duty to impart wisdom to the client to help bring about change. Strength-based practice views the youth as experts on their own lives; therefore, working together is productive, empowers the youth, and enhances the relationship.

Explore the youth's motivation to change

Our experience indicates that it is erroneous to believe that youth don't want to change. They try, and they try again. As previously stated, it is difficult to make changes without a sense of connection and support. High-risk youth often have little or no belief in themselves that change can occur. Setbacks are extremely difficult and reinforce the negatives they already believe about themselves. If these beliefs have not come from their family circumstances, they will arise from the labels that have been attached to them as they encountered human service systems such as medical, school, child welfare, and justice. They learn they are "problem children," that they have behavioural issues, are conduct disordered, ADHD, ADD, depressed, learning disordered, attachment disordered, anti-social and *high-risk!* They also hear it from peers who label them as "druggies," "criminals," "psychos," "sluts," "hookers," and/or "stupid." How does a youth find an identity through all of these labels? How does a youth find some measure of motivation through all of this "deficit-based" talk?

As our research and conversations with youth have shown, high-risk youth have very limited access to resources, little help to find resources, and a deep mistrust that such resources will result in a positive experience. A youth's mental health, internalized beliefs and addictions may be barriers that prevent them from meeting their basic needs, such as finding a place to live, escaping hunger, and even arranging transportation to appointments.

Finding solutions to these issues with the youth can be a monumental task requiring much patience. It takes time working with the youth to get permission to involve other resources whether a psychologist, a psychiatrist, a school, a life skills program, a placement, a physician, or a dentist. It can be very much a "seize the day" mentality in being ready to act when the motivation is evident. As tough as the youth may be on the street, this process can involve a lot of hand-holding, otherwise the appointments simply don't happen. For most youth, being pushed into a series of meetings means being put into a situation of repeatedly taking risks and this can be overwhelming. This doesn't reflect a lack of motivation by the youth, but rather that the process is moving at the pace of the worker rather than the youth. This speaks to the need of constant "checking in" with the youth to ensure they are feeling safe, have appropriate support, and can handle the speed at which events are unfolding.

Build relationships and community networks

By extending our own networks of support, we inevitably expand the networks of support for the youth. The youth are part of the community, so we in child welfare services need to be part of the community. Outreach workers and service agencies are working with high-risk youth in the community. Child welfare needs to be partners in the human service community. The community represents an important resource for youth, rich in wisdom, ideas, creativity and support resources.

In interacting with outreach and agency partners in Edmonton (Alberta), community members (professional and non-professional) have proven to be invaluable in their role in bridging the "disconnect" between the youth and the system. By developing partnerships with outreach and service agencies, there is the opportunity to expand the support network for youth to access a wider variety of services (mandated and non-mandated). It is also very important that the youth perceive their support people working together; that they have a team on their side.

The HRYU and the community work closely together and have developed a strong relationship. Concerns, criticisms, and constructive venting are put on the table to ensure all are accountable in best supporting the youth. Most referrals to the HRYU come from the community, which, in itself, shows a willingness to work with the child welfare "system" and an expectation that the voice of the youth will be respected. When working in partnership, the message to the youth is this: "These people (from the HRYU) are good people and they will go out of their way to help you." This can give permission to the youth to accept services and make connections. The partnerships promote the sharing of ideas, the use of natural resources in the community, and the importance of demonstrating to the youth that they have a team of support behind them.

Of particular importance is the connection with cultural supports and services for HRY. One such agency for the HRYU is Boyle St. Community Services. This Edmonton inner-city agency offers a continuum of services to meet individual, family, and community needs. This community partnership tries to ensure that work with Aboriginal youth is as culturally sensitive as possible, and that Aboriginal resources are accessed (slightly over 50 percent of the youth involved with the HRYU are Aboriginal). Boyle program manager Karen Bruno believes that, in working with Aboriginal clients, it is particularly important to know the community. She believes that the community values relationships, views life as a journey of discovery, sees strengths, and supports people to be successfully independent. Aboriginal cultural norms are acknowledged as strengths to incorporate in meeting the needs of youth.

CONCLUSION

We do not believe that we have all of the answers but, instead, continue to look to the youth who have articulated what *does not* work in the system. Through partnership with the community and others who share a passion in working with high-risk youth, attempts have been made to ensure that the voices of these youth are heard and their needs are better met by a child welfare system that has acknowledged a need for this to happen. Edmonton and Area Children and Youth Services, Region 6, and the community have started an initiative through the High Risk Youth Unit incorporating a harm reduction and resiliency/strength-based approach that relies on meaningful community engagement. Relationship-building is a key focus area in working with these youth, as outlined in the strategies discussed above.

Every youth that comes into the unit presents new challenges and new understandings, which encourages workers to ally with them and provide services creatively. This is our gift from the youth. Our gift to them is not to judge, but to listen, to try and understand what they are going through, to help them be accountable to themselves, to help create some happy memories, and to give them hope for the future.

FUTURE DIRECTIONS

There is very little research on child welfare practice with high-risk youth. As child welfare workers begin to partner with youth and work creatively with them, research will need to be done to evaluate outcomes and measure effectiveness for youth, families, communities and child welfare agencies. Until such time, work needs to continue in an effort to challenge traditional practice to better engage youth and build relationships.

The High Risk Youth Unit does not reach all high-risk youth in Edmonton and area, so work will continue to support the expansion of the initiative, and the philosophy behind it, both in Edmonton and throughout Alberta. This is not just about changing the way day-to-day practice is done, but also allowing for a non-traditional framework with this population of youth. This means giving caseworkers permission to think and act differently and to work creatively *with* the youth; this means providing access to appropriate training and allowing caseworkers time to grow comfortable in the role. In addition, the continuation of the development and modification of services and programs for this challenging population will aim to ensure that the voices of the youth are being heard.

REFERENCES

Alberta Child and Youth Services, Office of the Child and Youth Advocate (2007). *Word on the Street* (Video). Available from the Office of the Child and Youth

Advocate, Peace Hills Trust Tower, #803, 10011-109 St., Edmonton, AB, (780) 422-6056.

Bernard, B. (1991). *Fostering resiliency in kids: Protective factors in the family, school, and community.* Portland, OR: Northwest Regional Educational Laboratory.

Bishop, A. (2002). *Becoming an ally: Breaking the cycle of oppression in people,* 2nd Edition. Fernwood Publishing: Halifax, Nova Scotia.

Blundo, R. (2001). Learning strength-based practice: Challenging our personal and professional frames. *Families In Society, 82*(3), 296-304.

Capuzzi, D., & Gross, D. (2004). *Youth at risk: A prevention resource for counselors, teachers, and parents,* Fourth Edition. New Jersey: Pearson Education, Inc.

Elovich, R., & Cowing, M. (1993). Recovery readiness: Strategies that bring treatment to addicts where they are. National Health Care for the Homeless Council, National Harm Reduction Working Group Report. Retrieved August 15, 2007, from http://www.nhchc.org/Curriculum/module4/module4D/H8PrinciplesofHarmReduction.pdf

Hammond, W., & Nuttgens, N. (2007). Resiliency: Embracing a strength-based approach to service provision. Presentation at Joint Professional Development Day, City Centre Education Project, Edmonton, AB, November 14, 2007.

Kagan, R. (2004). *Rebuilding attachment with traumatized children: Healing from losses, violence, abuse, and neglect.* New York: The Haworth Maltreatment and Trauma Press.

Levy, T. M., & Orlans, M. (1998). *Attachment, treatment, and healing: Understanding and treating attachment disorder in children and families.* USA: Child Welfare League of America, Inc.

Madsen, W. C. (2001). Collaborative therapy with multi-stressed families: From old problems to new futures. New York: Guilford Press.

Masten, A. S. (1994). Resilience in individual development: Successful adaptation despite risk and adversity. In M. C. Wang & E. W. Gordon (Eds.), *Educational resilience in inner-city America: Challenges and prospects* (pp. 3-25). Hillsdale, NJ: Erlbaum.

Neufeld, G., & Mate, G. (2004). *Hold on to your kids: Why parents matter.* Alfred A. Knopf Canada.

Smyth, P., & Eaton-Erickson, A. (2007). Making the Connection: Working with high-risk youth. Prairie Child Welfare 4th Biannual Symposium, Regina, Saskatchewan (power-point presentation).

Smyth, P., and Eaton-Erickson, A. (1999). High-risk teen caseload: A pilot project. Edmonton. Edmonton and Area Child and Family Services, Region 6.

Smyth, P., Eaton-Erickson, A., Slessor, J., & Pasma, R. (2005). *The word on the street: How youth view services aimed at them. Edmonton.* High Risk Youth Task Force, Edmonton and Area Child and Family Services, Region 6.

Ungar, M. (2002). *Playing at being bad: The hidden resilience of troubled teens.* Nova Scotia: Pottersfield.

Ungar, M. (2004). *Nurturing hidden resilience in troubled youth.* Toronto: University of Toronto Press.

Ungar, M. (2005). Delinquent or simply resilient? How "problem" behaviour can be a child's hidden path to resilience. Voices For Children, www.voicesforchildren.ca/report-aug-2005.

Ungar, M. (2006). *Strengths-based counseling with at-risk youth.* Thousand Oaks, CA: Corwin Press

Werner, E. E. (1996). How children become resilient: Observations and cautions. *Resiliency in Action, 1*(1), 18-28.

Wharf, B. (Ed.). (2002). *Community work approaches to child welfare.* Canada: Broadview Press, Ltd.

Wilson, M., & Woods, L. (2006). Iatrogenic outcomes of the child welfare system: Vulnerable adolescents, peer influences, and instability in foster care arrangements. In K. A. Dodge, T. J. Dishion & J. E. Lansford (Eds.), *Deviant peer influences in programs for youth: Problems and solutions* (pp. 203-214). New York: Guilford Press.

Worden, M. (1999). *Family therapy basics* (second edition). Pacific Grove, CA: Brooks/ Cole Publishing Company.

CHAPTER 7

The Moving Forward Project: Working with Refugee Children, Youth, and their Families

Judy White and collaborators Dawn Franklin, Klaus Gruber, Cody Hanke, Bernadette Holzer, Nayyar Javed, Pat Keyser, Ashraf Mir, Ijeoma Udemgba, Mechilene Veszi, Clive Weighill

INTRODUCTION

The aim of this chapter is to present a discussion about some of the challenges faced by social workers and human service workers engaged in responding to the child welfare needs of refugee children and youth. Through a discussion referring to the Saskatchewan-based Moving Forward project, the chapter will highlight important aspects of this work: working with parents, building strong communities, understanding the needs and challenges facing refugee families. The Moving Forward project was sparked by two publications: *Post traumatic stress disorder: The lived experience of immigrant, refugee, and visible minority women of Saskatchewan* (Immigrant, Refugee, and Visible Minority Women of Saskatchewan,

SUGGESTED CITATION: White, J., Franklin, D., Gruber, K., Hanke, C., Holzer, B., Javed, N., et al. (2009). The Moving Forward project: Working with refugee children, youth, and their families. In S. McKay, D. Fuchs, & I. Brown (Eds.), *Passion for action in child and family services: Voices from the prairies* (pp. 143-164). Regina, SK: Canadian Plains Research Center.

2002), and *Women and post traumatic stress disorder: Moving research to policy* (Omorodion & White, 2003). The 2002 study discussed experiences that led to post traumatic stress and described symptoms of post traumatic stress (for example, flashbacks, hypervigilance, withdrawal, and depression). The studies reported the underutilization of "mainstream" mental health agencies. Both studies reported the concerns of refugee parents about the unaddressed needs of their children.

Despite the fact that Canada has boasted of a long tradition of humanitarian response to the needs of this population (Government of Canada, 2008), social workers and human service practitioners are still learning about how to respond to the needs of children and youth who have experienced trauma. Unlike the situation of immigrants, where there is some choice with respect to returning to their countries of origin, refugees have a real fear of returning to their countries of origin because of the situations of war, violence, oppression, and persecution (Immigration and Refugee Board of Canada, 2006). These experiences have resulted in post traumatic stress responses, and in calls for the development of programs, services, and interventions to address accompanying symptoms and negative outcomes that affect the lives of children and youth.

These children and youth may not have experienced traumatic events directly. However, they may experience secondary traumatization and its transgenerational effects (Kirmayer, Lemelson, & Barad, 2007). They may grow up hearing stories about the experiences of their parents, and may develop anxieties as a result (Kirmayer, Lemelson, & Barad, 2007). The impact of traumatic events extends to the wider community. Alexander (2004) (as cited in Kirmayer et al., 2007) and Robben and Suarez-Orozco (2000) (as cited in Kirmayer et al., 2007) have suggested that there is need to understand how "the interaction of individual and collective processes contribute to resilience and reconstruction in the aftermath of political violence" (Kirmayer, Lemelson, & Barad, 2007, p. 10). In short, as the literature concludes, child welfare work with refugee children and youth cannot be done in isolation, but within the context of community and family (Hurlock, McCullagh, & Schissel, 2004; Kirmayer, Lemelson, & Barad, 2007).

Various reports have already described some of the negative outcomes of trauma: the vulnerable situation of refugee and immigrant youth, including the potential for involvement in gangs, situations of violence, and drug trafficking (Baldwin, 2005; Federation of Canadian municipalities,

2004; CBC Sports, 2007; Van Ngo & Schleifer, 2005; Hurlock, McCullagh, & Schissel, 2004; Mellor, MacRae, Pauls & Hornick, 2005). These reports emphasize the need for ongoing knowledge building, and also the development of a social and health services infrastructure to serve this population (Cooper, Masi, Dababnah, Aratani, & Knitzer, 2007).

There have been some initiatives aimed at responding to these issues (Public Safety Canada, 2006; United States Conference of Catholic Bishops/Migration and Refugee Services, 2007); however, there is still a dearth of literature relating specifically to the needs of refugee children and youth living in the Prairies. It is hoped that this study will contribute to an understanding of the importance of including this literature within the domain of Canadian, but particularly Prairie, child welfare literature.

BACKGROUND

Immigration trends: Canada and Saskatchewan

One of the challenges of putting the topic of trauma and its impact on immigrants and refugees on the public agenda in Saskatchewan was that, prior to the 2000s, the number of immigrants and refugees arriving in Saskatchewan was relatively small (Christensen, 1999, 2003, 2005; Henry, Tator, Mattis, & Rees, 2000; Beaujot, 1996; Elliott, 2003; Mulder & Korenic, 2005). In addition, immigrant retention rates were relatively low (City of Saskatoon, 2004, 2007). Nevertheless, Saskatchewan's experiences with refugee resettlement have been more significant. Indeed, settlement work in Saskatchewan evolved from Saskatchewan residents' concerns about the needs of refugees. For example, the Open Door Societies, now the largest settlement agencies in the province, were first established in the 1980s to respond to the needs of refugees from Vietnam. Another interesting observation is that in the 2001 to 2002 period, the immigrant population to Saskatchewan tended to have larger numbers of children and youth than Saskatchewan-born residents (Elliott, 2003).

Saskatchewan's "economic boom" has resulted in some changes with respect to attitudes to newcomer settlement. "Economic boom" has resulted in labour market shortages in Saskatchewan, and immigrants and refugees are now being seen as a source from which to draw. In 2002, 229,000 immigrants arrived in Canada, with 1,665 of these arriving in Saskatchewan (Citizenship and Immigration Canada, 2006; City of Saskatoon, 2004, 2007). About 43 percent of the immigrants to Saskatchewan tend to settle in Saskatoon. In terms of refugees, there was an increase from 9.7 percent to 11.6 percent between 1996 and 2001. During this period, 21 percent of immigrants came under the family class, 46 percent under economic immigrant class, and 33 percent came under refugee class. Between 2001 and 2004, 22 percent came under the family class, 41 percent came under the economic immigrant class, and 35 percent came under the refugee class (Citizenship and Immigration Canada, 2006; City of Saskatoon, 2004).

There has also been a shift with respect to source countries. Prior to the 1970s, the majority of immigrants to Canada came from the United States, Britain and other European countries (Christensen, 1999, 2003, 2005). In more recent times, immigrants have been arriving in larger numbers from African, Asian, Caribbean, and Latin American countries (Beaujot, 1996; Mulder & Korenic, 2005). Many are coming from war-affected regions and regions of unrest. Host communities are faced with the goal of helping these families, children, and youth to settle in Canada and to build community and social relationships within their environments.

Project Design and Assumptions

The partners

The project was designed by International Women of Saskatoon (IWS) and Family Service Saskatoon. IWS (formerly Immigrant Women of Saskatchewan, Saskatoon Chapter) is a non-profit community-based organization that has been providing services to immigrant women and refugee women and their families for the past twenty years. Family Service Saskatoon is a non-profit community-based organization that has served the Saskatoon community for more than 75 years. The agency provides counseling services and programs for youth, young parents, couples, individuals, and families. The advisory committee included representatives from the settlement and immigrant serving agencies, the police, and the school sector. It was anticipated that social work practicum students would be involved in the project and therefore would also be invited to participate on the advisory committee.

Rationale and assumptions driving the project design

IWS decided to approach Family Service Saskatoon because IWS assumed that they themselves lacked the capacity to address the psychological needs of this population. While IWS had a long history of working with immigrant and refugee women, they did not believe that the agency had the professional knowledge and skills to address the issues of trauma adequately on their own. They were also committed to building bridges with "mainstream" organizations and building capacity within these organizations. Family Service Saskatoon's staff members were extremely enthusiastic about this partnership. The agency had a long history of counseling, including group work, and they made assumptions that their staff had the knowledge and skills to work competently with this population. The project was designed based on these assumptions: one agency assuming they could apply the Western model as their modus operandi; the second assuming that the other partner was the expert, with knowledge and skills that they did not have.

Goals of the project

The main goal of the project was to provide opportunity for building knowledge and skills among refugee children, youth, and their families to effectively address issues of trauma. A second goal was to build awareness of the services and programs available to immigrant and refugee families. A third was to enhance capacity among service providers so they could better respond to the needs of refugee children, youth, and their families.

Recruitment and group process

The project coordinator, in consultation with the group facilitators, was responsible for screening participants. No new group members were to be added to the group after the first group session. The intervention plan for the first intake included facilitating 6 group sessions with parents from 7-10 families from Afghanistan and Sudan, and 6 group sessions with children and youth from the same communities. The groups would be co-facilitated with at least one facilitator being a new Canadian, immigrant, or refugee woman.

The decision to focus on these two populations was supported by statistics that reported that 30 percent of government-assisted refugees were arriving from Sudan, and 25 percent from Afghanistan (Anderson, 2005). Advisory committee members who were connected with settlement agencies also supported this choice. It was anticipated that choosing participants from two countries only would minimize communication (language) challenges. Allowances were made within the budget to accommodate the use of interpreters if necessary.

The team planned on developing posters and pamphlets to advertise the project and to assist with recruitment. Other planned methods of recruitment included presentations to staff and clients at settlement agencies, schools, and ethnocultural associations. The team also planned to develop and disseminate resource materials on the topic of post traumatic stress. The team hoped that these resource materials would serve to engage refugee and immigrant families.

Orientation

Prior to the commencement of groups, the advisory committee planned an orientation for all staff and volunteers involved in the program. The aim of the orientation sessions was to expose participants to a broad range of topics relevant to working with refugee children, youth, and families. The orientation sessions included presentations by individuals from specific ethnocultural communities (focusing on those identified for recruitment). The aim of these presentations was to invite speakers to share information about the historical, political, economic, and social conditions in their countries of origin. Presenters were also invited to share personal stories about their experiences living in war-affected countries, in situations of extreme trauma, and in refugee camps. Other presentations focused on information about the journey, settlement, and integration experiences of refugees in general. Other key components of the orientation included presentations on the theme of post traumatic stress and post traumatic stress responses, and on cross-cultural communication. The orientation session always included a presentation on self-care for service providers.

HOW THE PROJECT UNFOLDED

Project components

The primary components of this project were education, intervention, resource development and dissemination. These components would be mutually inclusive of one another, reflecting a commitment to a holistic, integrated approach to program delivery. The project materials (for example, flyers, brochures, and pamphlets) were used for publicity, recruitment and education. These were developed in multiple languages in an attempt to reach as broad a cross-section of the immigrant and refugee community as possible. The team relied on group work in order to provide opportunity for participants to learn life skills topics such as the effects of trauma and stress on family dynamics, positive coping skills, and problem solving skills. Youth had an opportunity to use arts and crafts to assist with building communication and self-expression skills.

The education component was directed not only towards the immigrant and refugee children, youth, and families, but also towards service providers and professionals. For example, presentations were done to the Saskatoon Catholic Schools Professional Development Conference, to the 2007 Congress of the Social Sciences and Humanities Conference held in Saskatoon, and at the Prairie Child Welfare Consortium Symposium held in 2007 in Regina.

The advisory committee

Following receipt of funding, one of the first tasks of the team was to put together an advisory committee. Bimonthly meetings provided opportunity for input and guidance through brainstorming, project reports, reviews, and discussions. During the first intake, representation came primarily from the immigrant and refugee serving agencies. Following this intake the team was more intentional about reaching out to the school sector and used formal letters of introduction with telephone and face-to-face follow-up meetings to assist with networking. A representative from the public school system joined the advisory committee. Letters of invitation were also sent to the Saskatoon Police and to the Mennonite Central Committee. Both of these responded positively.

There are still individuals or sectors missing from this advisory committee; of particular note would be representation from the health and social services sectors. The team concluded that participation by the mental health sector would be a step towards addressing concerns about the underutilization and often non-utilization of traditional mental health services by refugee families, children and youth (Canadian Task Force on Mental Health Issues Affecting Immigrants and Refugees, 1988; Williams, 2002; White, 2007; Immigrant, Refugee, and Visible Minority Women of Saskatchewan, 2002; Omorodion & White, 2003). Another gap is the lack of direct participation or representation from the province's child welfare services. This is a major failing considering the fact that one of the stated reasons for the creation of the project was the vulnerability of refugee and immigrant youth and the potential for them to become involved in the child welfare system (risk of gang involvement, violence, drugs). The failure to reach out to these sectors reflects the general tendency of human services agencies to approach their work in a fragmented manner.

The orientation sessions

These orientation sessions have been invaluable, as reflected in the feedback following both orientations. The project team gained an understanding of the possible challenges they would face while working with the target group. The use of presenters from different countries allowed participants to listen to individuals who had survived challenging life experiences, and who were now giving back to their communities in many different ways. In some cases, the stories gave participants a glimpse of the depth of trauma experienced by individuals, the level of resilience, and also of the invisible and deep-rooted scars of trauma. Presenters spoke about the factors that led to strife, violence, and underdevelopment in their countries of origin. They would often share information about themselves, including information about the events or conditions that led to their leaving their countries of origin. These sessions put a human and local face to much of what participants may have learned about through books and the media. The sessions provided background preparation for all those involved in the project, as well as an opportunity for participants to begin the process of networking and sharing with one another.

Toseland and Rivas (1995) have argued that it is not possible for professionals to know everything about the background and cultures of all the individuals and families with whom they work. However, the authors acknowledge that there are many ways of building knowledge in this area. These include reading and researching, visiting agencies and communities that newcomers might frequent, and through the technique of social mapping. The Moving Forward project team continued to remain focused on providing an approach that would best meet the child welfare needs of this population and on encouraging professional development that would identify and respond to new and emerging issues and challenges.

Orientation sessions provide opportunity to build and enhance knowledge and skills among practitioners from varied backgrounds in order to provide the best possible and most comprehensive approaches.

This is supported in the literature, which suggests that interventions with refugee children and youth have often been fragmented and that it is important to ensure the "weaving together of intervention modalities by a multicultural, multidisciplinary, professional and paraprofessional team, preferably working at the primary prevention level" (Aldous, 1999, p. 49).

Recruiting refugee families

The team promoted the project and worked on recruitment through: telephone calls, correspondence, face to face meetings with management staff and English as a Second Language teachers at schools, home visits, presentations at adult group meetings and classes at settlement agencies, and other social events and gatherings where there would be potential parents and youth; print media, and on websites. Although the team initially assumed that they would recruit about 7-10 families from Afghanistan and Sudan, the first intake actually included families not only from these two countries but also from Burundi, China, Colombia, and Peru. Eighteen families participated in this first intake. Service providers from the settlement agencies referred individuals whom they assessed to be in tremendous need of services, and this list went beyond the anticipated target populations.

At the second intake, the team again tried to limit the number of country groups, still believing that this would help alleviate the difficulties that multiple languages posed. Again, because of demand, the team did not adhere to their plan. International Women of Saskatoon played a lead role in the recruitment process of the participants. This "flexibility" continued to create challenges for group facilitators and had an impact on the group process that will be discussed later in this chapter. Eighteen families from Colombia, Afghanistan, Sudan, Burma, Rwanda, Congo, Egypt, Mongolia, Bosnia, and Burundi participated in the project. In this final list, there were 4 families from Columbia, 7 from Afghanistan, 3 from Sudan, and 1 from each of the other countries.

There were distinct differences between the two intakes. Group sessions from the first intake took place at Family Service Saskatoon office while the second was school-based. The children and youth connected with the first intake were between the ages of 12 and 17; those from the second intake were between the ages of 12 and 22.

The group process with parents

Six week sessions were held with parents. The team provided transportation, childcare, and refreshments. During the design and planning stages, the assumption was that the groups would be closed (that is, not adding new members after the first session) (Toseland & Rivas, 1995). The different viewpoints in the literature demonstrate some of the challenges of making decisions about whether groups should be closed. Some authors suggest that while there is a place for open groups, constantly adding new members can be distracting (Daste & Rose, 2004). Daste and Rose (2004) cite literature suggesting that groups should be closed after the first sessions "to enhance cohesion of the group and to 'allow progressive work and promote good attendance" (p. 21). Toseland and Rivas (1995) note that groups where there are "frequent and extensive membership changes" (p. 86) usually remain at the formative stage. These authors argue that open groups usually do not lead to intimacy among members.

The notion of a closed group was not easily understood by the participants. The team had expectations about how the groups would evolve, but decided that the messages from the parents were compelling. These messages were that the parents were happy with an open group concept and process. The result was that in both intakes it took some time to build cohesiveness because of having to navigate through a maze of different languages. Participants were new to the country and often to one another. Nevertheless, this "open group" concept seemed to work for the participants. The facilitators accepted that parents would bring their friends to the group. They also learned to embrace the spontaneous dancing and singing that would emerge. They were flexible and were able to embrace the new members, while at the same time knowing that this meant they were entering "new territory" with respect to how they would run their groups.

It was always important to focus on the intent and benefits of the group process. First, the team drew on literature about the nature of the group experience (Ephross, 2004, p. 2). Individuals would be members based on being "social beings in continuous interaction with others who are both seen and unseen" (p. 2). With respect to understanding group principles, there was a belief that "a member's actions are socially derived and contributory" (p. 2). Participants would realize they were not alone in their experiences, and they could support and learn from one another. Parents would learn to identify and discuss the effects of trauma on themselves and on their children. The team anticipated that the group process would provide opportunity for giving information or educating (in this case education about trauma and other aspects of the healing journey) (Moursund & Kenny, 2002; Toseland & Rivas, 1995; Ephross, 2004).

Cooper, Masi, Dababnah, Aratani, and Knitzer (2007) note that the lives of refugee children and youth in Canada will be influenced by the experiences of their parents as they (the parents) go through the process of learning to live and cope with life in Canada. Hence, it was important to build knowledge and skills among parents so that they could begin to name and understand the challenges of life in Canada, and also begin to build and enhance relevant skills and capacities to assist them with communicating their needs and concerns with others and developing the kind of mutual aid and support networks that they might require (Moursund & Kenny, 2002; Toseland & Rivas, 1995; Ephross, 2004).

With respect to educative and informative goals, parents seemed to express more interest (especially at the start) in talking about how they could become a part of Canadian society, and less in talking about their past experiences of trauma. They did not want to relive memories, and wanted to make a fresh start in Canada. Nevertheless, there were opportunities for the facilitators to provide information about trauma and about responses to trauma. This included information about the impact of trauma and its effects on the family and on child development. This was consistent with the goals and objectives that the facilitator had presented to the participants.

Language, reading, and writing

Facilitating groups with parents proved to be extremely challenging, especially because of the assumption that presentations and discussions would be the primary activities during the groups. Language barriers made this difficult. Since participants did not want to have interpreters in the sessions, they acted as peer interpreters when necessary. A disadvantage of this was that there would be side conversations that could be distracting. Nevertheless, peer interpreting may not necessarily have taken more time than if professional interpreters had been used.

Lack of basic literacy skills in reading and writing was evident among some participants in the first cohort. This was even more apparent with the second cohort. This created challenges for facilitators who were not accustomed to having to address literacy issues. Once the team realized that not all participants had English language skills, they began to use more visual aids. Facilitators used flip charts to write out the names of emotions (sadness, anger, joy) in different languages. However, this had to be supplemented with peer support and interpreting, since not everyone could read (even in their own language). The team had to be creative and explore techniques that would best fit the group members.

One of the lessons was that knowledge could be expressed in various forms and that lack of ability to use traditional reading and writing did not necessarily mean a lack of understanding or knowledge about trauma, or an inability to engage in the healing journey. This suggests a need for both practitioners and newcomers (particularly refugees) to come together to share knowledge in their different "languages" and means of expression. This is consistent with UNESCO's definition of literacy and suggests that this might be an opportunity for practitioners in the helping profession to engage "clients" to use the modes of communication and healing that best fit them and that would achieve intended goals and objectives. The team has since informally discussed the potential for theatre, dance, art, and learning about other techniques and approaches that may have been used in other countries and settings (Pipher, 2002).

Group dynamics and follow-up

Some participants spoke to facilitators about still living in fear of the people from their own country. This extended to how they felt about participating in groups when there were individuals from their home country. This concern was more apparent among participants from Afghanistan and Columbia. At the conclusion of the adult group sessions, the facilitators reported to the advisory committee about the challenges they had encountered. In response, one of the members of the advisory committee made a presentation about aspects of life in Columbia, since this had not been done during the orientation sessions.

The group process with children and youth: A work in progress

The team hoped to be able to facilitate group sessions with children and youth. This component of the project remained very much in its infancy stage. During the first intake, there were two groups: one with female youth (ages 12 to 16), and another with male youth (ages 13 to 18). These groups took place at Family Service Saskatoon. The girls were involved in a mask-making exercise and were encouraged to talk about what the masks meant to them. The facilitators concluded that the participants were not ready to go very deeply into issues. Only one went a bit further when she said that she had put feathers across the eyes on the mask to express her feelings of not being understood. The feathers kept her hidden. The male participants talked about the issues that had an impact on their settlement process: language barriers and communication difficulties, finances, visas, passport, public transportation services, and adapting to the weather. They identified grief and losses including loss of relatives they had left behind. In many ways, the males seemed to take on the role of provider and were already striving to be independent adults.

During the second intake, a group of girls/young women from two schools were invited to participate in the groups. Both schools were geographically close to one another. The group sessions were held at times that were appropriate to the needs of the young people. Sharing a meal was an integral part of this process and so food was always provided. Participants were ages 15 to 18. Approximately 4 sessions were held with art and craft being the primary activity. The fact that the youth continued to return seemed to suggest that the facilitators were able to engage them, and that artistic and creative approaches worked well with youth.

There were several challenges: getting parental consent, schools' consent, schools' willingness to participate, school/academic schedules, privacy issues, diverse personal interests of youth, availability. This was compounded by the fact that the youth were reluctant to express their pain and feelings. They wanted to fit in, and would not venture into any activity that would make them appear to be "different." Another challenge was the perception by some school counselors that participation in any group session would result in re-traumatizing and reliving of experiences which would have negative effects. Some school counselors wanted to be a part of the entire group process as a condition of the school's participation in the project.

As already mentioned, this is an area that needs much more reflection and planning. One might speculate that the expansion of the advisory team to include creating safe spaces, nurturing relationships, community building, and having fun representation from other sectors such as Child and Youth (mental health) services and the Child Welfare sector might help to strengthen this component of the project. Another is the need to allow time for building relationships with and among youth.

CONCLUSIONS

The gathering: The first step

The Moving Forward team assumed that there would be a screening process for participants, that the groups would be closed, that they would
build awareness about the issue of trauma, and that the parents would
begin to develop some knowledge and skills to help them address their
own issues of trauma. The team also hoped that this insight would help
parents to assist their children with their healing and growing needs.
What evolved was the creation of a space where parents could meet, feel
safe, laugh, cry, and build new relationships (especially relationships
of trust). The facilitators' willingness to be flexible and to comply with
the parents' move to the open group concept helped in the creation of
this safe space. This is consistent with the literature which stresses the
importance of creating safe spaces, nurturing relationships, community
building, and having fun (Pipher, 2002). The team considered factors
such as user friendly administrative processes, warm and welcoming
physical environments, and practical issues such as ensuring that posters were available in multiple languages (Pipher, 2002). As Pipher (2002)
concludes, "Therapy is very much about the construction of a space for
people to think, talk, and work out their problems" (p. 298).

In reflecting on how the groups evolved, some team members suggested that what had emerged at each intake was a Gathering; and that
it was totally acceptable to consider that this was a necessary concept or
method of professional response. In many ways, this Gathering or creation of a space where parents could come together to address the issue
of trauma in their own way is consistent with what the literature has
identified as relevant to healing. The themes of trust and safety, for example, which are also aspects of safe space, run through the literature on
trauma (Herman, 1992; Rousseau & Measham, 2007; Pipher, 2002). The
importance of community, which is created by the Gathering, is also discussed in the literature (Herman, 1992; Hurlock, McCullagh, & Schissel,
2004; Kirmayer, Lemelson, & Barad, 2007).

Herman (1992) has suggested that survivors recognize how much
their own self-worth is connected to their relationships with others or
"depends on a feeling of connection to others" (p. 214). Group solidarity
is therefore a strong factor in the healing journey of trauma survivors
(Herman, 1992, p. 214). When survivors become a part of a group whose

members share, embrace, give to, listen, hug, care for and take care of one another, these human acts create a sense of connection to others, and help members to reconnect with the world around them. Herman has referred to this as the "restoration of social bonds" (p. 215).

Barter (2001, 2005) has emphasized the importance of understanding the contexts of the lives of children defined as "at risk." He draws on the work of Schorr (as cited in Barter, 2001, 252) and notes that children at risk are "growing up in families whose lives are out of control, with parents too drained to provide the consistent nurturance, structure, and stimulation that prepares other children for school and life" (Barter, 2001, p. 252). One of the remarkable aspects of working with refugee families was being able to recognize the parents' commitment and devotion to ensuring that their children have "successful" lives in Canada. Many live for their children. Yet, their lives have been so disrupted that they themselves have a difficult time helping their children. Therefore, an important aspect of addressing the needs of refugee children and youth is responding to the needs of their parents.

In many ways, the Gathering seemed to represent the first stage of healing for the participants. This appears to be the equivalent to what Herman (1992) describes as the third stage group. She suggests that third stage groups are those that "concern themselves primarily with reintegrating the survivor into the community of ordinary people" (p. 217). The Gathering comprised individuals who had lived in refugee camps or who had survived differing kinds of traumatic experiences. Most had come as refugees and had embraced Canada as their new homeland. They were interested in building community, learning about life in Canada, making Canadian friends. During the first session, when the facilitators were doing introductions, they asked about the expectations of the parents. Why had they come? What did they want from the sessions? Despite the fact that the parents had been informed about the intent of the program, their responses related to settlement issues such as finding jobs, learning English, learning about how to live as Canadians. What distinguished members from those of other groups was the recognition of the traumatic experiences that they had survived, that there would be times when they would have to cry together, but often it was about moving forward together from places of grief and trauma.

On the other hand, closed groups appeared to be more appropriate for the youth who lived at a developmental stage where peer influence and support were particularly important. During the recruitment stage, the team paid attention to group affiliation, to existing cliques and relationships, to age and age differences, life experiences, and to other factors that might influence group formation and bonding. These issues were recognized during the recruitment with parents, but did not have the same impact on the actual recruitment and group process.

An important lesson for child welfare workers and policymakers was the value of creating safe spaces and opportunities for community- and relationship-building, since these are vital for successful integration and creation of sense of home. While one might approach working with children and youth differently from working with adults, the overall goals of prevention and empowerment remain the same.

Implications for social work practice and education, and human service intervention

One of the biggest lessons for the team was that of flexibility. The team entered this project with assumptions that were strongly influenced by a Eurocentric approach to helping, and found they had to redefine what intervention would mean in this context. One of the common comments was: "It's different work ... it's different." In this case, it was important to listen to participants, and take cues from them, especially as this related to how the program would evolve.

Another lesson was one with which settlement agencies have long grappled: the importance of supports such as childcare and transportation. During the first intake the team had not anticipated that most families would be large and had assumed that some families could carpool. Instead, the team had to focus on ensuring that vans were sent to pick up families since these could accommodate large-sized families.

A second lesson was that family size would have an impact on the requirements for childcare. This was a hard lesson for the team during the first intake because they were not prepared for the numbers of children. Interaction with the children allowed team members to begin to build relationships with children and families. It also gave team members a glimpse into some of the needs of these families. Providing a school-based program (as occurred at the second intake) helped with child-minding, since the team now had access to gym and recreational facilities. Another factor related to family size was deciding if several siblings would be in the same group, and then determining how to respond to the specific needs of each child or youth. The team relied on members of the advisory committee (for example, the Settlement Support Workers in Schools [SS-WIS] to assist with making decisions about recruitment.

Lessons for social work practicum students

The team was able to involve practicum students from the Faculty of Social Work, University of Regina. During this process, students interacted with the participants, and often became anxious about how their relationships with the families were evolving. One of the biggest concerns of students was that their relationships with participants seemed to extend beyond the boundaries of what they had been taught was appropriate. Sometimes families would invite students to tea or coffee or they would want to hug students, and students were nervous that they were violating professional boundaries.

Team members continually stressed the importance of relationship-building, of being genuine, and about using good judgment. This was difficult for students who seemed to have very rigid notions of what their relationships should "look like." Indeed, this is an area that needs to be discussed in social work education. What does it mean to have genuine relationships with newcomers and other clients? How rigid do these boundaries need to be? What is the intent of the "professional boundary"? The team realized that participants generally trusted them and women would disclose incidents of abuse and violence with individual facilitators. Many of the women seemed to come from traditions where women found ways of supporting one another, and they evidently considered the facilitators as individuals whom they could also trust to support them in the same way. They were not always ready to leave or report incidents of abuse and violence. but clearly wanted to talk. Students learned to take cues from the women about what kind of physical responses (hugs, etc.) would be appropriate. In the case of children and youth, this was more difficult because it seemed to take a long time for these young people to go beyond superficial discussions. Facilitators tended to be relatively rigid with the rules about physical contact with young people.

Another lesson for practicum students was that while the team engaged in group work, the work was also about community-building: community development. Community developers usually know that there are tasks that need to get done and they quickly go about doing them. Group work practitioners are also aware of the details they have to address as part of setting up groups. These include ensuring that facilities are appropriate and adequate, and ordering or preparing refreshments. These may also include ensuring that transportation and childcare arrangements are addressed.

All of the social work practitioners and community workers involved in the project assisted with these tasks. At the start, it was evident that not all social work practicum students considered these tasks as social work duties, despite the fact that the practitioners modeled behaviour. Nevertheless, since its inception, there has been a significant change in attitudes, and social work students now work alongside community workers and social workers to ensure that the tasks are completed. That is, in any kind of community development work, everyone participates and does what is necessary to ensure success of projects. This group work project was also built on community development principles, and consistent with the focus on building safe community.

FINAL COMMENTS

If one considered that a goal of the project was to enhance accessibility and utilization of traditional mainstream agencies, then in many ways this project made significant progress in achieving this goal. One step in doing this was to build awareness among service providers, professions, and immigrant and refugee children, youth, and their families about the kinds of programs and services that are available within the community. Another was to build relationships with the participants so that they become more comfortable with service providers and with using mainstream services. The relationships with practitioners that emerged from this project have had important outcomes.

Graduates from the project have contacted facilitators and other team members for support and advocacy when child welfare protection agencies have become involved with the families, and when other personal crises have arisen. One of the facilitators made this comment: "We are their Canadians," which could also be interpreted to mean that the team had achieved another goal of helping participants to begin to build relationships and bridges with Canadians. There has also been greater conversation and interaction between settlement workers and workers from Family Service Saskatoon. An important lesson for the team was one that came with years of community work: the importance of integrating food, fun and especially celebration into the project.

Some of the challenges for facilitators may be related to the notion that professionals trained within Western settings have certain expectations of how to provide service to their "client populations." This project exposed the strong influence of these Western ways of "doing and thinking," and challenged the team as a whole to rethink how one might provide service in contexts where populations are becoming increasingly culturally diverse and where migration has been a strong influence on these changes. Clearly, services to address the child welfare needs of refugee children would reflect a commitment to prevention, and to creating the kinds of strong community supports and infrastructures that would enhance access and utilization of refugee children, youth, and their families, for example, encouraging the participation of refugee families in parent education groups, in families and schools together (FAST) programs, and in other group and community activities.

There have been other offshoots of this project. The team has presented reports about their work at several conferences. The feedback has been positive and has resulted in requests for more information and also for team members to lead other workshops or provide educational materials. The team has developed educational material focusing on the topic of post traumatic stress among immigrants and refugees. These have been well received by the participating schools. At the end of the two intakes, parents wanted to continue to meet. There have been several ways in which International Women of Saskatoon responded to these requests. These have included the development of women's drop-in programs and activities based on the requests of women (for example, craft-making sessions; presentations and sessions on self-care and self-esteem; yoga, cooking and other recreational activities). The organization, often in partnership with Family Service Saskatoon has continued to work to ensure that participants strengthen relationships within the community and build new communities of support. Both agencies have partnered with schools and other agencies frequented by newcomers, to develop programs and activities aimed at social integration and social inclusion.

The project has exposed the importance of working holistically with newcomer families who come from war-affected regions. There are now plans to build on this by engaging in further research and evaluation, in partnership with refugee families, to address the needs of this population. An area that is being explored is the development of a participatory action research evaluation study with refugee and immigrant families to determine the impact of projects such as these, and to make recommendations for future action. The Moving Forward project represents a journey that once begun, is hard to leave.

REFERENCES

Aldous, J. (1999). Immigrant and refugee children and adolescents: Expanding the vision of possibilities. In G. Lie & D. Este (Eds.), *Professional social service delivery in a multicultural world* (pp. 49-74). Toronto: Canadian Scholars Press.

Anderson, A. (2005). Population trends. In *The Encyclopedia of Saskatchewan* (pp. 699-708). Regina: Canadian Plains Research Center.

Baldwin, J. (2005). The rights connection. *Connections* (Manitoba Human Rights Commission) 5(10) (October), 1.

Barter, K. (2001). Services for vulnerable children: A conceptualization. In J. C. Turner & F. J. Turner (Eds.), *Canadian social welfare* (4th ed., pp. 250-264). Toronto: Pearson.

Barter, K. (2005). Community capacity building: A re-conceptualization of services for the protection of children. In J.C. Turner & F. J. Turner (Eds.), *Canadian social welfare* (pp. 270-288). Toronto: Pearson.

Beaujot, R. (1996). *The demographic perspective*. Ottawa: Metropolis.

Canadian Task Force on Mental Health Issues Affecting Immigrants and Refugees (1988). *After the door has been opened: Mental health issues affecting immigrants and refugees in Canada*. Ottawa: Health and Welfare Canada and Author.

CBC Sports (2007, July 5). Winnipeg immigrants hope to kick off 'newcomers' soccer league. Retrieved March 17, 2008, at http://www.cbc.ca/sports/soccer/story/2007/07/04/soccer-day-manitoba.html

Christensen, C. (2003). Canadian society: social policy and ethno-racial diversity. In A. Al-Krenawi & J. Graham (Eds.), *Multicultural social work in Canada* (pp. 70-97). Toronto: Oxford University Press.

Christensen, C. (2005). Immigrant groups in Canada. In J. C. Turner & F. J. Turner (Eds.), *Canadian social welfare* (pp. 167-195). Toronto: Pearson.

Christensen, C. (1999). Multiculturalism, racism and social work: An exploration of issues in the Canadian context. In G. Lie & D. Este (Eds.), *Professional social service delivery in a multicultural world* (pp. 293-310). Toronto: Canadian Scholars Press.

Citizenship and Immigration Canada (2006). Facts and figures 2006, Immigration overview: Permanent residents (Canada-permanent residents by top source countries). Ottawa: Author.

City of Saskatoon (2007). Immigration council report. March. Saskatoon: Author.

City of Saskatoon (2004). Proposal for the development of City of Saskatoon immigration and refugee resettlement plan. November. Saskatoon: Author.

Cooper, J. L., Masi, R., Dababnah, S., Aratani, Y., & Knitzer, J. (2007). Strengthening policies to support children, youth, and families who experience trauma. Unclaimed children revisited Working Paper No. 2. July. New York: National Centre for Children in Poverty, Columbia University, Mailman School of Public Health.

Daste, B. M., & Rose, S. R. (2004). Group work with cancer patients. In G. L. Greif & P. H. Ephross (Eds.), *Group work with populations at risk*, 2nd Edition (pp. 18-30). New York: Oxford University Press.

Elliott, D. (2003). Demographic trends in Saskatchewan: A statistical analysis of population, migration, and immigration. A report for Saskatchewan Intergovernmental and Aboriginal Affairs, August 2003. Retrieved June 28, 2008, from http://www.gr.gov.sk.ca/PDFs/Demographic_Trends.pdf

Ephross, P. H. (2004). Social work with groups: Practice principles. In G. L. Greif, & P. H. Ephross (Eds.), *Group work with populations at risk*, 2nd Edition (pp. 1-12). Toronto: Oxford University Press.

Federation of Canadian municipalities (2004). Youth violence and youth gangs: Responding to community concerns. Retrieved March 12, 2008, from http://ww2.ps-sp.gc.ca/publications/policing/199456_e.asp

Government of Canada (2008). Citizenship and immigration Canada: Refugees. Author. Retrieved July 1, 2008 from http://www.cic.gc.ca/english/index.asp

Henry, F., Tator, C., Mattis, W., & Rees, T. (2000). *The colour of democracy: Racism in Canadian society*. Toronto: Harcourt Brace Canada.

Herman, J. (1992). *Trauma and recovery*. New York: Basic Books.

Hurlock, D., McCullagh, K., & Schissel, C. (2004). *Conversations for change: An overview of services for immigrant children and youth in Calgary*. Calgary: Author.

Immigrant, Refugee and Visible Minority Women of Saskatchewan (2002). *Post traumatic stress disorder: The lived experience of immigrant, refugee, and visible minority women of Saskatchewan*. Project # 24. Winnipeg: Prairie Women's Health Centre of Excellence.

Immigration and Refugee Board of Canada (2006). *Immigration and Refugee Board: An overview*. Ottawa: Communications Directorate, Immigration and Refugee Board of Canada.

Kirmayer, L. J., Lemelson, R., & Barad, M. (2007). Introduction: Inscribing trauma in culture, brain, and body. In L. J. Kirmayer, R. Lemelson, & M. Barad (Eds.), *Understanding trauma: Integrating biological, clinical, and cultural perspectives* (pp. 1-20). New York: Cambridge University Press.

Mellor, B., MacRae, L., Pauls, M., & Hornick, J.P. (2005). *Youth gangs in Canada: A preliminary review of programs and services.* Ottawa, ON: Public Safety and Emergency Preparedness Canada. Accessed on June 22, 2009 at http://www.ucalgary.ca/~crilf/publications/Youth_Gang_Report.pdf

Moursund, J., & Kenny, M. C. (2002). *The process of counselling and therapy,* 4th Edition. New Jersey: Prentice Hall.

Mulder, M., & Korenic, B. (2005). *Portraits of immigrants and ethnic minorities in Canada: Regional comparisons.* Edmonton: Prairie Centre of Excellence for Research on Immigration and Integration.

Omorodion, F., & White, J. (2003). *Women and post traumatic stress disorder: Moving research to policy.* Project #61. Winnipeg: Prairie Women's Health Centre of Excellence. Under the auspices of Immigrant, Refugee and Visible Minority Women of Saskatchewan.

Pipher, M. (2002). *The middle of everywhere: Helping refugees enter the American community.* Toronto: Harcourt.

Public Safety Canada (2006, July 19). Minister Day announces funding for youth prevention projects in Calgary. Retrieved March 15, 2008, from http://www.publicsafety.gc.ca/media/nr/2006/nr20060719-en.asp

Rousseau, C., & Measham, T. (2007). Posttraumatic suffering as a source of transformation: a clinical perspective. In L. J. Kirmayer, R. Lemelson, & M. Barad (Eds.). *Understanding trauma: Integrating biological, clinical, and cultural perspectives* (pp. 275-293). New York: Cambridge University Press.

Statistics Canada (2004). Study: Immigrants in Canada's urban centres. The Daily, Wednesday August 18. Retrieved July 1, 2008, from www.statcan.ca/Daily/English

Toseland, R.W., & Rivas, R.F. (1995). *An introduction to group work practice.* New Jersey: Allyn & Bacon.

United States Conference of Catholic Bishops/Migration and Refugee Services (2007). Bridging Refugee Youth and Children's Services. Retrieved March 17, 2008 from http://www.brycs.org/

Van Ngo, H., & Schleifer, B. (2005). Immigrant children and youth in focus. *Canadian issues* (Spring), 29-33.

White, J. (2007). Enhancing and developing policies, models and practices to address the mental health needs of immigrant and refugee women in Saskatchewan. Unpublished doctoral thesis, University of Manitoba, Manitoba, Canada.

Williams, C. (2002). A rationale for an anti-racist entry point to anti-oppressive social work in mental health services. *Critical Social Work, 2*(2) (Fall), 26-31.

CHAPTER 8

Passion for Those Who Care:
What Foster Carers Need

Rob Twigg

Those researching and writing about child and family services generally focus on the needs of the children coming into care. Some expand that focus to include the children's families, and others include the social systems that impact on them. The needs of those who provide services to these children and their families are rarely the focus of research, writing, or policy. This chapter looks at the needs of one group of service providers: foster carers and their own children. The thesis of this chapter is that fostering can and must become a service that successfully meets the needs of both those who need the service (foster children and their families) and those who provide the care, including foster carers and their families. The chapter focuses on the implications of the needs identified, and on how child and family services agencies could modify the way in which they work with foster carers for the improvement of the system.

SUGGESTED CITATION: Twigg, R. (2009). Passion for those who care: What foster carers need. In S. McKay, D. Fuchs, & I. Brown (Eds.), *Passion for action in child and family services: Voices from the prairies* (pp. 165-184). Regina, SK: Canadian Plains Research Center.

THE GROWTH OF FOSTER CARE
IN THE CHILD WELFARE SYSTEM

Child welfare services are currently being asked to provide out-of-home care for a large number of children.[1] Across North America and the United Kingdom from the 1970s through the 1990s, there was a significant increase in the number of children and youth entering the child welfare system (Hochmann, Hochmann, & Miller, 2003). The most recent available references are that an estimated 33,000 children were in care in the United Kingdom (Wilson, Sinclair, & Gibbs, 2000) and 500,000 in the United States (Gibbs & Wildfire, 2007; Hochmann et al., 2003; Redding, Fried, & Britner, 2000). In Canada (not including Quebec), there were 76,000 children in care between 2000 and 2002 (Farris-Manning & Zandstra, 2003), an increase from 36,080 in 1997 (Human Resources Development Canada, 1997, cited in Farris-Manning & Zandstra, 2003).

Children who cannot be kept in their family homes, even with the provision of support services, find their way into out-of-home care and, most often, into foster care. While current Canadian data is not available, foster care has traditionally been the major service provider for this population (Twigg, 1991), providing as much as 60 percent of out-of-home care (Gibbs & Wildfire, 2007; Wilson et al., 2000). Wilson et al. noted that, although the number of children in care in the United Kingdom has not changed since 1997, the proportion of children in state care who are being fostered has nearly doubled. While kinship care is a growing subset of foster care—the number of children living in kinship care homes in the U.S. increased 40 percent between 1980 and 1990 (U.S. Bureau of Census, 1991)—this chapter focuses on foster care in non-relatives' homes.

PROBLEMS IN PROVIDING FOSTER CARE

Cashen (2003) and Manning and Zandstra (2003) both reported that there is a shortage of foster care spaces across Canada due in part to the challenges faced in recruiting and retaining foster families. Manning and Zandstra further noted that an increased length of stay in placement is contributing to this lack of space. A U.S. study showed that the length of stay of children in foster care increased during the 1990s and remained at high levels, with most stays being between 21-35 months (Barbell &

---

1   While recognizing that those coming into the child welfare system range in age from birth to 16, the term children will be used throughout this paper.

Freundlich, 2001). Fuchs, Burnside, Marchenski, & Mudry (2007) stated that children with disabilities in Manitoba remain in care for long periods of time "not because of ongoing risk of maltreatment, but because they have intensive needs for care as a result of their disabilities which communities and services are unable to fully meet" (p. 128).

One outcome of this shortage of foster care spaces is the growing number of children being served through group care and institutional/residential treatment. One study showed that the number of children placed in group and institutional forms of out-of-home care increased by 58 percent in the 1990s (Barbell & Freundlich, 2001). This increase in the use of other forms of out-of-home care implies that there is a shortage of family-based resources, an interpretation that seems valid given the constant attempts by foster care providers to recruit more carers.[2]

Throughout its history, foster care has had its critics. One of the most common criticisms is the treatment children receive in the foster home. In 1994, Van Biema wrote that "foster care is intended to protect children from neglect and abuse at the hands of parents and other family members, yet all too often it becomes an equally cruel form of neglect and abuse by the state" (p. 144). A recent U. S. study (Doyle, 2007) found that children who remained with their parents, regardless of the issues the family faced, experienced fewer delinquencies and teen births and did better in the job market as adults than did children who were placed in care.

It is a bitter irony that a system designed to provide safe and loving homes to children in need of such often places them in as much risk as did the homes from which they were removed. Many reasons can be offered to explain this irony, but these certainly include: not adequately screening newly recruited foster carers; not providing sufficient support and training for them; placing more children in carers homes that they could reasonably be expected to care for; lack of adequate reimbursement for foster carers (Rosenthal et al., 1991, cited in Kendrick, 1994); social work caseloads that are too high for the social workers to be able to adequately support the carers (Cashen, 2003); and often a silo approach to service

2   Providers of in-home care will be called foster carers in this chapter. While the term foster family is most often used in North America, I have chosen to use the British term foster carer, as I feel it more accurately reflects the variety of carers, including single persons.

provision that leaves one social worker responsible for the child in care, one for the foster carer, and one for the child's family.

Concerns are also raised about the level of training in child welfare that social workers receive in their academic programs. Tracy and Pine (2000) discussed the challenges facing child welfare education in both agencies and universities. At the university level they cited differences in areas of concentration among schools, with some allowing students to concentrate their learning on child welfare, others focusing on other areas of social work practice and still others taking a generalist practice approach. Armitage, Callahan, & Lewis (2001) discussed the "creative tension" that existed between social work faculties in British Columbia and the provincial government, as the latter tried to ensure that all child welfare social workers would have a Bachelor of Social Work degree, one of the recommendations of the Gove inquiry into the death of Mathew John Vaudreuil, age 5 1/2 years (Government of British Columbia, 1995). Armitage et al. suggested that, in this instance, social work education struggled with a dilemma "… as old as its origins. Does it prepare students for practice under these conditions, or does it prepare students to protest against them?" (p. 11). Recruitment of social workers lacking the necessary academic training to adequately do the work for which they are hired means that, even if the other challenges described above were to be miraculously overcome, an adequate level of care still could probably not be guaranteed. As Allen and Bissell (2004) stated about the U. S. child welfare system:

> In too many states, neither the child welfare agencies nor the courts have the trained staff, skills, or resources necessary to make decisions about the care and treatment that is appropriate to meet the individual needs of children and their families. (p. 64)

Although there is less written about the Canadian child welfare system than is written about its counterpart in the United States, conversations with social workers and foster carers suggest that the same statement can be made about the situation in Canada in 2008.

One of the reasons for this shortage of resources and adequately educated staff is the changing needs of the children being fostered. Child welfare in the 1980s was characterized by an emphasis on maintaining children in their familial homes. This emphasis temporarily reduced the number of children coming into care but meant that those coming into foster care entered care with special needs that presented the foster carers with new challenges (Brown & Calder, 2000; Redding et al., 2000; Wilson et al., 2000). Writing of the situation in Manitoba, for example, Fuchs et al. (2007) stated that "the number of children involved with mandated child welfare agencies who have medical, physical, intellectual, and mental health disabilities has increased dramatically over the last decade" (p. 128). Cashen (2003) found that 66.2 percent of the foster families she interviewed felt that "children's behaviour is more difficult now than ever before" (p. 143).

Many of the children with special needs are cared for in treatment foster care (TFC) programs designed to address these needs.[3] Treatment foster care is more costly than regular foster care and requires a high level of psychological skills on the part of all staff, including those who provide the family-based treatment. In addition, all members of the TFC team, including the carers, need adequate training and support to deal with the children needing this level of care. For these reasons, TFC has always made up no more than a minority of foster care placements (Twigg, 2006).

As TFC placements fill, children needing similar accommodation are placed in regular foster homes. As these homes fill, child welfare programs can be forced to place children in motel and hotel units. Support and supervision may be provided in these settings, but hotel life is not family life. It does not provide the setting in which new and more appropriate parenting styles can be practiced and children raised in a normalized environment, which is the implicit goal of state interventions that remove children from their parents.

As we have seen, the ability of the child welfare system to provide successful family-based living arrangements for children in need of such is hampered by several factors, one of which is a significant lack of foster carers. This lack has been documented throughout the history of foster care, with the reason for the shortage most often identified as social changes, such as both parents working outside of the home, affecting family life (Testa & Rolock, 1999; Twigg, 1991).

---

3   Treatment foster care programs are known by many names, the most common being treatment family care, therapeutic foster care, specialized foster care, family based treatment, intensive foster care, and parent therapist program.

Foster care programs have responded to this chronic lack of carers in the same way decade after decade, by recruiting new carers. Funding is allocated for recruitment drives, which generally are sufficiently successful to justify continuing them. Most foster care systems have policies that require potential carers to meet certain standards. For example, police checks may be required, work histories and financial statements assessed, family histories studied, and candidates psychologically screened (Anderson, 1982, cited in Kendrick, 1994; Francis, 1991, cited in Kendrick, 1994; Government of Alberta, 2007). Policies are typically in place requiring carers to have a certain level of training before they first take a child into their home. Unfortunately, when these policies hamper the ability to provide placements for kids, the screening and training process is often truncated.

What the emphasis on this front end challenge, the recruitment of foster carers, fails to address is the dropout rate of experienced foster carers. Whatever success the recruitment drives have is diminished by the number of carers retiring. Christian (2002) reported that some agencies have foster carer turnover rates of between 30 percent and 50 percent a year. Although interviews with carers who have retired or who are considering retiring from fostering are rarely done, the information found in the literature discussed to this point suggests that carer views are almost universally shared, and that they leave for reasons that can be grouped under the headings of lack of support, lack of recognition, lack of training, and lack of adequate financial compensation. The remainder of this chapter, after an initial discussion on the development of foster care, expands upon these four needs of foster caregivers. Following this, suggestions are made about ways to deal with these needs, with a view to reducing the loss of trained and experienced carers.

DEVELOPMENTAL TRAJECTORY OF FOSTER CARE

Discussion of the needs of foster carers must start with a discussion of the role of the foster carer in the child welfare system. Foster care, as currently practiced, has its roots in the child-saving movement of the late 1880s. Hutchison and Charlesworth (2000) argued that this was the time of the transition from the economically useful, and even necessary, child to the economically useless, but emotionally priceless, child. Prior to the Industrial Revolution, children from a very young age had a role to play in the family economy and were valued for this. Parents also expected that their children would provide for them when they were too old or ill to care for themselves, by carrying on the family business and/or providing a place to live and the care needed to sustain life.

The Industrial Revolution brought families into the cities, where increasing numbers of new industrial jobs were emerging. At first, children remained economically necessary as there were many jobs for children— jobs that their size and physical dexterity made them ideal candidates for, regardless of the inherent drudgery and physical danger. Wages were such that, in many instances, the combined income of father, mother, and all children in the family was barely enough for survival.

As the Industrial Revolution continued, children's jobs began to disappear and were taken over by more sophisticated machines. At the same time, social reformers raised public concern about children's working and living conditions, and steps were taken to make changes. Employers were required to provide education for the children they employed, primitive safety standards were introduced and, ultimately, child labour was abolished. This progressive step forward left many unsupervised children on the streets where they were, rightly or wrongly, seen as a nuisance and a menace. Those concerned with the plight of these "street urchins" thought their best interests would be served by removing them from the negative influences of the cities and sending them to rural areas. Placement was with farmers and others who needed extra hands to complete their labours.

In reaction to the criticism of the child protection system that grew as the plight of these "saved" children was recognized, those who took children into their homes were expected to do so out of love for children rather than for any hope of adequate remuneration, whether "in kind" through child labour, or monetarily through the placement agency. Over time, this policy was revised so that the basic cost of raising a child was provided to foster carers by child welfare agencies. This was generally considered to be acceptable, since the philosophy of foster care was that children were placed with loving parents who were motivated by affection and a sense of charity rather than cash. Supervision of the foster placement, when it happened, was rudimentary. Often, the children in care never met the supervisor.

Over time, and as foster care became less of a private venture and more of a state run enterprise, standards for the care of children the state was responsible for were developed, and foster carers were expected to adhere to those standards. Beginning in the late 1970s, public concern about physical, and later sexual, abuse and corporal punishment meant both that more and more children came into care as a result of their parents abusing or maltreating them[4] and that the monitoring of foster homes increased. Standards were put in place to forbid carers from physically touching children both because of the fear of abuse and the recognition that abused children might well misinterpret the carer's behaviour. Concerns about the living environment of the child in care led to policies regarding living space, the number of children allowed to be fostered by one family, play space, fire safety, and others.

Concerns about nutrition found their way into foster care policies, and nutritional standards for meals served to children in care were set. The growing awareness of the importance of maintaining one's religious and/or cultural heritage—and the political struggles that ensued from this—placed expectations on the carers to be aware of, sensitive to, and supportive of the religious/cultural heritage of the children residing in their homes (Brown & Calder, 2000). The fostering paradigm shifted from exclusive to inclusive fostering, setting out expectations that foster carers would be ready and able to work with the biological parents of the children in their care (Brown & Calder, 2000; Ryan, McFadden & Warren, 1980; Wilson et al., 2000).

The shifting social and political motivation behind many of these changes has led some to describe child welfare policy as being a pendulum (Finholm, 1996; Patterson, 1999; Trocmé & Chamberland, 2003; all cited in Dumbrill, 2006). Dumbrill reported on how child welfare in Ontario shifted in 10 years from being based on the "rule of optimism," which is a strengths-based approach to practice (Dingwall, Eekelaar & Murray, 1983, cited in Dumbrill, 2006, p. 6) to the "rule of pessimism" (Reder et al., 1993, cited in Dumbrill, 2006), which is based on a deficit model.

This developmental trajectory of the regulation of foster care has created a debate as to whether foster carers are volunteers or professionals. Although policies and standards affecting foster carers, and public

---

4   Although public attention has been focussed on the plight of sexually abused children, that population has never made up much more than 25 percent of children brought into state care. Neglect is by far the most common reason for removing children from their parents' care.

expectations of what they should and should not do, have been growing over the years, foster carers are still seen in many places as volunteers fostering for the love of the child. This debate is beyond the scope of this chapter, but it should be noted that the place of the foster carer subsystem within the larger foster care system does influence the decisions made regarding support and recognition, the topics foster carers identify as most important to them. Redding et al. (2000) indicated that these factors not only contribute to satisfied foster carers but also to successful placement outcomes, the goal of the foster care system.

This chapter is based on the assumption that foster carers are professionals and deserve to be treated as such. Foster carers are a significant subsystem of the foster care system (Twigg, 1991). They provide 24-hour care for the children in their care and have insights and understandings based on that care that need to be recognized. Whatever the long term goal of the placement, whether return to the biological family, adoption, institutionalization, or independent living, providing the child with the support, role modeling, and often the training needed to meet that goal is done most regularly and most consistently in the foster home and by the foster carers.

FOUR NEEDS OF FOSTER CAREGIVERS

Need for Support

Critics of the foster care system often point to the lack of support foster carers receive from the placement agencies as one of the main reasons foster carers give for retiring from fostering (Cashen, 2003; Chamberlain, Moreland, & Reid, 1992; Martin, Altemeier, Hickson, Davis, & Glascoe, 1992; Walter, 1993). Gibbs and Wildfire (2007) reported that a less-than-satisfactory working relationship with foster care agencies is "the most commonly cited factor affecting foster parents' decision to cease foster parenting" (p. 588). Rindfleisch, Bean, & Denby (1998) found that seven of the fourteen factors they identified as predicting why foster parents would leave fostering were related to the relationship between foster parents and the agency. Brown and Calder (2000) asked foster carers what they need to be good foster carers. One set of answers clustered around "support from social services." Wilson et al. (2000) stated that "the provision of effective support becomes a moral imperative; irrespective of any effects it may have on recruitment, effectiveness, and retention of foster carers" (p. 207).

As has been noted, fostering has become more challenging over the decades, both because of the increasing needs of the children brought into care, the increased expectations placed on the carers, and the monitoring of their work both by foster care agencies and the general public. These increasing demands need to be balanced by the creation of an environment in which carers receive the training, understanding, reimbursement and personal and familial support they need (Redding et al., 2000)

Foster carers need a place where they can debrief after serious issues and where they can celebrate successes. Wilson et al. (2000) identified six potentially stressful fostering events for which foster cares need support: "(placement) breakdowns or disruptions, allegations, relations with birth parents, family tensions, 'tug of love' cases, and other disagreements with social services" (p. 193).

Foster carers need to be able to relate to others who will understand the nature of fostering and be able and willing to support them (Redding et al., 2000; Twigg, 1991; Wells & D'Angelo, 1994). For example, they need support in grieving the loss of a child from their home, whether from graduation, placement failure, allegations of abuse, or death. Edelstein, Burge & Waterman (2001) suggested that unresolved grief caused by the lack of recognition of and support for the foster carers' grief is a reason many carers retire from fostering.

Family units are generally thought of as being subsystems of larger family systems. These larger family systems are often sources of support for families as they go through the challenges of living. Brown and Calder (2002) found that foster families reported that having supportive extended families contributed to their success and longevity in fostering. Practice experience shows that many foster families do not have such supportive extended families. Foster care agencies can provide the forum for such support through ongoing support/training groups for foster carers. Brown and Calder (2002) found that the foster parents they studied indicated that they valued the support they received from other foster parents. Social workers can also provide such support if they are trained to recognize the need and are mandated to provide the support.

One challenging area in which foster carers need support is that of allegations of abuse, whether physical or sexual (Wells & D'Angelo, 1994; Wilson et al., 2000). Wilson et al. reported that an estimated one in six foster carers in the United Kingdom will have to deal "with a complaint or allegation" (p. 195) at some time in their fostering career and that this incidence rate is growing. As far back as 1992, researchers (e.g., Carbino, 1992) found that foster carers were more likely to be reported for allegations of child abuse and neglect than were biological families. Brown and Calder (2002) found that 70 percent of the families they studied were concerned about being accused of abusing children in their care. Rindfleisch et al. (1998) found that this concern was one of the factors that influenced the decision of some foster carers to retire from fostering.

Some children who come into the foster home as victims of abuse or neglect behave in ways that contribute to their revictimization in the foster home. Some of these children may also pose risks for the abuse of other children in the home, both foster and biological children. The foster carers, including their children and their support network (e.g., respite care, extended family, friends) need training and support in how to recognize and respond to such behaviour. They also need support during the investigation of complaints against them, something that neither the agency nor the social workers can legally provide in most North American jurisdictions. In the United Kingdom, a program titled the National Foster Care Agency (National Foster Care Association, 1993; Robertson & Moody, 2007) provides such training and support. No such support exists in North America.

Need for Recognition

One of the consequences of being given the status of volunteer in what has become an increasingly professional child welfare system is that the foster carer is seen as someone whose contribution is highly valued, but someone without the credentials to make a valuable contribution to a professional dialogue (Seaberg & Harrigan, 1999; Wells & D'Angelo, 1994). As one foster parent stated, "The chain of command doesn't lead to the people who can actually change the problems in the system. We (foster parents) have no input, we either have to accept the way things are or get out" (cited in Cashen, 2003, p. 144). This lack of recognition leaves the foster carer either excluded from case conferences and other planning meetings, or grudgingly granted the status of observer at such meetings. Gibbs and Wildfire (2007) reported that having no voice in planning for the children in their care was a reason cited in their study for leaving fostering. Brown and Calder (2002) found that most of the foster parents they studied wanted to be involved in making decisions that affected children in their care. Only half felt they were treated as professionals.

Foster carers repeatedly complain of being overlooked and of their voices not being heard when decisions are to be made regarding the children in their care. Gibbs and Wildfire (2007) reported that social workers who do not clearly communicate their expectations and treat foster carers in a "condescending manner" are two of the primary reasons foster carers give for leaving fostering. This lack of recognition makes the foster carers feel insignificant and lacking in validation for their commitment to the child. In addition, lack of recognition for their efforts while working with more difficult children under the increasing scrutiny of the foster care agency is a recipe for disillusionment, placement failure, burnout, and retirement from fostering.

An example of this lack of recognition and its impact on the recruitment and retention of foster carers is the status of foster carers' own children, called the "unknown soldiers of foster care" by some (Twigg, 1994). Foster carers told Brown and Calder (2000) that among the supports they need to be good foster carers was support for their own children. Concerns about the impact of fostering on their children are one of the main reasons carers give for retiring from fostering (Twigg, 1994; Twigg & Swan, 2007). Children of foster parents report that social workers don't know their names and show no interest in them when they come to visit the foster child. If social workers don't know the names of the foster carer's own children, how can they help the carer and his/her children to deal with the challenges of fostering? Indeed, how can they expect to retain the foster family? One study (Swan, 2002) showed that as many as one-third of the foster carers' children interviewed indicated that they would not consider becoming foster carers because of the way they were treated by the social workers. Thus, the lack of recognition by social workers of foster carers' own children both contributes to the retirement of foster carers and significantly reduces one pool of potential foster carers, a pool of people with first-hand experience of the challenges of fostering.

Need for Addressing Financial Concerns

The financial concerns expressed by foster carers are of three varieties: 1) lack of adequate reimbursement for the work that they do (Brown &

Calder, 2002; Gibbs & Wildfire, 2007; Rindfleisch et al., 1998); 2) lack of adequate compensation for expenses associated with fostering (Brown & Calder, 2000); and 3) a frustrating bureaucracy that makes it difficult to get approval for expenses associated with fostering and creates delays in receiving reimbursement (Rindfleisch et al., 1998).

The question of adequate reimbursement for the work being done is directly related to the previous discussion of the status of the foster carer in the foster care system. If carers are volunteers who work for the love of the child, they need no material reimbursement. If they are recognized as part of the foster care system, the reimbursement should be consistent with their status in the system and what is expected of them. If they are professionals, they should be paid a wage in keeping with the requirements of the job.

As in all forms of employment, the rate of pay is understood to reflect the value the employer, and thus society, places on the job, in this case fostering. Brown and Calder (2002) reported that 44 percent of the foster parents they studied felt they were not adequately compensated for their services. Cashen (2003) found that many of the foster parents she interviewed felt that the "current per diem rates were an insult to foster parents who provide exceptional care to children" (p. 147). If the rate of pay foster carers receive both fails to cover the actual costs of fostering and is not competitive with wages paid in the workplace, many will not be able to enter fostering, and many foster carers will have to retire in order to achieve an income adequate to support their desired lifestyles and work in a field with more public recognition.

It is the lack of fit between what they receive and what they are expected to do that seems to be at the heart of the reimbursement issue (Seaberg & Harrigan, 1999; Wilson et al., 2000). Foster carers are most often paid on a per diem basis, where they receive reimbursement for the number of children they have in their home per day. Some are paid on a contract basis where their services are contracted for the period of time the child is in the home; others are paid on a salary basis, where they are seen as employees of the foster care agency. Per diem rates rarely cover more than the anticipated costs of fostering, contracts sometimes include benefits, and salaries usually include benefits. It is increasingly common for the demands of fostering to require that a carer be at home, or at least on call, 24 hours a day, making it impossible for them to work outside of the home, alongside of fostering. To the extent that the rate received for fostering is less than the income they could receive in the workplace, it often becomes financially impossible for the carers to continue fostering.

Which of these reimbursement models is the best and what the proper amount of reimbursement should be is beyond the scope of this chapter and may well vary given the geographical area the fostering is being carried out in and the nature of the children in care. However these decisions are made, the process should be transparent and the reimbursement should accurately reflect the nature and value of the work provided.

The issue of reimbursement for expenses related to fostering should be dealt with by each fostering agency so that what is considered a reimbursable expense is clearly spelled out and accurately reflects and adequately covers the expenses related to fostering. The reimbursement system should also be clearly understood by all and should contain no unnecessary impediments. It should also be recognized that unexpected expenses may be incurred, sometimes on an emergency basis.

Need for Training

Its stands to reason that the need to provide adequate training for the carers increases as the needs of the children entering the foster care system become more challenging, as more is known about how to care for the varying physical, mental, and emotional challenges these children bring with them into the foster home, and as the expectations about how to manage a foster home have increased (Twigg, 1991). As discussed previously, this need has been addressed at the policy level, but reports from the foster carers indicate that the product being delivered is inconsistent, not sufficiently ongoing, and, all too often, too little, too late (Gibbs & Wildfire, 2007; Wells & D'Angelo, 1994).

In most if not all North American jurisdictions, training is to begin before the carers first have a child placed in their home. This initial training tends to be focussed on the policies and expectation of the agency and is seen as orientation. Some training may be given regarding how to identify, understand, and respond to the needs of the children to be cared for. As we have seen, the realities of the demands for placements often truncates this process so that carers have a child placed with them before going through basic orientation. Ongoing training is also hampered by many factors such as lack of resources, scheduling problems, transportation issues especially for those fostering in rural areas, and a lack of priority given to training by the foster care system.

Redding et al. (2000) reported regarding treatment foster care programs that

> [W]ithout appropriate and sufficient training for foster parents, early termination is likely. Studies have found that training reduces the number of unsuccessful placements and increases the retention of TFC parents in the program, with the probability of a desired outcome increasing in direct relation to the amount of specialized training received. (p. 439)

The lack of timely, consistent, and relevant training is a contributing factor to both carers retiring from fostering and the complaints made against carers for improper treatment of children in their care. It seems likely that a proper training program has many benefits, including support and supervision for the carers, In addition, a proper training program provides accountability—the agency is more accountable for the services it provides to the carers, and the carers are more accountable for meeting the agency's standards.

As mentioned earlier, one area of increasing concern for foster carers, and one that reflects both support and training needs, is allegations of abuse in the home. Both the allegations and incidence of abuse in foster care are significant, with some researchers suggesting that the incidence of abuse in foster homes is at least as great as that in the homes of the general public. These allegations and incidents can involve a foster carer, carer's child, extended family member, alternate caregiver (e.g., respite care), or other foster child. Kendrick (1994) documented this issue as it was 14 years ago, referencing both Canadian, U.S., and U.K. studies that addressed the need both for adequate training to deal with what can become a sexualized relationship within the foster home and how to deal with the aftermath of the relationship—the investigation, possible closure of the foster home, and possible criminal charges. In the U.K., the National Foster Care Association provides both training in how to handle allegations and support for carers who are alleged to have abused or allowed abuse to occur in their homes (National Foster Care Association, 1993; Robertson & Moody, 2007). Although North American foster carers face similar issues, a body similar to the NFCA does not exist on this continent.

WHAT TO DO

This chapter has presented the items that foster carers indicate influence their decision to leave fostering, as reported in the few published foster carers' exit interviews, the author's experience in the field, and anecdotal reports. These three knowledge bases show that the same concerns are voiced by those considering leaving and by those who give no indication that they are considering leaving fostering. If fostering is to survive as a means of providing out-of-home care, it is necessary that these concerns be recognized by the foster care system and steps be taken to bring about the necessary changes.

As many of these concerns relate to the status of the foster carer in the foster care system, how that question is addressed is critical. Foster carers are facing increasing demands on their time, resources, and skills, as the needs of the children they are being asked to care for increase and as the scrutiny they undergo by the placement agency, the government, and the general public increases. In spite of this, their place in the foster care system all too often remains one of a volunteer, a service provider whose service is valuable but who do not have a place at the decision-making table.

If the carers' role were seen as significant and if they were seen as being at least as expert about the way to best provide daily care for the foster child as the other professionals in the system are about their own areas of expertise, many positive changes would likely occur. First, the carers would be more satisfied with their work and would be less likely to retire. Second, it would be easier to recruit new carers as reports of satisfaction from existing foster carers would significantly influence the decision-making of those considering fostering. Finally, and most importantly, the services provided to the foster child would improve; the outcomes of being in care would be more positive, and the long term personal, inter-personal, and societal consequences of fostering failure reduced.

Reimbursement is another issue regularly raised by the carers. Carers need to be adequately reimbursed for their time and work. The per diem system still used in many programs was designed at a time when society expected one middle-class parent, usually the wife, to remain home in a care-giving role. Currently, it is possible, and even necessary, for both spouses to work outside the home to maintain middle-class status. Thus, a reimbursement system based on one member making a "living wage" is out-of-date.

The increasing demands on foster carers also make it necessary to revisit the reimbursement scheme. Reimbursement systems such as contract work and part or full employment need to be seriously considered, and the state, whose children are being cared for by the foster care system, needs to provide the resources necessary to provide adequate care for its children. Once the state makes this commitment, the foster care agencies will be in a better position to properly reimburse the carers.

Training of foster carers is another area of concern that is often reported. As the demands on the foster family increase, the support services available to them must be increased accordingly (Twigg, 1991). Redding et al. (2000) summarized a series of studies that show foster carers are more satisfied with their work if they have a supportive group experience. One of these support systems is ongoing and relevant training.

There are many challenges to be faced in making such training possible, including finding adequate training materials, competent trainers, and a mechanism for providing training that is responsive to such things as schedule conflicts and fostering in rural and remote locations. On-line programs, chat rooms, and distance education facilities could be used to overcome some of these challenges.

FINAL WORD

As long as the child welfare system remains as it is, it can be expected that 60 percent of children in care will be in foster care. If the needs of these children and their families are to be met, a trained and dedicated cadre of foster carers is required. This cadre can only be successfully recruited and retained if the needs addressed in this chapter are met. Until they are, we will continue to struggle with the challenges of recruiting and retaining qualified carers. Those carers who remain will continue to struggle with the various forms of stress discussed in this chapter, all of which are caused by this poorly structured and under-funded service.

REFERENCES

Allen, M., & Bissell, M. (2004). Safety and stability for foster children: The policy context. *Children, Families, and Foster Care, 14*(1), 49-73.

Armitage, A., Callahan, M., & Lewis, C. (2001). Social work education and child protection: The B.C. experience. *Canadian Social Work Review, 18*(1), 9-24.

Barbell, K., & M. Freundlich. (2001). *Foster care today.* Washington, DC: Casey Family Programs.

Brown, J., & Calder, P. (2000). Concept mapping the needs of foster parents. *Child Welfare, LXXIX*(6), 729-746.

Brown, J., & Calder, P. (2002). The needs and challenges of foster parents. *Canadian Social Work, 4*(1), 125-135.

Carbino, R. (1992). Policy and practice for response to foster families when child abuse or neglect is reported. *Child Welfare, LXXI*(6), 497-509.

Cashen, C. (2003). Foster parent satisfaction in Nova Scotia. *Canadian Social Work, 5*(2), 138-150.

Chamberlain, P., Moreland, S., & Reid, K. (1992). Enhanced services and stipends for foster parents: Effects on retention rates and outcomes for children. *Child Welfare, 71*, 387-401.

Christian, S. (2002). Supporting and retaining foster parents. NCLS State Legislative Report: Analysis of state actions on important issues, 27(11). Retrieved June 3, 2008, from http://www.ncsl.org/programs/cyf/fosterparents.pdf

Doyle, J. (2007). Child protection and child outcomes: Measuring the effects of foster care. Forthcoming, American Economic Review. Retreived April 29, 2008, from http://www.mit.edu/~jjdoyle/doyle_fosterlt_march07_aer.pdf

Dumbrill, G. (2006). Ontario's child welfare transformation: Another swing of the pendulum? *Canadian Social Work Review, 23*(1-2), 5-20.

Edelstein, S., Burge, D., & Waterman, J. (2001). Helping foster parents cope with separation, loss and grief. *Child Welfare, LXXX*(1), 5-25.

Farris-Manning, C., & Zandstra, M. (2003). Children in care in Canada: A summary of current issues and trends with recommendations for future research. Ottawa, ON: Child Welfare League of Canada. Retrieved April 29, 2008, from http://www.nationalchildrensalliance.com/nca/pubs/2003/Children_in_Care_March_2003.pdf

Fuchs, D., Burnside, L., Marchenski, S., & Mudry, A. (2007). Children with disabilities involved with the child welfare system in Manitoba: Current and future challenges. In I. Brown, F. Chaze, D. Fuchs, J. Lafrance, S. McKay, & S. Thomas-Prokop (Eds.), *Putting a human face on child welfare: Voices from the prairies* (pp. 127-145). Prairie Child Welfare Consortium www.uregina.ca/spr/prairiechild/index.html / Center of Excellence for Child Welfare www.cecw-cepb.ca

Gibbs, D., & Wildfire, J. (2007). Length of service for foster parents: Using administrative data to understand retention. *Children and Youth Services Review, 29*(5), 588-599.

Government of Alberta. (2007). Becoming a foster parent. Retrieved May 14, 2008, from http://www.child.alberta.ca/home/884.cfm

Government of British Columbia. (1995). Executive summary: Report of the Gove Inquiry into child protection in British Columbia. Retrieved May 18, 2008, from http://www.qp.gov.bc.ca/gove/govevol1.htm

Hochmann, G., Hochmann, A., & Miller, J. (2003). Foster care: Voices from the inside. Commissioned by the Pew Commission. Retrieved January 18, 2008, from http://pewfostercare.org/research/voices/voices-complete.pdf

Hutchison, E., & Charlesworth, L. (2000). Securing the welfare of children: Policies past, present and future. *Families in Society, 81*(6), 576-585.

Kendrick, A. (1994). Fostering assessment in the context of child sexual abuse: A literature review. Retrieved May 25, 2008, from http://www.sircc.strath.ac.uk/research/kendrick.html

Martin, E. D., Altemeier, W. A., Hickson, G. B., Davis, A., & Glascoe, F. P. (1992). Improving resources for foster care. *Clinical Pediatrics, 31*, 400-404.

National Foster Care Association. (1993). *Making it work.* London: National Foster Care Association.

Redding, R., Fried, C., & Britner, P. (2000). Predictors of placement outcomes in treatment foster care: Implications for foster parent selection and service delivery. *Journal of Child and Family Studies, 9*(4), 425-447.

Rindfleisch, N., Bean, G., & Denby, R. (1998). Why foster parents continue and cease to foster. *Journal of Sociology and Social Welfare, 25*(1), 5-24.

Robertson, S., & Moody, S. (2007) Managing allegations—can we make a difficult experience more positive? The Fostering Network, Scotland. Workshop presented at the International Foster Care Association 2007 European Training Seminar, Malta, November 18, 2007.

Ryan, P., McFadden, E., & Warren, B. (1980). Foster families: a resource for helping parents. In A. Maluccio & P. Sinanoglu (Eds.), *The challenge of partnership: Working with parents of children in foster care* (pp. 189-199). Washington, DC: Child Welfare League of America.

Seaberg, J., & Harrigan, M. (1999). Foster families' functioning, experiences and views: Variations by race. *Children and Youth Services Review, 21*(1), 31-55.

Swan, T. (2002). The experience of foster caregivers' children. *Canada's Children,* Spring, 13-17.

Testa, M., & Rolock, N. (1999). Professional foster care: A future worth pursuing? *Child Welfare, LXXVIII*(1), 108-124.

Tracy, E., & Pine, B. (2000). Child welfare education and training: Future trends and influences. *Child Welfare, LXXIX*(1), 93-113.

Twigg, R. (1991). The next step in foster care. *Journal of Child and Youth Care, 6*(1), 79-85.

Twigg, R. (1994). The unknown soldiers of foster care: Foster care as loss for the foster parents' own children. *Smith College Studies in Social Work, 64*(3), 297-313.

Twigg, R. (2006). *Withstanding the test of time: What we know about treatment foster care: A Monograph on treatment foster care.* Hackensack, NJ: Foster Family Based Treatment Association.

Twigg, R., & Swan, T. (2007). Inside the foster family: What research tells us about the experience of foster carer's children. *Adoption and Fostering, 31*(4), 49-61.

U.S. Bureau of Census. (1991). *Current population reports: Marital status and living arrangements: March 1990* (Series P-20, No. 450). Washington, DC: U.S. Government Printing Office.

Van Biema, D. (December 2, 1994). The storm over orphanages. *TIME Magazine, 144.*

Walter, B. (1993). *In need of protection: Children and youth in Alberta.* Edmonton, AB: Children and Youth Advocate.

Wells, K., & D'Angelo, L. (1994). Specialized foster care: Voices from the field. *Social Service Review, 68*(1), 127-144.

Wilson, K., Sinclair, I., & Gibbs, I. (2000). The trouble with foster care: The impact of stressful 'events' on foster carers. *British Journal of Social Work, 30,* 193-209.

CHAPTER 9

Children with FASD Involved with the Manitoba Child Welfare System: The Need for Passionate Action

Don Fuchs, Linda Burnside,
Shelagh Marchenski, and Andria Mudry

Meeting the needs of children with disabilities creates significant challenges for child welfare agencies in Manitoba. Because of additional risk factors associated with disability, these already vulnerable children have a greater potential than other children for requiring the support or protection of a child welfare agency. In Manitoba, one-third of children in care fall within a broad definition of disability (Fuchs, Burnside, Marchenski, & Mudry, 2005). Significantly, 17 percent of children in care were affected by a particular disability: diagnosed or suspected Fetal Alcohol Spectrum Disorder (FASD) (Fuchs, Burnside, Marchenski, & Mudry, 2007). Children with a diagnosis of FASD present agencies with an array of complex and variable needs arising from the children's compromised neurological biology, the family systems they live in, and the many

SUGGESTED CITATION: Fuchs, D., Burnside, L., Marchenski, S., & Mudry, A. (2009). Children with FASD involved with the Manitoba child welfare system: The need for passionate action. In S. McKay, D. Fuchs, & I. Brown (Eds.), *Passion for action in child and family services: Voices from the prairies* (pp. 185-206). Regina, SK: Canadian Plains Research Center.

resulting psychosocial and environmental problems that result for them and for their families. Meeting the needs of these children in an effective way begins with an understanding of the nature of their relationship with child welfare agencies. In particular, it is important to understand *when* these children come into care and to understand their experiences *while* they are in care.

To broaden the understanding of the relationship between children with FASD and child welfare agencies, this chapter reports on the results of a study that was aimed at gathering data on the placement and legal status histories of children with FASD in care and comparing those histories to the histories of children with other disabilities and children with no disabilities. The chapter includes a brief review of FASD literature to provide a contextual background for the research. In addition, to illustrate the magnitude of concern for the risk of continued growth in the numbers of children with FASD coming into care, the chapter reports the results of a study of women of child-bearing age receiving service from Addictions Foundation of Manitoba. The implications for policy, practice and research are discussed and the chapter puts forward some directions for further research.

THE FETAL ALCOHOL SPECTRUM DISORDER CONTEXT

The term Fetal Alcohol Spectrum Disorder (FASD) encompasses a range of conditions that are caused by maternal alcohol consumption during pregnancy and that have lifelong implications for the affected person, the family, and society. Considered to be a completely preventable condition (Nulman, Ickowicz, Koren, & Knittel-Keren, 2007; Zevenbergen & Ferraro, 2001), the adverse effects of maternal consumption of alcohol have been noted throughout history but were first described as a pattern of disabling effects under the term *Fetal Alcohol Syndrome* in the early 1970s (Overhoser, 1990). Although there are no national statistics on the rates of FASD in Canada, the incidence of FASD in Manitoba has been estimated at 7.2 per 1,000 live births (Williams, Obaido, & McGee, 1999) to as high as 101 per 1,000 live births (Square, 1997). American incidence rates of 9.1 per 1,000 lives births have been reported (Sampson et al., 1997), but it should be noted that diagnosis of FASD may be delayed or missed entirely, affecting the accuracy of such statistics (Chudley et al., 2005).

Because of the range of effects that result from prenatal alcohol exposure, diagnosis of FASD can be complex (Chudley et al., 2005; Hay,

1999; Wattendorf & Muenke, 2005; Zevenbergen & Ferraro, 2001). Indicators include physical characteristics such as distinct facial features and inhibited growth, neurodevelopmental problems such as impaired fine motor skills, and behavioural and cognitive difficulties that are inconsistent with developmental level, such as learning difficulties, poor impulse control, or problems in memory, attention and/or judgment. Diagnosis is somewhat facilitated if there is a confirmation of maternal alcohol use. Diagnosis is often made between the ages of 4 and 14 (Lupton, Burd, & Harwood, 2004), and early diagnosis with accompanying intervention is recommended to ameliorate the problematic effects of FASD, through the provision of cognitive stimulation, speech and language therapy, educational supports, and other interventions (Sonnander, 2000).

The effects of FASD are manifested throughout the individual's lifespan (Streissguth, Barr, Bookstein, Sampson, & Olson, 1999; Zevenbergen & Ferraro, 2001). Infants who have been exposed to alcohol may show decreased arousal, sleeping problems, irritability and feeding difficulties. Difficulties with speech, language development, and attention span are often identified in preschool years. Poor attention, impulsivity, and hyperactivity often persist throughout childhood and adolescence, leading to behavioural problems in school settings, which only exacerbate the academic challenges that stem from learning disabilities and other cognitive impairments related to FASD. These academic and social difficulties often contribute to low self-esteem, conduct problems, and delinquent behaviours in adolescence. As adults, individuals with FASD are vulnerable to mental health problems, conflict with the law, alcohol and drug issues, and problems with employment (Streissguth, Barr, Koga, & Bookstein, 1996).

In addition to the effects of FASD on the individual, the impact of FASD on society is profound (Lupton et al., 2004). Individuals with FASD often require high levels of medical care, residential services, special education supports, adult vocational services, and other social services throughout their lifetimes. The increased risk for deleterious outcomes in adulthood as a result of FASD (i.e., unemployment, homelessness, poverty, criminal activity, incarceration, and mental health problems) all have a social cost in terms of the support services, organizational structures, and associated financial costs that must be provided to respond to the needs of this vulnerable population (Lupton et al., 2004).

Given the difficulties facing individuals affected by FASD, it is not surprising that families who are caring for a child with this condition experience significant challenges. Little research exists with regard to the needs of families parenting a child with FASD (Wilton & Plane, 2006), although there is a growing body of literature examining the experiences of substitute caregivers (foster parents and adoptive parents) who increasingly are responsible for the care of children with FASD through the child welfare system (Barth, 2001; Brown, Bednar, & Wiebe, 2004; Brown, Sigvaldason, & Bednar, 2006; Gammon, 2002; Jones, 2004; McCarty, Waterman, Burge, & Edelstein, 1999; Warner, 1999). Because parental substance abuse and its relationship to child abuse and neglect is one of the major reasons for the involvement of the child welfare system with families (Barth, 2001; Bartholet,1999), it is not surprising that many children with FASD come into out-of-home care, often on a permanent basis (Jones, 1999). Increasingly, child and family services systems across Canada are recognizing the need to assist youth with FASD as they transition into adulthood, given the high risks they face as a result of their disabilities and the inability of adult support services to meet their particular needs and challenges (Child and Youth Officer for British Columbia, 2006; Reid & Dudding, 2006; Schibler & McEwan-Morris, 2006).

In their study of children in care with disabilities in child and family services agencies in Manitoba, Fuchs et al. (2005) concluded that 17 percent of all children in care were affected by FASD. An overwhelming majority (89 percent) of children with FASD were in permanent care of an agency and had limited contact with biological parents. Consequently, child welfare agencies in Manitoba have a significant care responsibility for these children until their age of majority, requiring agency staff and caregivers to be cognizant of the special needs of this population during childhood and adolescence and through the transition to adulthood. There is a good deal of evidence to indicate that this is similar to other jurisdictions in Canada and the United States (Brown et al., 2006).

RESEARCH CONTEXT AND OBJECTIVES

This study is a second phase of the original research by Fuchs et al. (2005) identifying children in care with disabilities. It looks more closely at children with FASD and their history as they enter the child welfare system and come to rely on the parenthood of the state. It was conducted by the

Faculty of Social Work, University of Manitoba, and the Child Protection Branch of the Manitoba Department of Family Services and Housing under the auspices of the Prairie Child Welfare Consortium. Funding was provided by Health Canada with the support of the Centre of Excellence for Child Welfare.

In recognition of the high care needs and the over-representation of children with disabilities in the Manitoba child welfare system, as identified in the previous research of Fuchs et al. (2005), this study was aimed at developing a fuller understanding of the pathways into care for children with disabilities. In addition, the 2005 study found First Nations and Métis children were significantly over-represented in the population of children in care with disabilities. Because of the significant proportion of Manitoba children in care identified with a diagnosis of FASD, and because of the over-representation of First Nations children, understanding the relationship between this population and child welfare agencies is particularly important. Information on the evolution of child welfare interventions—from an initial admission into care resulting in a first legal status, to subsequent legal statuses, including the possibility of a permanent order of guardianship—has implications critical to prevention, intervention, and permanency planning for children with disabilities. It is also important to understand the role of Voluntary Placement Agreements (VPAs) as a tool for intervening with children with disabilities.[1] Analysis of placements and a comparison of the pattern of placements of children with and without disabilities would provide valuable information that had not previously been examined in depth. Information on the placement and legal status histories of children and comparative analysis of children with and without disabilities is useful at all levels of the service delivery system, from practitioners to policy-makers, for enhancing capacity to meet the needs of children with disabilities.

Using the population of children identified in Manitoba's Child and Family Service Information System (CFSIS) as having a disability, this study was designed to examine the legal status and placement history of those children and compare that history to the general child in care (CIC) population. More specifically, this project aimed to:

---

1   Voluntary Placement Agreements are agreements in which children come into care and parents give up custody of their child but retain guardianship.

1. Analyze the histories of children in care with disability, especially FASD, to determine their length of time in care, their age at coming into care, their placement history and their legal status history.
2. Compare the legal status history of children who are permanent wards and those in care under Voluntary Placement Agreements.
3. Compare the history of involvement with an agency of children with and without disabilities.

With these objectives in mind, it is important also to consider the legislative context within which decisions around children's placements in agency care are made. The *Child and Family Services Act* (1985) in Manitoba details requirements regarding the duration of time that children can remain in temporary care before an agency is required to make a more permanent plan for the child, particularly focusing on the needs of younger children to have timely opportunities for stable, consistent caregiving relationships within which attachments can form. As such, children who are admitted to care under the age of five are permitted to be in temporary care for a shorter period of time, with fewer allowable renewals for temporary care, before a permanent plan must be made, requiring either that children be safely reunified with parents or become permanent wards of the state.

Voluntary placements, although they are contractual arrangements negotiated between parents and a child welfare agency, are also subject to time constraints when pertaining to the placement of younger children to ensure that their rights to permanence are not compromised. Exceptions are allowed for children whose medical care needs or significant mental health conditions of a permanent nature warrant placement in a specialized setting to better meet their care demands. Similarly, exceptions are considered for children over the age of 14—presumably of an age where attachment issues are less predominant compared to younger children—who can be placed in care under a series of annual VPAs until age of majority at age eighteen.

These legislative requirements can have a significant impact on the length and type of involvement children have with the child and family services system, especially when young children are in need of protective services related to parental functioning (as was found to be the case for the majority of Manitoba children with disabilities in care in the 2005 study by Fuchs et al.) or require supportive services as a result of the child's care needs. Therefore, it is important to view the findings of this study within this legislative context, as children who are admitted to care at preschool ages may be predisposed to different care trajectories than school-age children and adolescents.

DESIGN AND METHODOLOGY

This project sought to examine the legal status and placement histories of children with disabilities and compare this to the histories of children without a recorded disability in the care of mandated child protection agencies in Manitoba as of December 1, 2005. The researchers were able to use as a study population a cohort of children in care with and without disabilities who were identified in their previous research and who were still in care (Fuchs et al., 2005). This helped ensure that there were two discrete groups for comparison purposes.

Using CFSIS, two groups of children in the care of mandated child protection agencies in Manitoba were created: 1) children with a disability, and 2) children without a disability as recorded on their CFSIS file. To create comparable groups for further examination, the children were further divided into subgroups based on legal status and disability. Children were sorted by disability into three exclusive categories: children with either diagnosed or suspected FASD (FASD); children with a disability other than diagnosed or suspected FASD (CWD No FASD); and children without a disability (No disability).

Legal status provided an additional dimension to the groupings. Groups of children were divided according to their legal status as either a permanent ward (PW) or a child under a Voluntary Placement Agreement (VPA) as of December 1, 2005. The PW group also included children who were PWs but were currently in transition planning. Children with other legal statuses, such as those under apprehension or temporary wards as of December 1, 2005, were not examined as they may not have had sufficiently detailed legal and placement histories.

This method created 6 study groups:
1. FASD PW (permanent wards with FASD)
2. FASD VPA (voluntarily placed children with FASD)
3. CWD PW no FASD (permanent wards with a disability that was not FASD)

4. CWD VPA no FASD (voluntarily placed children with a disability that was not FASD)
5. No disability PW (permanent wards with no disability)
6. No disability VPA (voluntarily placed children with no disability)

From the six mutually exclusive comparison groups that were created, six random samples were drawn. To make the amount of data manageable within the resources available for this project, 25 percent of those in each group were chosen randomly from lists generated by the CFSIS system to create the sample. The sample groups are shown in Table 1.

Table 1. Random Sample Group Sizes		
Disability status	Random Sample (25% of Total)	
	PW n	VPA n
FASD	122	18 or 20*
CWD No FASD	94	38
No Disability	329	165

*Due to the small size of the FASD VPA group, all children who had adequate information on their CFSIS files were included. Sample size differs for analysis of legal status (20) and placement (18) due to the availability of file information.

When comparing the random sample groups, it was important to consider the impact of the wide variation in group size. The strategy of using a randomly chosen sample of 25 percent of the population for 5 of the 6 groups maintained the comparative size difference between the disability and legal status groups of children in care. This difference must constrain any conclusions drawn from comparing groups that range in size from 18 or 20 children to 329 children.

FINDINGS

Comparing In-care Trajectories of Children with Disabilities and Children with No Disabilities

For the purposes of this phase of the research project, only children who were permanent wards or were under VPAs on December 1, 2005, were examined as part of the 6 comparison groups. Although they were all either permanent wards or under a VPA on that date, their legal status histories could consist of a variety of legal statuses and may have included Apprehension, Temporary Ward, Permanent Ward (PW), Transition Planning, Voluntary Placement Agreement (VPA), Voluntary Surrender of Guardianship (VSG) and/or Unknown legal statuses. The legal status of children was derived from the recordings in CFSIS.

Children with permanent ward status were further examined to determine the length of time from their first legal status to the time they became permanent wards. The FASD PW population had the shortest period of time between the two legal statuses (M = 2.11 years). At just over 2 years on average between their first legal status and becoming a permanent ward, this was almost a year shorter than other children who became permanent wards. The No disability PW group was just over 3 years (M = 3.05 years), as was the CWD PW no FASD group (M = 3.29 years). This may be partially due to the legal status legislative requirements under the *Child and Family Services Act* (1985) that apply to children who are involved with the child welfare system at different ages, as discussed earlier. Since the PW FASD group on average is first involved with the system at 2.49 years of age, the amount of time they can be in care under temporary status is less than children who are older than 5 years of age when they first come into care.

Because the age of children is a factor that influences the length of their total time in care, a more accurate comparison of the relative time spent in care by the legal status disability groups could be made by comparing the children's time in care as a proportion of their ages. Again it was found that children under a VPA were in care for a shorter proportion of their life, while children who were permanent wards spent a greater portion of their lives in care. A finding that was particularly important to note was that children with FASD spent over 70 percent of their lives in care of a child welfare agency in Manitoba.

Although the legal status and placement status of children are linked, there may be differences between the amount of time children have a legal status and the amount of time they are actually in an agency-supported placement. The history of a child with an agency may involve a variety of placement arrangements, and it was important to understand whether the placement history of children varied by their disability.

The mean length of time in placements of children in the six legal status by disability groups was determined and compared. As expected, permanent wards spent the longest time in placement. However, of the permanent wards, those with FASD spent the most time in child welfare agency placements (M = 7.20 years, SD = 2.97), compared to permanent wards with other disabilities (M = 5.98 years, SD = 2.98), and permanent wards with no disabilities (M = 5.08 years, SD = 3.12). The VPA groups did not follow the same pattern. Children with FASD in care under a VPA were in placements much less time (M = 2.72 years, SD = 1.70) than other children with disabilities (M = 4.73 years, SD = 4.16), although their time in placement was greater than children with no disabilities (M = 1.69 years, SD = 1.43).

The total time in placement for each child was divided by their total number of placements to determine the mean length of placements for each child. A mean of those means was calculated for the established legal status disability groups and a comparison was made across groups. The children who were permanent wards tended to have longer placements than children in care under a VPA.

The total length of time each child had spent in an agency placement was calculated as a proportion of their age at December 1, 2005. A mean of the proportions was determined for each disability legal status group. The comparison of mean proportions showed that children with FASD spent on average greater than 70 percent of their lives in care (M = 73.14%). This was a higher proportion than permanent wards with no disabilities (M = 59.22%), and considerably higher than permanent wards with other disabilities (M = 53.08%) (See Table 2).

It is clear from these findings that permanent wards who receive a diagnosis of FASD have come into care for the first time at a younger age (2.5 years) than children with no disability (3.6 years) and at a considerably younger age than children with other disabilities (4.3 years). The

Group	Sample N	Mean Years in Placement as % of Age	SD	Median %
No Disability VPA	165	19.91	22.76	12.19
FASD VPA	18	21.36	13.72	15.70
CWD VPA No FASD	38	34.45	28.62	22.95
CWD PW No FASD	94	53.08	23.09	52.34
No Disability PW	329	59.22	26.68	58.35
FASD PW	122	73.14	23.57	76.52

Table 2. Mean Years in Placement as a Proportion of Age

data also demonstrated that children in the FASD group became permanent wards more quickly than children in either of the other permanent ward groups. Their time from first legal status to a permanent order was approximately 2 years, compared to 3 years for other children. This fast track, compounded by an earlier initial legal status, results in the children with FASD becoming permanent wards at a much earlier age, at approximately 4 years of age, compared to 6 years of age for children with no disabilities and over 7 years of age for children with other disabilities.

Given the shorter time period between first legal status and the granting of permanent guardianship, one would expect that the FASD permanent ward group would have a lower mean number of legal status changes.[2] That is precisely what the data demonstrated. Fewer opportunities were occurring for these children to be re-united with their families of origin. Once the children were in care, they moved comparatively quickly and directly to becoming permanent wards. As previously discussed, this shortened pathway into care for children with FASD may be entirely a consequence of the conditions imposed by the *Child and Family Services Act* (1985). What this research demonstrates is that the conditions specified in the Act appear to have a greater impact on the legal status history of children with FASD, as a result of their younger age at admission to care.

The placement history of permanent wards mirrors their legal status history. PWs with FASD spent the longest time in placements, on average more than 2 years longer than children with no disability. Possibly as a consequence of being in care longer, they have a higher number of placements than other permanent wards.

Finally both the legal and placement histories confirm that permanent wards with FASD were spending, on average, approximately three quarters of their lives in the care of an agency, about 15 percent more than any other children who are permanent wards.

Although the sample of children with FASD in care under a Voluntary Placement Agreement is very small compared to the other groups, it does include the entire population of children in Manitoba in that group for whom legal and placement histories were complete. Clearly, VPAs are seldom used by families of children with FASD. When VPAs were

---

2   Although there are rare exceptions to this rule, it is generally true that once a child becomes a permanent ward, he/she will have no more legal statuses.

used, they tended to be used for less time for children with FASD than for children with other disabilities but for longer than children with no disability.

There are some notable differences between children with FASD who become permanent wards and those whose relationship with an agency is proscribed by a Voluntary Placement Agreement. The age of first legal status is markedly different. Permanent wards with FASD had their first legal status on average at age 2.5 years and VPAs with FASD did not have a legal status until 6 years later at a mean age of 8.6 years.

The mean number of legal statuses for children under a VPA (6.6) was also greater than the mean number for children who became permanent wards (4.8). Although the VPA group had more legal statuses, the amount of time they spent with a legal status or in a placement was significantly less than children in the permanent ward group.

In summary, children with FASD who become permanent wards in Manitoba tended to become children in care of an agency at a much earlier age than other children with disabilities or children with no disabilities. Once in care, they were more likely to continue in agency placements than other children. They became permanent wards more quickly than other children. While VPAs provide a means of supporting families of children with other disabilities, they are not commonly used for children with FASD.

Women of Child-Bearing Age with Alcohol Problems in Manitoba and the Risk for Children with FASD Coming in Care

Recognizing the significant number of alcohol-affected children in the child welfare system, the researchers felt it was important to learn more about the possible number of children in Manitoba who might be similarly affected, and about the women who might give birth to them. There were no reliable provincial statistics identifying the number of children with FASD in the general population, as there are in all probability many women using alcohol during pregnancy who are not known to the social services, medical, or legal professions. Still, to begin to develop an awareness of the scope of this issue, information on one particularly vulnerable group of women was obtained from the Addictions Foundation of Manitoba (AFM): women of child-bearing age (19 to 45 years) who were involved with an addictions program in 2005-2006, the year of the study. This sample is not intended to be representative of Manitoba women who might have children affected by FASD, but rather to serve as an example of one group, among many, of women who appear to be at risk for having such children.

AFM provided summary data on women who participated in screening for addictions-related programs. Many of the women who sought treatment were compelled to seek treatment, either because of a probation order or as a requirement for the return of their children from care. The screening tool is a self-report questionnaire completed by all potential AFM clients. AFM reported that in 2005-2006 the number of women in the 19-45 age group who participated in screening was 1,212. The number of respondents varied from item to item in the screen with a range for general questions from a high of 1,212 answering the question "How may children do you have?" to a low of 584 answering "Have you ever attempted suicide?" The average number of respondents to general questions was 1,084. Although women might be involved with AFM for any addiction, over 90 percent reported feeling a need to cut down on alcohol or drug use.

Of particular interest to this study is the potential number of children in situations of maternal alcohol abuse. In this population, 65 women (6 percent of respondents) were pregnant at the time they filled out the screen. The number of women who responded to the question "How many children do you have?" was 1,239. Of those, 312 reported no children, 230 had one child, 264 had two children, 207 had three children, 104 had four children, 70 had five children, and 52 had six or more children. Based on their report and using six as the maximum number of children, we can conclude that these mothers account for at least 2,457 children. Although 312 women reported having no children, 669 women indicated that they had no children living with them.

Although there may be other explanations for children not living with their mothers, many of these mothers have, at least temporarily, lost custody of their child/ren to an agency. Child and Family Services (CFS) was noted as the referral source for 234 women. When asked about specific events that occurred in the past year, 370 women reported the loss or apprehension of a child to a CFS agency. It is not possible from the information provided to determine how many children were involved or whether there were previous apprehensions. However, the screening tool does gather information on current involvement with the legal system. Of 479 women who indicated being involved with the legal system, 156 reported a child & family services order as the nature of that involvement. When asked if alcohol was related to their involvement in the court system, 291 women indicated that it was. In summary, there is evidence that approximately one-third of women screened for acceptance into an AFM program have been involved with a child and family service agency.

It is possible from the data collected to describe the main socio-demographic characteristics of the group of women 19-45 years completing the AFM screening in 2005/06. The majority, approximately 70 percent, were from the Winnipeg region, which includes the city of Winnipeg and extends as far west as Portage la Prairie and includes all of southeast Manitoba. Approximately half of the women (615 or 51%) had not completed high school: 181 (15%) had less than grade 9 education, and 434 (36%) had incomplete high school. Of the remaining half, 244 (20%) had completed high school, 203 (17%) had some college or university, and 99 (8%) had a college or university degree.

Only 309 (26%) of these women were employed: 202 (17%) were employed full-time and 107 (9%) part-time. Women most commonly described themselves as unemployed (578 or 49%). Another 119 (10%) described themselves as homemakers. For those completing this item, household incomes were generally low, with 365 (31.7%) reporting an income of less than $10,000 and 175 (15%) citing the $10,000 to $19,000 category. Only 244 women (21%) reported household incomes above $20,000, with 88 of those in the $20,000 to $29,000 range. This item was poorly completed: 287 (25%) responded "don't know" and another 80 (7%) declined to answer.

Present marital status was single for 661 (57%), married/common law for 283 (25%), divorced/separated for 164 (14%), and widowed for 10 (1%). Half of the women (541) described themselves as having been seen at some time for emotional or mental health issues, and 594 (53%) have at some time been prescribed antidepressant medications. Emotional or mental health issues were serious enough to have resulted in hospitalization for 231 (22%). Violent behaviour when either sober or straight was reported by 329 women (29%) and self-reports of violent behaviour increased to 620 (55%) when using alcohol or other drugs. An overdose of drugs or alcohol was reported by 339 (31%) women in the group; this had occurred within the past 12 months to 157 women.

In summary, in Manitoba in 2005-06, more than 1,200 adult women of child-bearing age were screened for services related to addictions at the Addictions Foundation of Manitoba, which is only one of the service providers for women of child-bearing age in Manitoba. These women tended to be single, unemployed, and of low economic status. Many have less than a high school education and half of them have had a history of emotional or mental health issues. They were mothers to 2,500 children but were not currently custodial parents to all of their children. In addition it is important to note that there were 312 women who reported having no children.

IMPLICATIONS FOR CHILD AND FAMILY SERVICE POLICY AND SERVICE PROVISION

The data reported in these two studies suggests that FASD presents a significant issue for child welfare agencies in Manitoba. Large numbers of children with FASD find themselves in the care of a child welfare agency. They spend a greater proportion of their lives in agency care than other children. Of the groups of children examined in this study, this group (children with FASD) are the most reliant on the state to serve as their parents. Therefore, their needs must be anticipated and strategically addressed by child and family service agencies. This creates a range of implications for service delivery, policy, and prevention.

Social workers need to be aware of the possibility that children for whom they are providing service may be alcohol-affected. Workers need to know the characteristic physiology and behaviour patterns that are an indication of the condition and should pursue formal assessment for children they suspect may have FASD. In addition to understanding how this disability affects the child's functioning and service needs, workers need to be trained to recognize and help alleviate the additional stressors faced by families caring for a child with FASD. Because children with FASD come into care earlier and spend more of their life in placement, workers must recognize the even more critical role of permanency planning for them. There are some services available in the community for children with FASD and/or their families. Workers need to know about the availability of services in their region and be able to advocate for FASD-related services for both children in care and children in danger of coming into care and their caregivers.

Similarly, expertise related to FASD is critical for foster parents and other direct service providers. They must be prepared to manage the unique needs of children with this condition. Recognizing the long-term placement needs of these children, foster parents need to be able to make a long-term commitment to their care. They must be aware of the additional stresses that may result from caring for children with FASD and must develop some reliable stress-management strategies.

It is not enough to plan for the needs of children while they are in care. It is important to begin planning for life *after care* for these children, beginning while they are still *in care*. Every year increasing numbers of children who have been identified with FASD will be transitioning out of care and into the community. The shift to independence is difficult for all children with disabilities. This is due in part to the significant differences in the structure of service delivery for children and adults. The move to independence for persons with FASD is further complicated by the nature of their disability. They are often not eligible for services related to cognitive impairments because their level of intellectual functioning is above the eligibility criteria. There are few if any adult services directly related to FASD. As adults, their disability tends to be invisible, but their behaviour can present many challenges. Long-term planning for children with FASD needs to include special attention to their transition into adulthood and conceptualization and consideration of lifespan planning should begin in childhood.

In summary, workers, foster parents and other service providers must be prepared to provide the kind of care that best supports children presenting with this configuration of needs. Connections to FASD expertise must be made to adequately provide for the needs of alcohol-affected children. Whether this means increasing the expertise within CFS or integrating FASD services with other service providers, it is essential to have knowledge and skills related to FASD available to every affected child in care.

The review of the number of women of child-bearing age who are involved with AFM gives a cursory indication of the scope of addiction issues among women in the province of Manitoba. The potential for children to be affected by alcohol both biologically as a result of prenatal exposure, and environmentally as a result of postnatal exposure, is significant. The child welfare system appears to be a primary intervener with this high-risk population. CFS policy direction and resource alloca-tion must recognize the prevalence and complex needs of this group.

Beyond the scope of Child and Family Services, the AFM data em-phasized the importance of prenatal alcohol prevention programs and the potential need for supports for women and families. It is also an indi-cation of the continued importance of early childhood intervention and identification of children and families requiring support.

The availability of FASD diagnostic services throughout the province for children of all ages is fundamental to service planning and provision. Manitoba has high quality assessment services, but is lacking in quantity. Assessment services at the Clinic for Alcohol and Drug Exposed Chil-dren are based in a central clinic in Winnipeg with limited accessibility for rural or northern residents. Working to capacity, the central clinic is able to focus only on children under the age of 12 years.

The potential exists in many jurisdictions to develop a service model across divisions that would encompass the provision of early childhood intervention and child care, family supports, vocational/employment strategies, independent living supports, and affordable housing. In-tegrated service delivery on this scale would make social inclusion of persons with FASD possible. An integrated approach would reduce the demand on the overly subscribed child welfare system in Manitoba and provide greater access to the range of appropriate services required by the children and families with FASD disabilities.

CONCLUSIONS AND DIRECTIONS IN FUTURE RESEARCH

A number of important questions arise from this research. They are re-lated to preferred practices in service provision, policy and prevention. Although children in care with FASD have now been identified and their legal and placement histories described, they are still largely unknown. What are the reasons they come into care, what is the nature of their re-lationship with their family of origin, their siblings, and their extended family? What are the social problems experienced by the biological moth-er / father that contribute to the need for care? Are there opportunities for maintaining family relationships? What are needs of sibling group-ings of children with FASD? What are the factors that make it possible for some placements to be sustained over long periods of time? What is their success in achieving independence? A longitudinal study of a cohort of children from families dealing with addictions would offer an opportunity to obtain information of immeasurable value.

The knowledge that children with FASD in Manitoba are spending such a large proportion of their lives in care makes it even more important to understand their needs and be able to meet them. Most children in care in Manitoba are in foster homes. What are the support needs of foster families who are fostering children with FASD? If children are in long-term foster care, what is the best way to increase the stability of their placements?

As children with FASD enter adulthood, it is clear that they will need some continuing support. What is the most effective way to assist them in their transition out of agency care? What is happening in other jurisdictions?

The research identified two groups of children with FASD in Manitoba: one group that became permanent wards at a young age and a second much smaller group that remained out of care for many years longer than the permanent ward group. The second group spent a shorter period of time in care via the use of a VPA(s). What variables account for the different age of admission to care among the two groups? What differences in these populations make one group more successful in the community than the other? Can these differences provide instruction that will lead toward improving practice with children with disabilities and their families?

The findings show that children with FASD come into care in Manitoba earlier and become permanent wards more quickly than other children. This raises the question of the efficacy of the permanency planning provision of the Act in relation to children with FASD. It appears that the Act's intention to meet the needs of children for a stable permanent home have a particular impact on children with FASD because they enter the child welfare system in Manitoba at an earlier mean age than other children. If there was more time to support families struggling with addictions, would it be possible for more children with FASD to return to their families of origin? This issue may not be adequately addressed without a concurrent increase in community addiction services to better and more quickly support these families when children first come into care. In a related question, can voluntary placement agreements be used more effectively to maintain parental involvement in the care of children with FASD?

It is said that, of all disabilities, FASD is the one that is most pre-ventable. The information from AFM identifies a high-risk population of women. What type of prevention programs would be most success-ful in addressing a high-risk population? Although beyond the scope of the child and family services system such prevention programs would nonetheless be of great importance to CFS because they would prevent children coming into care by preventing the incidence of FASD.

FASD is a disability that has significant impacts on the legal status and placement histories of children in care in Manitoba. Because children with FASD enter the child welfare system at a younger age and spend a greater proportion of their lives in care than other children, their needs present an additional challenge to the child welfare system. The data on the increasing number of children coming into care and the prevalence data from the Addictions Foundation of Manitoba indicate that there is a growing degree of urgency for health, education and child welfare systems to develop effective integrated health and service policy and programs to respond to the increasing numbers of children and fami-lies with FASD and to develop a broad cross-sectoral preventive strategy. Truly, there is great need for much more passion for action to address this complex and compelling social issue.

REFERENCES

Barth, R. P. (2001). Research outcomes of prenatal substance exposure and the need to review policies and procedures regarding child abuse reporting. *Child Welfare, 80*(2), 275-296.

Bartholet, E. (1999). *Nobody's children: Abuse and neglect, foster drift, and the adoption alternative.* Boston: Beacon Press.

Brown, J., Bednar, L., & Wiebe, B. (2004). Motives of currently licensed Manitoba fos-ter parents. *Envision: The Manitoba Journal of Child Welfare, 3*(2), 1-13.

Brown, J. D., Sigvaldason, N., & Bednar, L. M. (2006). Motives for fostering children with alcohol-related disabilities. Journal of Child and Family Studies. Retrieved January 20, 2007, from http://www.springerlink.com.proxy2.lib.umanitoba.ca/content/p30ll1662x70m271/fulltext.pdf

Child and Youth Officer for British Columbia. (2006). A bridge to adulthood: Maxi-mizing the independence of youth in care with fetal alcohol spectrum disorder. Retrieved November 29, 2006, from http://www.gov.bc.ca/cyo/ down/cyo_fasd_sept28.pdf

Chudley, A. E., Conry, J., Cook, J. L., Loock, C., Rosales, T., & LeBlanc, N. (2005). Fetal alcohol spectrum disorder: Canadian guidelines for diagnosis. *Canadian Medical Association Journal, 172*, 1-21.

Fuchs, D., Burnside, L., Marchenski, S., & Mudry, A. (2005). Children with disabilities receiving services from child welfare agencies in Manitoba. Retrieved December 1, 2006, from http://www.cecw-cepb.ca/DocsEng/DisabilitiesManitobaFinal. pdf

Fuchs, D., Burnside, L., Marchenski, S., & Mudry, A. (2007). Children with FASD: Involved with the Manitoba Child Welfare System. Retrieved January 11, 2007, from http://cecw-cepb.ca/files/file/en/FASD%20Final%20Report.pdf

Gammon, H. (2002). Fetal alcohol disorders, stress, and the female caregiver. *Envision: The Manitoba Journal of Child Welfare, 1*(2), 43-53.

Hay, M. (1999). A practical roadmap for the imperfect but practical-minded clinician. In J. Turpin & G. Schmidt (Eds.), *Fetal alcohol syndrome/effect: Developing a community response* (pp. 26-43). Halifax, NS: Fernwood.

Jones, K. (1999). The ecology of FAS/E: Developing an interdisciplinary approach to intervention with alcohol-affected children and their families. In J. Turpin & G. Schmidt (Eds.), *Fetal alcohol syndrome/effect: Developing a community response* (pp. 80-87). Halifax, NS: Fernwood.

Jones, K. (2004). Successfully raising resilient foster children who have fetal alcohol syndrome: What works? *Envision: The Manitoba Journal of Child Welfare, 3*(1), 1-18.

Lupton, C., Burd, L., & Harwood, R. (2004). Cost of fetal alcohol spectrum disorders. *American Journal of Medical Genetics Part C, 127C*, 42-50.

McCarty, C., Waterman, J., Burge, D., & Edelstein, S. B. (1999). Experiences, concerns and service needs of families adopting children with prenatal substance exposure: Summary and recommendations. *Child Welfare, 78*(5), 561-577.

Nulman, I., Ickowicz, A., Koren, G., & Knittle-Keren, D. (2007). Fetal alcohol spectrum disorder. In I. Brown, & M. Percy (Eds.), *A comprehensive guide to intellectual and developmental disabilities* (pp. 213-227). Baltimore: Paul H. Brookes Publishing.

Overhoser, J. C. (1990). Fetal alcohol syndrome: A review of the disorder. *Journal of Contemporary Psychotherapy, 20*(3), 163-176.

Reid, C., & Dudding, P. (2006). *Building a future together: Issues and outcomes for transition-aged youth.* Ottawa, ON: Child Welfare League of Canada.

Sampson, P. D., Streissguth, A. P., Bookstein, F. L., Little, R. E., Clarren, S. K., Dehaene, P., Hanson, J. W., & Graham, J. M. (1997). Incidence of fetal alcohol syndrome and prevalence of alcohol-related neurodevelopmental disorder. *Teratology, 56*(5), 317-326.

Schibler, B., & McEwan-Morris, A. (2006). Strengthening our youth: Their journey to competence and independence. Retrieved December 1, 2006, from http://www.childrensadvocate.mb.ca/English/Assets/Strengthening%20Our%20Youth%20-%20Final%202006.pdf

Sonnander, K. (2000). Early identification of children with developmental disabilities. *Acta Paediatrica, 434,* 17-23.

Square, D. (1997). Fetal alcohol syndrome epidemic on Manitoba reserve. *Canadian Medical Association Journal, 157*(1), 59-60.

Streissguth, A. P., Barr, H. M., Bookstein, F. L., Sampson, P. D., & Olson, H. C. (1999). The long-term neurocognitive consequences of prenatal alcohol exposure: A 14-year study. *Psychological Science, 10*(3), 186-190.

Streissguth, A. P., Barr, H. M., Koga, J., & Bookstein, F. L. (1996). *Understanding the occurrence of secondary disabilities in clients with FAS and FAE.* Seattle, WA: University of Washington Fetal Alcohol and Drug Unit.

The Child and Family Services Act. (1985). Government of Manitoba. Retrieved July 14, 2008, from http://web2.gov.mb.ca/laws/statutes/ccsm/c080e.php

Warner, K. (1999). Parenting children with fetal alcohol syndrome. In J. Turpin & G. Schmidt (Eds.) *Fetal alcohol syndrome/effect: Developing a community response* (pp. 14-25). Halifax, NS: Fernwood.

Wattendorf, D. J., & Muenke, M. (2005). Fetal alcohol spectrum disorders. *American Family Physician, 72*(2), 279-285.

Williams, R. J., Obaido, F. S., & McGee, J. M. (1999). Incidence of fetal alcohol syndrome in northeastern Manitoba. *Canadian Journal of Public Health, 90*(3), 192-194.

Wilton, G., & Plane, M. B. (2006). The family empowerment network: A service model to address the needs of children and families affected by fetal alcohol spectrum disorders. *Pediatric Nursing, 32*(4), 299-306.

Zevenbergen, A. A., & Ferraro, F. R. (2001). Assessment and treatment of fetal alcohol syndrome in children and adolescents. *Journal of Developmental and Physical Disabilities, 13*(2), 123-136.

CHAPTER 10

Physical Punishment in Childhood: A Human Rights and Child Protection Issue

Ailsa M. Watkinson

> How can we expect children to take human rights seriously and to help build a culture of human rights, while we adults not only persist in slapping, spanking, smacking and beating them, but actually defend doing so as being 'for their own good'? Smacking children is not just a lesson in bad behaviour; it is a potent demonstration of contempt for the human rights of smaller, weaker people.
>
> *Thomas Hammarberg, cited in Pinheiro, 2006, p. 11*

On the evening of January 10, 2008, a member of Parliament (MP) from Ontario was interviewed on the Canadian Broadcasting Corporation (CBC) program *As It Happens*. The MP, Ruby Dhalla, had been on a trip to the Punjab Region in India and, while performing an official duty, her

SUGGESTED CITATION: Watkinson, A. (2009). Physical punishment in childhood: A human rights and child protection issue. In S. McKay, D. Fuchs, & I. Brown (Eds.), *Passion for action in child and family services: Voices from the prairies* (pp. 207-226). Regina, SK: Canadian Plains Research Center.

assistant's purse was stolen. The police reacted and recovered the purse, which had been stolen by two children, five and nine years of age. The event came to public attention after a local television station in the Punjab reported that the children, when found by the police, were "beaten black and blue" (Fatah, 2008). Although the actual facts are still in dispute, the issue that is significant here is the MP's description in the CBC interview of what happened to the children. She said she had been shown "horrific pictures" of the children struggling with the police and that they had been beaten. She described this as a physical and severe "reprimand." She was asked by the interviewer what she meant by "physical reprimand," but did not answer the question directly.

If the police treated an adult in the manner described, it is unlikely that the encounter would have been depicted as a "reprimand." It would probably have been framed as an assault, a beating, or even police brutality. It is this distinction between the naming of an assault on children as a "reprimand" versus the naming of an assault on an adult as a "beating" that is central to the discussion that follows. Reprimanding a child in some non-violent way is normal to help shape positive development, but too often we view the use of physical force against children as a reprimand rather than as the assault that it is.

A recent United Nations global study on violence against children found that the magnitude of violence against children worldwide is substantial (Pinheiro, 2006). The report described the violence as a serious global problem that "occurs in every country in the world in a variety of forms and settings and is often deeply rooted in cultural, economic and social practices" (p. 6). Corporal punishment (sometimes referred to as physical punishment) is identified in the United Nations report (Pinheiro, 2006) as one of the most extensive forms of violence experienced by children. Corporal punishment is defined by the United Nations' Committee on the Rights of the Child as "any punishment in which physical force is used and intended to cause some degree of pain or discomfort, however light" (Pinheiro, 2006, p. 52, citing Committee on the Rights of the Child, 2006, para. 11).

According to Pinheiro (2006), only 2.4 percent of children worldwide are provided legal protection from corporal punishment in all settings, including the home and school. In Canada, all adults are provided legal protection from corporal punishment. Children are not.

The purpose of this paper is to consider the current social and legal positioning of children in Canada regarding the use of physical punishment[1] and its correlation to the intersection of child protection and children's rights. The physical punishment of children in Canada has been a topic widely discussed for decades. I will review the meaning of child maltreatment as it relates to physical punishment and physical abuse. In addition, I will discuss the first major children's rights case under the *Canadian Charter of Rights and Freedoms* that challenged the use of physical punishment on children. The case was eventually heard by the Supreme Court of Canada. Finally, I will review the Supreme Court's decision and report on findings from a study flowing from the decision. The study was conducted to determine the public's knowledge of the changes to the interpretation of the law following the Supreme Court's decision.

The findings of this study and others referred to in this paper support the need for advocacy by social workers to ensure that child protection policies and parental programming reflect Canada's international obligations to its children, namely to "explicitly prohibit all forms of violence against children, however light, within the family, in schools and in other institutions where children may be placed" (Committee on the Rights of the Child, 2003, para. 33).

CHILD MALTREATMENT AND
S. 43 OF THE *CRIMINAL CODE OF CANADA*

A useful definition of child maltreatment is "the harm, or risk of harm, that a child or youth may experience while in the care of a person they trust or depend on, including a parent, sibling, other relative, teacher, caregiver or guardian" (Jack, Munn, Cheng, & MacMillan, 2006, p. 1). Child maltreatment includes: physical abuse, sexual abuse, neglect, emotional harm and exposure to family violence (Trocmé et al., 2005). Although all forms of maltreatment harm children and their development in many ways (Finkelhor, 1994; Gershoff, 2002; McGillivray & Durrant, 2006; Pinheiro, 2006), this paper will focus solely on physical abuse—the

---

[1] Throughout the paper I will use the phrases 'physical punishment' and 'corporal punishment' interchangeably. For the purposes of this discussion they have the same meaning—"the intentional use of force to cause pain or discomfort."

only form of child maltreatment that sometimes can be legally excused.

There is an ongoing debate about the distinction between physical punishment and physical abuse. "Definitions vary, as one person's view of what constitutes abuse—'hitting'—is another person's method for disciplining her or his child—'spanking'" (Vine, Trocmé, & Findlay, 2006, p. 147). These attempts at drawing distinctions is confounded by child protection mandates, children's human rights, and s. 43 of the *Criminal Code of Canada*.

Each Canadian province and territory has it own legislation that deals with child welfare and protection (see Centre of Excellence for Child Welfare, 2008, for summaries). In Saskatchewan, for example, the legislation is the *Child and Family Protection Act*. Legislation for each province and territory is accompanied by regulations and protocols. The common benchmark used in child physical abuse cases investigated by child protection agencies, however, is physical injury or "demonstrable harm" (Trocmé et al., 2005, p. 16), which is described as injuries such as bruises, cuts, burns, bite marks and other injuries that appear to indicate various stages of healing (Saskatchewan Provincial Child Abuse Protocol, 2006).

The latest report on child maltreatment across Canada estimated that in 2003 the child welfare system substantiated over 31,000 incidents of physical maltreatment[2] (Trocmé et al., 2005). As the authors point out, the estimates of child maltreatment are based on reported cases and do not include cases that were never reported, cases that were screened out before the investigation, and those cases investigated only by the police (Trocmé et al., 2005). Most cases of substantiated child physical abuse that come to the attention of child protection agencies stem from an escalation of child physical punishment (Durrant & Ensom, 2006). In fact, one of the findings arising from the 2003 *Canadian Incidence Study of Reported Child Abuse and Neglect* was that "[p]unishment accounted for 75% of substantiated incidents in which physical maltreatment was a primary category for investigation" (Durrant et al., 2006). Fifty-nine Canadian children under the age of eighteen were killed in 2003, and 31 of these children were

---

2   These numbers are national estimates derived from the sample used in the study. The CIS tracked 14,200 child maltreatment cases investigated by 63 Child Welfare Agencies across Canada. "Weighted national annual estimates were derived based on these investigations" (Trocmé et al., 2005, p. 1). For information on the method used, see Appendix H in Trocmé et al., 2005, p. 129.

killed by a family member (Canadian Centre for Justice Statistics, 2005).

In 1989, the United Nations adopted the *Convention on the Rights of the Child*, "which signals clearly that children are holders of human rights and acknowledges their distinct legal personality and evolving capacities" (Pinheiro, 2006, p. 33). All members of the United Nations (except the United States and Somalia) have ratified the *Convention*. The United Nations' Committee on the Rights of the Child, established to review each country's compliance with the *Convention,* has consistently interpreted the *Convention* to mean that corporal punishment is incompatible with its principles and goals. In 2006, it issued a special report on the issue of corporal punishment and said:

> Addressing the widespread acceptance or tolerance of corporal punishment of children and eliminating it, in the family, schools and other settings, is not only an obligation of States parties under the Convention. It is also a key strategy for reducing and preventing all forms of violence in societies. (Committee on the Rights of the Child, 2006, para. 3)

Recently, the United Nations' Committee on the Rights of the Child responded to Canada's report on its compliance with the *Convention on the Rights of the Child* saying:

> The Committee recommends that the State [Canada] party adopt legislation to remove the existing authorization of the use of "reasonable force" in disciplining children and explicitly prohibit all forms of violence against children, however light, within the family, in schools and in other institutions where children may be placed. (Committee on the Rights of the Child, 2003, para. 33)

The Committee was referring to section 43 of the *Criminal Code of Canada*. This section provides parents, teachers and others charged with the care of children with a defence should they be charged with assault when they use force (physical punishment) to "correct" a child's behaviour.

Legally, it is considered a violation of Canada's *Criminal Code* to apply force upon another person without his or her consent—such force is considered an assault. Section 265 (1) of the *Criminal Code of Canada* states:

A person commits an assault when:

a) without the consent of another person, he applies force intentionally to that other person, directly or indirectly;
b) he attempts or threatens, by an act or a gesture, to apply force to
   another person, if he has, or causes that other person to believe
   on reasonable grounds that he has, present ability to effect his
   purpose; or
c) while openly wearing or carrying a weapon or an imitation thereof, he accosts or impedes another person or begs (*Criminal Code of
   Canada*, 1985)

However, there are times and circumstances in which using force on
another person is justified, and the *Criminal Code* provides defences that
can be applied to justify their actions. For example, section 37 provides
a defence to persons who use force to defend themselves and others
under their protection as long as the force used is no more than is necessary; section 38 provides a defence for those who use force to protect
their property as long as no bodily harm is caused to the trespasser; and
section 45 protects those who perform skilled and careful surgical opera-
tions for the benefit of the patient. Section 43 is another defence available
to parents, teachers and others acting in their place who use force to correct a child's behaviour.[3]

Section 43 states:

> Every school teacher, parent or person standing in the
> place of the parent is justified in using force by way of
> correction toward the pupil or child, as the case may be,
> who is under his care, if the force does not exceed what is
> reasonable under the circumstances.

The use of the word "force" in section 43 of the *Criminal Code* has been
interpreted, in the legal context, to mean force "for the benefit of the education of the child" (*Ogg-Moss v. The Queen*, 1984, p. 132).

---

3   In addition, there are common law defences, those that have arisen through
     court decisions. One is the defence of *de minimis non curat lex* (the law does not
     care for small or trifling matters; see *Canadian Foundation*, para. 200). Another is
     the defence of necessity, which recognizes human weaknesses and the fact that
     at times humans may be compelled by self-preservation or that of others, see
     Canadian Foundation, para. 196.

Corporal punishment, as described earlier, is the use of physical force, "however light" which is intended to cause pain or discomfort (Pinheiro, 2006, p. 52, citing Committee on the Rights of the Child, 2006, para. 11). Corporal punishment describes many actions, including hitting with the hand or with objects such as a belt, wooden paddle, or ruler. It also includes actions that do not involve hitting but cause discomfort for the child—for example, requiring a child to remain in an uncomfortable position, kneel on hard objects, experience forced physical exertion, be isolated in a confined place, or have foul-tasting substances placed in the mouth (Durrant & Ensom, 2006).

Restraint differs from physical or corporal punishment in that the intent is not to cause pain or humiliation. It may be used to prohibit or remove a person from causing harm to himself or others. Restraint is defined variously as "physically restricting movement" (Mohr, Petti, & Mohr, 2003, p. 330) and "the application of external control, not to punish, but to protect the child or others from physical pain and harm" (Durrant & Ensom, 2006, p. 2).

Section 43 provides those who use force on children with a defence if they can show that the force was used for correction and was reasonable under the circumstances. In the first case by the Supreme Court of Canada to consider the impact of s. 43 (heard in 1984), former Chief Justice Brian Dickson of the Supreme Court wrote:

> [T]he overall *effects* of that section are clear, no matter how its terms are defined. It exculpates the use of what would otherwise be criminal force by one group of persons against another. It *protects* the first group of persons, but, it should be noted, at the same time it *removes* the protection of the criminal law from the second [emphasis in the original]. (*Ogg-Moss v. The Queen*, 1984, p. 182)

Over the years, leading up to the *Charter* challenge, section 43 had been used to defend incidents of correction that stretch the boundaries of what we might consider to be "reasonable under the circumstances." Some of the many cases that found the correction to be reasonable included a teacher who used karate chops to the face and shoulders of students (*R. v. Wetmore*, 1996), a foster mother who hit three 2-year-olds on their diapered bottoms with a belt, leaving red marks (*R. v. Atkinson*, 1994), a

father who struck his 4-year-old son—who at the time had an ear infec-
tion that eventually required medical attention—across the face leaving
an imprint on his face (*R. v. Wood*, 1995), and a teacher who grabbed a
12-year-old student by the throat with both hands and "cuffed" him in
the stomach (*R. v. Caouette*, 2002). In 1995, s. 43 was successfully used as
a defence in a case involving allegations of child sexual abuse in which,
in one incident, a stepfather ordered his twelve-year-old stepdaughter
to remove her pants and underwear and lie across his knees so that he
could spank her bare bottom (*R. v. W. F. M.*, 1995).

THE *CHARTER* CHALLENGE TO S. 43

In 1982, Canada's *Charter of Rights and Freedoms* came into effect. It guar-
antees all citizens, including children, fundamental rights and freedoms,
including the right to security of their person (s. 7), the right to be free
from cruel and unusual punishment (s. 12), and equality rights (s. 15).
In addition, in 1991 Canada became a signatory to the United Nations'
Convention on the Rights of the Child. The *Convention* affirms that children
are endowed with inherent rights, including the right to freedom from
physical punishment (Articles 3, 19, 28 & 37).

   The Canadian *Charter* and the United Nations' *Convention on the Rights
of the Child* form an impressive combination in promoting the rights of
children. Armed with these two powerful human rights documents, the
author and others began a legal challenge to section 43, arguing that the
use of physical force on children was a violation of their right to dignity
and physical integrity.

   Another motivating factor that influenced our decision to take the
challenge forward was the overwhelming evidence of the harm caused
to a child's development and overall physical and mental well-being,
even when subjected to what we might consider "mild" corporal punishment. The research was synthesized in an important meta-analysis
conducted by Gershoff (2002). Gershoff reviewed all studies into the effects of corporal punishment on children conducted over 50 years. She
selected 88 of those studies that focused only on mild to moderate corporal punishment, excluding all studies that looked at the outcomes of
serious physical abuse. Her findings concluded that mild to moderate
corporal punishment reliably predicts decreased moral internalization,
increased child aggression, increased child delinquent and antisocial

behaviours, decreased quality of relationships between parent and child, poorer child mental health, increased risk for being a victim of physical abuse, increased adult aggression, increased adult criminal and antisocial behavior, poorer adult mental health, and increased risk for abusing one's own child or spouse (Gershoff, 2002). She concluded: "Corporal punishment was associated with only one desirable behaviour, namely, increased immediate compliance" (Gershoff, 2002, p. 544). Similar conclusions have been drawn from other reviews since (Grogan-Kaylor, 2004; Mulvaney & Mebert, 2007; Pinheiro, 2006).

The case of the *Canadian Foundation for Children, Youth and the Law v. Canada (Attorney General)* challenging the s. 43 defence was instigated by the author through the Court Challenges Program[4] and eventually carried forward by the Canadian Foundation for Children, Youth and the Law.[5] Our arguments were that s. 43 violated the *Charter* rights of children under three sections. First, we claimed that s. 43 infringed s. 7 of the *Charter*, which protects all citizens from invasions on their personal security, and that the infringement could not be justified within the prin-

---

4   The Court Challenges Program was a federal program designed to assist individuals and groups who faced no other alternative but to challenge federal laws and policies that violated their constitutional equality rights. It was a program that gained international praise through the United Nations but was dismantled by the Conservative Party of Canada in 2006. The *Canadian Foundation* case, discussed here, was often referred to by the Conservative Government as an example as to why the Court Challenges Program should be dismantled.

5   I applied for funding from the Court Challenges Program to research the constitutionality of s. 43 as it relates to the equality rights of children. Consequently, I was successful in obtaining $45,000 to challenge this section. However, I could not take the case forward on my own and was required to find an organization that had a history of working with children and youth and experience in equality rights cases. I selected the Canadian Foundation for Children Youth and the Law, an Ontario-based organization, since there was no other organization that I knew of with a history in both areas. In fact, they had tried twice to intervene at the Supreme Court level on cases involving the physical punishment of children so as to challenge the constitutionality of s. 43. The cases were *R. v. Halcrow*, (1993), 24 British Columbia Appeal Cases (affirmed on appeal to the Supreme Court: [1995] 1 Supreme Court Reports, 440) and *R. v. K.(M.)* (1992), 16 Criminal Reports (4th) 122 (due to the death of the defendant, the Supreme Court did not hear the case).

ciples of fundamental justice.[6] We also argued that s. 43 violated a child's rights under s. 12, which prohibits cruel and unusual treatment.[7] Finally, we argued that s. 43 is contrary to the equality rights proclaimed under s. 15, which protect all citizens from inequality in law and in the protection afforded by law.[8]

The majority of the Supreme Court judges sided with the Government of Canada, the Canadian Teachers' Federation and the Coalition for Family Autonomy[9] and found that, although the defence available to parents and teachers under s. 43 violates a child's "security of the person" rights under s. 7, it is not done in contravention of the principles of fundamental justice. They found that s. 12 of the *Charter* was not offended by s. 43 since s. 12 applies to the actions of governments and their agents—not to parents. Since teachers are considered agents of the state, the Court ruled that s. 12 did not apply, as the only force teachers could use on students was force that was not, according to the standard they had just constructed, "cruel and unusual" (Watkinson, 2006; Watkinson, in press).

Finally, the Court found that s. 43 did not constitute discrimination against children. They acknowledged that s. 43 "permits conduct toward children that would be criminal in the case of adult victims" (para. 50), but the distinction on the basis of age is, they said, designed to protect children by not criminalizing their parents and teachers. Chief Justice McLachlin, writing for the majority said:

6   Section 7 states: Everyone has the right to life, liberty and security of the person and the right not to be deprived thereof except in accordance with the principles of fundamental justice.

7   Section 12 states: Everyone has the right not to be subjected to cruel and unusual treatment or punishment.

8   Section 15 (1) states: Every individual is equal before and under the law and has the right to the equal protection and equal benefit of the law without discrimination and, in particular, without discrimination based on race, national or ethnic origin, colour, religion, sex, age or mental or physical disability.

9   The Coalition is made up of Focus on the Family (Canada) Association, Canada Family Action Coalition, the Home School Legal Defence Association of Canada, and REAL (Realistic, Equal and Active for Life) Women of Canada.

> The decision not to criminalize such conduct [the physical
> punishment of children] is not grounded in devaluation
> of the child, but in a concern that to do so risks ruining
> lives and breaking up families—a burden that in large
> part would be borne by children and outweigh any benefit
> derived from applying the criminal process. (para. 62)

Although the Court was not prepared to find s. 43 a violation of a child's *Charter* rights, it did limit significantly the scope of s. 43. Chief Justice McLachlin of the Supreme Court stated that Section 43 "exempts from criminal sanction only minor corrective force of a transitory and trifling nature" (para. 40). Further, its use can only be considered "reasonable" and used as a defence in cases when corporal punishment is used "for educative or corrective purposes" (para. 24) and when the "non-consensual application of force results neither in harm nor in the prospect of bodily harm. This limits its operation to the mildest forms of assault" (para. 30).

The Court expanded on the limitations, specifically listing the following actions that will not be considered "reasonable" under s. 43, and thus s. 43 would not be available as a defence to parents, teachers or others acting in their place. These actions enter what the Court called a "zone of risk." The "zone of risk" includes using corporal punishment on children under two years of age, because they do not have the capacity to understand "why they are hit" (para. 25 & 40). Also, a child with a "disability or some other contextual factor" will not be capable of learning from the application of force (para. 25). The Court said, "[I]n these cases, force will not be 'corrective' and will not fall within the sphere of immunity provided by s. 43" (para. 25), since children must be capable of learning and have the capacity to successfully correct their behaviour (para. 25). Corporal punishment is not to be used on teenagers, as it can induce aggressive or antisocial behaviour (para. 37, 40). Corporal punishment cannot be justified under s. 43 when an object or weapon is used, such as a ruler or belt (para. 37 & 40), in cases involving slaps or blows to the head (para. 37 & 40), when the force is "degrading, inhuman or harmful conduct" (para. 40), when it is applied in anger stemming from "frustration, loss of temper or abusive personality" (para. 40), or when it is used by teachers (para. 38 & 40).

The impact of the decision was that actions considered by some to be normal child-rearing practices one day, such as slapping a thirteen-year-old or using a wooden spoon to spank a 4-year-old, were considered criminal the next day.

STUDY ON ADULT KNOWLEDGE AND NEEDS

Eighteen months after the Supreme Court issued its decision, the author conducted research into the public's knowledge of the case to determine:

a) The degree to which the participants know and understand the limits placed on them.

b) Whether the limits on the use of corporal punishment interfere with the particpants' cultural, religious or other traditional values or beliefs.

c) What participants thought parents need in order to abide by the limits placed on their use of corporal punishment.

Method

The study involved four focus groups held in rural and urban settings. The first group consisted of nine university students in a northern urban centre, the second group consisted of seven rural mothers, the third consisted of ten urban mothers, and the fourth group consisted of eight mothers who were recent immigrants to Canada. Two participants were male. Forty-seven percent of participants were members of cultural minority groups: six identified themselves as Aboriginal, five as Afghani, four as Asian Canadian, and one as African Canadian. Seventy-four percent described themselves as being associated with some religious/spiritual group: six were Catholic, eight Protestant, four Traditional Spiritual, four Muslim, two New Age, and one Hindu. Six of the participants were not parents.

First, each focus group member was given a questionnaire to complete. The questionnaire gathered demographic information on the age, sex, cultural and religious backgrounds of the participants, where they lived and the number and ages of their children. The questionnaire then asked participants questions concerning the Supreme Court decision in order to determine their familiarity with it. They were asked if they were aware of the Supreme Court of Canada's decision on the use of physical punishment (spanking) of children and, if so, to list any of the changes to the law on spanking that they knew about such as: changes with regard to the ages of children who may be physically punished or where on the child's body physical punishment could be applied?[10] Finally, if they were aware of the changes to the law, they were asked how they found out about them. Suggestions were provided, such as through the newspaper, radio, television and so on. If English was not the first language of participants, the group facilitators or other group participants read the questions to them and recorded their responses.

The principal researcher then described the Supreme Court decision and the manner in which it limited the scope of s. 43. This process provided information to the participants about the decision in a relaxed and non-threatening way. Following this discussion, participants were asked to answer, in writing, whether the decision interfered in any way with their religious, cultural or traditional beliefs. Then a discussion was held to discuss, first, the implications of the decision on their religious, cultural or traditional beliefs and, second, what the participants felt they needed in order to comply with the limitations placed on parental physical punishment of children. The discussion was audiotaped and transcribed.

Findings

Only 12 of the 34 participants (33.3%) said they were aware of the Supreme Court's decision limiting the defence for parents who use physical punishment on children. There was no discernable difference between rural and urban participants in this regard: 3 of the 8 rural participants (37%) and 9 of the 26 urban participants (35%) were aware of the Supreme Courts decision.

Twenty-two of the participants (65%) could not provide any correct information about how the law regarding the physical punishment of children had changed. Of the 12 who answered "yes" to the question— "Are you aware of the Supreme Court's decision on the use of physical punishment?"—only 5 (41.7% of that group; 14.7% of the total sample) had any correct information on the changes. Of the three rural participants who said they knew about the decision, two could not recall any specifics. They responded with comments such as, "I don't know," or "I don't really remember—kind of vague." Of the urban participants, four

---

10   The question was: "Please list any of the changes to the law on spanking that you know about. For example, were there changes in regards to the age of a child; where on the child's body physical punishment can be applied, etc?"

out of nine provided some correct information. Thus, a minority of participants said they knew of the decision, and few (5 of 34) could partially
explain the decision, and even then only in a very limited way. For example, one of the five knew that physical punishment could not be used in
anger and that only an open hand could be used to apply physical force
on a child. Another knew that parents may not hit a child on the head
and that physical force on a toddler was prohibited, but nothing more.

Among the other seven participants who said that they knew about
the decision, one said that only mild force could be used (which is correct)
but thought it could be used only on children under five years of age (it is
limited to children between 2 and 12 years of age); four gave incorrect information, such as saying the court ruled it was permissible to hit a child
on the face; two thought the Court had said there was to be no hitting of
children at all. Another participant, a recent immigrant to Canada who
was not aware of the Supreme Court's decision and therefore could not
provide any examples of how the law had changed, reported being told
by Immigration authorities that children cannot be spanked in Canada.

Participants were asked whether the Court's limits on the use of
physical punishment interfered in any way with their cultural, religious
or other traditional values or beliefs. This question was asked in response
to concerns that any changes to the law concerning the physical punishment of children could be seen as violating the religious, cultural or
traditional practices of parents. The Old Testament is often relied upon to
justify the use of corporal punishment on children (for example, Proverbs
22:1) and researchers have found that members of Conservative Protestant denominations support corporal punishment more strongly than
others (Bottoms, Shaver, Goodman, & Qin, 1995; Ellison, Bartkowski, &
Segal, 1996). As well, other research has found strong support for the use
of corporal punishment within certain cultural groups (Fontes, 2005).

Although 47 percent of participants were members of cultural minority groups, and 74 percent described themselves as being associated
with some religious/spiritual group, none of the participants found that
the limitations interfered with any religious, cultural, or other traditional values or beliefs. Nor were any concerns raised by the participants
regarding how the law has changed. In fact, three of the participants believed the law had always prohibited the use of physical punishment on
children.

What do parents need?

The participants discussed what they thought parents need in order to abide by the changes to the law. The most common theme was parental support. The participants talked, in some cases, very freely about the frustration they feel when dealing with their children. One participant described the frustration as being "on my last nerve …. I really think there is a need for support and I'm not exactly sure where it's supposed to come from when you're on your last nerve." There was an identified need for respite for parents "just to sit for a moment." Some suggested a drop-off centre for kids to go to so as to allow time for the parent to "de-stress." The establishment of such a facility would acknowledge that others share the frustrations and intensities of child rearing and "you wouldn't feel so alone." However, others worried that if they took part in such a service it might "red flag" them. There was the fear that by asking for help you are drawing attention to a weakness. One parent said, "That fear is there. We know we need this extra support in being able to parent our children in a wonderful, healthy way. But that stigma is out there and it makes us fearful to ask for the help that we know we need."

Another common theme was the need for parenting classes. The suggestions included ensuring that parenting classes be held at various times throughout the day so that they are available to working parents as well as to non-working parents, that parenting skills be front and centre in school curricula from grades K-12, and that the health system, the one common denominator in the lives of children and their parents, take the lead in the dissemination of information on healthy child-rearing practices.

Many of the mothers discussed the need to be recognized for the work they do. One group discussed the idea of monetary compensation for parents. Others seemed satisfied with any recognition of the importance and stress associated with the work they do in raising small children. Each focus group raised the need for more public education on physical punishment and its impact, as well as on the Supreme Court's decision.

DISCUSSION OF FINDINGS

Eighteen months after the Supreme Court decision, which brought about important changes to the law defining "reasonable force" with children, only 15 percent of this sample could provide accurate information on even some of these changes. Their lack of knowledge not only places them at risk for prosecution if they use force that is no longer considered reasonable; it also places their children at risk for assault because the law cannot have its intended inhibitory effect on parents' behaviour if parents do not know about it. Perhaps most worrisome is the fact that not one participant knew that the degree of force used may not exceed what is deemed transitory and trifling.[11] So, even those few parents who know that they can only hit with their hands do not know that they can only cause minor discomfort to the child.

Overall, the focus groups highlighted the role of stress in the interaction between parent and child. Its manifestations could be mitigated by providing a "time out" for parents, parenting classes, more recognition of their contribution, including pay, and the need for public education on all of these issues, including the direction arising from the Supreme Court decision.

Supporting and extending this research

Toronto Public Health conducted a structured national survey between January and March 2006, exploring Canadians' knowledge of the Supreme Court's decision on the use of physical punishment of children (Toronto Public Health, 2007). The study was conducted through telephone interviews of 2,451 respondents over the age of 18. The findings were consistent with those found in the study reported upon here. For example, two-thirds of the respondents were not aware of the Supreme Court's decision and, of those who were aware of the decision, "less than one in five knew the legal limitations placed on its use by the Supreme Court" (p. 1). One of the most startling findings in the Toronto Public Health study was the fact that those who were aware of the Supreme Court decision, compared to those who were not, were "more likely to believe that parents are allowed to physically punish their children and less likely to feel unsure that this is allowed" (Toronto Public Health, 2007, p. 9). The study concludes that " the law is ineffective in protecting children in the way the Court had intended, and it also places caregivers at risk of prosecution for acts that they do not know are criminal offences" (p. 11).

---

11   The Court did not define "transitory and trifling"; however, the phrase is found in the Criminal Code of Canada.

Children in Canada are not fully protected from physical punishment, and neither are their parents protected from prosecution. The 2004 Supreme Court decision limited the use of physical punishment based on the severity, age and location on the child's body, but it did not prohibit it outright. In fact, by focusing on the form of physical punishment used rather than its use *per se*, the Court gave its implicit approval to the use of physical punishment on children, thereby maintaining, rather than reducing, the likelihood of physical violence against children (Durrant, Covell, McGillivray, Watkinson, & McNeil, 2008). In so doing, the Court reinforced the idea that physical punishment of children is a normative act.

In a recent study on the intergenerational transmission of approval of physical punishment, the authors found that the best predictor of approval is one's belief that it is normative (Durrant et al., 2008). This variable was a better predictor than the frequency and severity of physical punishment experienced in childhood, the emotional impact of one's experiences of physical punishment over the short and long terms, and the disciplinary context (inductive, power assertive, emotionally abusive or emotionally supportive) in which one's experiences of physical punishment took place. Therefore, the Supreme Court lost an opportunity to decrease approval of physical punishment, which is the most powerful predictor of its use (Durrant et al., 2008) by re-defining physical punishment as an assault, rather than as a normative act.

SUGGESTED SOLUTIONS

With this in mind, it is important to consider means to interrupt the "normativeness" of physical punishment. Such interruptions may include alternatives in legislation, education, and parental supports that mirror the rights of children as stated in the *Convention on the Rights of the Child*.

For example, Canada could follow the lead of more than twenty countries that prohibit all physical punishment of children, no matter how light,[12] to send a clear message that physical punishment is no longer

---

12   The countries that have prohibited all corporal punishment of children are: Costa Rica (2008); Spain (2007); Chile (2007); Venezuela (2007); Uruguay (2007); Portugal (2007); New Zealand (2007); Netherlands (2007); Greece (2006); Hungary (2005); Romania (2004); Ukraine (2004); Iceland (2003); Germany (2000); Israel (2000); Bulgaria (2000); Croatia (1999); Latvia (1998); Denmark (1997); Cyprus (1994); Austria (1989); Norway (1987); Finland (1983); and Sweden (1979).

the "norm." Many of the countries that have prohibited all use of physical punishment have replaced their legislation with positive statements about the entitlements of children to care and a loving environment. For example, Sweden enacted the following law in 1979:

> Children are entitled to care, security and a good upbringing. Children are to be treated with respect for their person and individuality and may not be subjected to corporal punishment or any other humiliating treatment. (*Parenthood and Guardianship Code*, 1983, cited in Durrant & Ensom, 2006, p. 24)

We could also amend all provincial and territorial child protection legislation so that the need for evidence of "demonstrable harm" is removed and instead is replaced with an assurance that all forms of physical punishment, "however light," are prohibited.

Other strategies for reducing the perceived normativeness of physical punishment, and thus preventing the physical and emotional harm it can engender (Gershoff, 2002), include undertaking educational initiatives on the rights of children that are geared to children themselves, their families, and others who work with children; amending education acts to reflect every student's positive entitlement to respect and dignity; supporting parents in adopting positive disciplinary approaches; and providing parental respite. Finally, we need to take a stand as professional organizations and Faculties of Social Work in supporting and promoting initiatives that affirm children's inherent rights and dignity, and work together to end the most common—but least visible—form of violence against children.

REFERENCES

Bottoms, B. L., Shaver, P. R., Goodman, G. S., & Qin, J. (1995). In the name of God: A profile of religion-related child abuse. *Journal of Social Issues, 51*, 85-111.

Canadian Centre for Justice Statistics. (2005). *Family violence in Canada: A statistical profile 2005*. Ottawa, ON: Statistics Canada. Cat. No. 85-224-XIE, 2005.

Canadian Foundation for Children, Youth and the Law v. Canada (Attorney General) [2004] S.C.R. 76.

Centre of Excellence for Child Welfare. (2008). *CECW information sheets*. Retrieved April 14, 2008, from http://www.cecw-cepb.ca/pubs/infosheets_e.html

Committee on the Rights of the Child (27 October 2003). Concluding observations of the Committee on the Rights of the Child: CANADA, CRC/C15/Add.215.

Committee on the Rights of the Child (2006). General Comment No. 8. The right of the child to protection from corporal punishment and other cruel or degrading forms of punishment (articles 19, 28(2) and 37, inter alia), CRC/C/GC/8.

Convention on the Rights of the Child. (1989). U.N. Doc. A/RES/44/25 (1989). Retrieved May 8, 2008, from http://www.unhchr.ch/html/menu3/b/k2crc.htm

Criminal Code of Canada, R.S.C. 1985, c. C-46.

Durrant, J. E., Covell, K., McGillivray, A., Watkinson, A. M., & McNeil, J. (2008). *"It didn't do me any harm": Explaining the intergenerational transmission of approval of child physical punishment*. Department of Family Studies, Faculty of Human Ecology, University of Manitoba, Winnipeg, MB. Manuscript submitted for publication.

Durrant, J. E., & Ensom, R. (2006). *Joint statement on physical punishment of children and youth*. Ottawa, ON: Coalition on the Physical Punishment of Children and Youth.

Durrant, J. E., Trocmé, N., Fallon, B., Milne, C., Black, T., & Knoke, D. (2006). Punitive violence against children in Canada. Centre of Excellence for Child Welfare. Retrieved May 8, 2008, from http://www.cecw-cepb.ca/files/file/en/PunitiveViolence41E.pdf

Ellison, C. G., Bartkowski, J. P., & Segal, M. L. (1996). Conservative Protestantism and the parental use of corporal punishment. *Social Forces, 74*(3), 1003.

Fatah, N. (Producer). (2008, January 10). *As It Happens* [Radio Broadcast]. Toronto, ON: Canadian Broadcasting Corporation.

Finkelhor, D. (1994). Children as victims of violence: A national survey. *Pediatrics, 94*, 413-420.

Fontes, L. A. (2005). *Child abuse and culture: Working with diverse families*. New York: The Guilford Press.

Gershoff, E. T. (2002). Corporal punishment by parents and associated child behaviours and experiences: A meta-analytic and theoretical review. *Psychological Bulletin, 128*(4), 539-579.

Grogan-Kaylor, A. (2004). The effect of corporal punishment on antisocial behavior in children. *Social Work Research, 28*(3), 153-162.

Jack, S., Munn, C., Cheng, C., & MacMillan, H. M. (2006). *Child maltreatment in Canada: Overview paper*. Ottawa, ON: National Clearinghouse on Family Violence, Public Health Agency of Canada.

McGillivray, A., & Durrant, J. E. (2006). Child corporal punishment: Violence, law, and rights. In R. Alaggia & C. Vine (Eds.), *Cruel but not unusual: Violence in Canadian families* (pp. 177-200). Waterloo, ON: Wilfred Laurier University Press.

Mohr, W. K., Petti, T. A., & Mohr, B. D. (2003). Adverse effects associated with physical restraint. *Canadian Journal of Psychiatry, 48*(5), 330-337.

Mulvaney, M. K., & Mebert, C. J. (2007). Parental corporal punishment predicts behaviour problems in early childhood. *Journal of Family Psychology, 21*(3), 389-397.

Ogg-Moss v. The Queen, [1984] 2 S.C.R., 173.

Pinheiro, P. S. (2006). *World report on violence against children.* Geneva: United Nations Secretary General's Study on Violence against Children.

R. v. Atkinson, [1994] W.W.R. 485 (Manitoba Provincial Court).

R. v. Caouette, [2002] Q.J. No 1055 (Quebec Criminal Court).

R. v. W. F. M. (1995), 169 A.R. 222 (Court of Appeal).

R. v. Wetmore, (1996). 172 N.B.R. (2d) 224 (Queen's Bench).

R. v. Wood (1995), 176 A.R. 223 (Provincial Court).

Saskatchewan Provincial Child Abuse Protocol. (2006). Retrieved May 9, 2008, from http://www.socialservices.gov.sk.ca/child-abuse-protocol.pdf

Toronto Public Health. (March 2007). *National survey of Canadians' knowledge of the law on physical punishment of children (Section 43 of the Criminal Code of Canada).* Retrieved May 8, 2008, from http://www.toronto.ca/health/ssl_index.htm

Trocmé, N., Fallon, B., MacLaurin, B., Daciuk, J., Felstiner, C., Black, T. (2005). *Canadian incidence study of reported child abuse and neglect – 2003: Major findings.* Ottawa, ON: Minister of Public Works and Government Services Canada.

Vine, C., Trocmé, N., & Findlay, J. (2006). Children abused, neglected, and living with violence. In R. Alaggia & C. Vine (Eds.), *Cruel but not unusual: Violence in Canadian families* (pp. 147-176). Waterloo: Wilfred Laurier University Press.

Watkinson, A. M. (2006). Supreme Court of Canada stands behind corporal punishment—sort of .... *International Social Work Journal 49*(4),531-536.

Watkinson, A. M. (in press). Corporal punishment and education: Oh Canada! Spare us! In M. Manley-Casimir & K. Manley-Casimir (Eds.), *The courts, the charter and the schools: The impact of the Charter of Rights and Freedoms on educational policy and practice, 1982-2007.* Toronto, ON: University of Toronto Press.

CHAPTER 11

Complex Poverty and Home-grown Solutions in Two Prairie Cities

Jim Silver

> The kind of real poverty that once existed in Canada (and that can be found elsewhere in the world today) has been largely defeated.

Winnipeg Free Press, lead editorial, September 15, 2007

A central argument of this chapter is that the above claim is false. What the *Free Press* calls "real poverty" exists in western Canadian cities like Winnipeg and Saskatoon. It takes a particular form—spatially concentrated racialized poverty—that is about much more than a shortage of income and that is deeply entrenched and resistant to quick or easy solutions. This chapter will argue, secondly, that despite the complexity and tenacity of this form of poverty, out of its midst are emerging community-based solutions that are innovative and effective, that embody a 'passion for action', and that have significant potential for overcoming poverty.

SUGGESTED CITATION: Silver, J. (2009). Complex poverty and home-grown solutions in two Prairie cities. In S. McKay, D. Fuchs, & I. Brown (Eds.), *Passion for action in child and family services: Voices from the prairies* (pp. 227-246). Regina, SK: Canadian Plains Research Center.

These community-based solutions will be described, with examples. Third, the chapter will argue that in order for these community-based solutions to become truly transformative in communities plagued by spatially concentrated racialized poverty, additional policy measures are needed. The chapter concludes by offering some thoughts on what these might be.

That high rates of poverty and of racism and the ongoing impact of colonization correlate strongly with matters related to child welfare has been well documented. Ross and Roberts (1999, p. 3) examined the correlation between family income and 27 different elements of child development, and found that for each of the 27 variables, "children living in families with lower incomes are found to be at a greater risk of experiencing negative outcomes and poor living conditions than those in higher-income families." In a similar study, focused on children and youth in Saskatchewan, Schissel (1997, p. 1) found that "... living in poverty reduces the emotional well-being of children and youth, places their physical and emotional health at risk, and impairs their satisfaction with and success in the educational system." With respect to educational outcomes, the Manitoba Centre for Health Policy (Brownell et al., 2004) found that 81 percent of students in high socio-economic neighbourhoods in Winnipeg graduated from grade 12, while 37 percent of students in low socio-economic neighbourhoods graduated from grade 12, and only 22 percent of students from the north end of Winnipeg's inner city—where poverty and the city's Aboriginal population are particularly concentrated—graduated from grade 12. Low educational attainment, in turn, correlates strongly with future poverty, thus feeding a vicious cycle from which children suffer in a variety of ways. Studies of child abuse, for example, have found a strong correlation between poverty and inadequate housing, and reported incidence of child abuse and neglect (Trocmé, Fallon, MacLaurin & Neves, 2005), and the combination of poverty, racism and the ongoing impact of colonization produces similar outcomes for Aboriginal children (Blackstock & Trocmé, 2005). Poverty and racism, and community-based strategies for their alleviation (Blackstock and Trocmé, 2005), are central concerns for those working in child welfare.

A PARTICULARLY DAMAGING FORM OF POVERTY

While it will be a central feature of the argument of this chapter that the poverty that is characteristic of Prairie cities is about much more than

a shortage of income, nevertheless the shortage of income is an important aspect of poverty, and in many respects it has been getting worse. A
study of poverty in Winnipeg's inner city using 1996 Census of Canada
data found, for example, that just over 50 percent of households had incomes below the Statistics Canada Low-Income Cut Off (LICO), and that
just over 80 percent of Aboriginal households, an astonishing four in every five of such households, had incomes below the LICO, and that in
some inner-city school catchment areas more than 80 percent of parents
with school-age children had incomes below the LICO (Lezubski, Silver,
& Black, 2000, pp. 38-40). The study found further that a very high proportion of those with incomes below the LICO were *far* below the LICO.
That continues to be the case. The gap between the average incomes of
those below the LICO, and the LICO itself, was $10,000 in Manitoba and
$8,100 in Saskatchewan in 2004 (Social Planning Council of Winnipeg,
2006). More recently, social assistance rates have plummeted far below
the LICO. In 2005 single employable recipients of social assistance received an amount equivalent to 25 percent of the LICO in Manitoba,
and 37 percent of the LICO in Saskatchewan; a couple with two children
on social assistance received 53 percent and 58 percent of the LICO in
Manitoba and Saskatchewan respectively (National Council of Welfare,
2006). Further, welfare incomes declined in real terms between 1989 and
2005 in Manitoba and Saskatchewan, and reached historic lows in Manitoba in the period 2000-2005 (National Council of Welfare, 2006), while
in Saskatchewan the shift to Transitional Employment Assistance (TEA)
for most social assistance recipients has produced even lower levels of
support than is provided by social assistance (Hunter & Donovan, 2005).
Many people in Prairie cities face a shortage of income. In a market-
based economy this is a *huge* problem; in a wealthy country like Canada
it is unconscionable.

But we need to go beyond such data to understand the complex form
of poverty—the spatially concentrated racialized poverty—that now
prevails in Prairie cities, as exemplified by the cases of Winnipeg and
Saskatoon.

This poverty is spatially concentrated in that certain neighbourhoods, typically inner-city neighbourhoods, have a particularly high
concentration of low-income households. For example, in Saskatoon's
core neighbourhoods in 2001, 21 percent of families had incomes below
$20,000, compared to 9 percent for Saskatoon as a whole; the average

income was $32,475 compared to $62,451 for Saskatoon as a whole; 21 percent of families were one-parent families; compared to 11 percent for Saskatoon as a whole; and 13 percent of individuals had less than grade 9, compared to 6 percent for Saskatoon as a whole. The same pattern prevailed in Winnipeg's inner city: 24 percent had incomes below $20,000, compared to almost 15 percent for Winnipeg as a whole; the average income was $42,477 compared to $63,657 for Winnipeg as a whole; 30 percent of families were lone-parent families compared to 19 percent for Winnipeg as a whole; and just over 12 percent of individuals had less than grade 9, compared to almost 8 percent for Winnipeg as a whole (Silver, 2008). These data suggest that poverty and related conditions are spatially concentrated. While the degree of concentration is not as great as in many American urban centres, the spatial concentration of poverty has been found to produce a host of particularly negative effects (Wilson, 1987).

A high degree of residential mobility may add to these negative effects. There is a great deal of mobility within the urban Aboriginal population, both back and forth between urban and rural communities (Clatworthy, 2000, 1996), and within urban settings (Skelton, 2002). High rates of residential mobility have been found in inner-city neighbourhoods in Winnipeg. A 1995 study by Manitoba Health (1995), for example, found that:

> Migrancy (frequent movers) is a particular problem for inner city children .... In a 1992 review of inner city schools, the lowest migrancy rate (proportion of children moving per year in the school population) was 40.6 percent. The highest rate was 84.7 percent .... Some children have been in 13 schools by 11 years of age .... In a nine-month period in 1992/93, there were 3,058 single-parent family moves out of a possible 3,553. (pp. 107-108)

In addition, this spatially concentrated poverty is racialized poverty in that a high proportion of those who are poor are Aboriginal. In Saskatoon's core neighbourhoods almost 26 percent of the population self-identify as Aboriginal, compared to almost 10 percent in Saskatoon as a whole, while in Winnipeg the comparative percentages are just over 19 percent compared to just over 8 percent (Silver, 2008). A 2005 evaluation of five Winnipeg inner-city neighbourhoods found that Aboriginal people comprised from 27.5 to 54.9 percent of the population, and that Aboriginal people plus visible minorities comprised a majority in four of the five inner-city neighbourhoods, from 51.5 percent to 66 percent, and were 42.5 percent in the fifth neighbourhood (Distasio, Dudley, Johnson, & Sargent, 2005, p. 23). Much the same is the case in Saskatoon's core neighbourhoods. In Pleasant Hill and Riversdale, two of the five core neighbourhoods, 48.4 percent and 43.5 percent of the population respectively were Aboriginal (Anderson, 2005, pp. 15, 19).

The result is that Prairie cities like Winnipeg and Saskatoon are segregated. This is something rarely talked about openly, rarely acknowledged, and perhaps not recognized by many. These cities are, however, both spatially and socially segregated. People can live their entire lives in the suburbs and rarely see Aboriginal people. Many non-Aboriginal people will never have socialized with Aboriginal people; most Aboriginal people will never have been invited to a social function in a non-Aboriginal home. Many students at the University of Winnipeg where I teach have never physically set foot in the inner city, and many are fearful of going into the inner city. A recent study (Berdahl, 2007, p. 17) found that in six major western Canadian cities, including Winnipeg and Saskatoon, "Most residents feel that there are unsafe parts of their cities; when asked to rate their agreement with the statement, 'There are parts of the city I am scared to set foot in', 7 in 10 strongly or somewhat agreed."

How did this happen? How have Prairie cities like Winnipeg and Saskatoon come to take this form?

THE EMERGENCE OF SPATIALLY CONCENTRATED RACIALIZED POVERTY

The form and character of the poverty that prevails in Prairie cities has taken shape over decades and can be seen to be the product of four broad socio-economic forces: suburbanization, de-industrialization, in-migration, and colonization.

Starting early in the post-Second World War period, those who could afford to do so moved from locations close to the geographic centre of cities, where houses were the oldest, to the suburbs, where new and larger houses were being built on much larger lots. This process of **suburbanization** was a continent-wide phenomenon (Jackson, 1985). As people moved to the suburbs, businesses followed. Inner cities were 'hollowed out.' This process of suburbanization was fueled by massive government subsidies, in the form of the construction of highways and bridges and other infrastructure to service the new communities, and government support for mortgages for the buyers of new homes. By contrast, relatively little public investment was directed at the hollowed-out inner cities (Silver, 2006b). The result was that those who stayed behind in inner cities were disproportionately those who could not afford to move to the suburbs, and their older homes and neighbourhoods suffered a relative lack of government investment. As people moved out of inner cities, demand for housing fell, driving prices down. Many older homes, their values in decline, were bought by absentee landlords, at least some of whom used them as revenue properties—investing little in maintenance and repair, and cramming in as many renters as possible, often in the form of rooming houses. Thus inner cities became areas of cheap housing, which then attracted those with lower incomes in search of housing that they could afford, thus contributing to the spatial concentration of poverty.

Starting in the late 1960s a second broad socio-economic force affected urban centres—the process of **de-industrialization**, a central part of what has come to be called 'globalization.' Global economic forces have promoted a massive shift in the character of the labour market, that is, in the kinds of jobs available to people in industrial countries generally, and more specifically for our purposes, in Prairie cities. There has been a steady attrition of mass-production industries—factories, industrial jobs symbolized by the assembly line. This is a process that continues today— witness the continued loss of jobs in southern Ontario's auto industry. These were the kinds of jobs that someone with a high school education or less could raise a family on. They were jobs that were unionized, offered steady employment, were full-time and included benefits. These kinds of jobs have been replaced by jobs in the service sector that are disproportionately low-wage, part-time, non-union jobs with neither benefits nor security. They are typically *not* the kinds of jobs that one can support a family on. The result for inner cities has been that not only have many jobs relocated to the suburbs, but also those that are left in inner cities are disproportionately 'contingent' jobs (Teeple, 2000; Broad, 2006). This has had a huge impact on young people with limited education and has been an important factor in the creation of the persistent and complex form of poverty found especially in inner cities.

The third broad socio-economic force contributing to the form of poverty that now exists in Prairie inner cities has been the very large **in-migration** of Aboriginal people from rural and northern communities to urban centres, starting in the 1960s. In Winnipeg, for example, there were 1,082 Aboriginal people in 1961; in 2006 there were 63,380, almost a 60-fold increase. During that time Winnipeg's total population grew from 476,543 to 694,668, which is less than a 1.5-fold increase. In Saskatoon there were 207 Aboriginal people in 1961; in 2006 there were 21,535, more than a 100-fold increase. During the same period Saskatoon's total population grew from 95,564 to 233,923, which is almost a 2.5-fold increase (Peters, n.d.; Statistics Canada, 2008). The vast majority of these in-migrants located in inner-city neighbourhoods, at first because rents were lowest there, as the result of suburbanization and the age of the housing stock, and as time passed because other Aboriginal people were already located there. However, they arrived just as the good jobs were leaving: for the suburbs, as part of the process of suburbanization; or out of the country altogether, as part of the process of de-industrialization. The kinds of jobs that had sustained in-migrants before them were rapidly disappearing, replaced by low-wage service sector jobs. At the same time, these newcomers faced a wall of racism and job discrimination. Newspaper accounts of the time make this very evident (Silver, 2006b, pp. 19-20); formal interviews with Aboriginal people repeatedly cite incidents of job-related discrimination (Silver, 2006a, pp. 62-64).

The fourth historic force contributing to the form and character of inner-city poverty in Prairie cities has been the historic legacy and enduring impact of **colonization**. This process can be described as follows. Canadians of European descent pushed Aboriginal people off their Prairie lands in the late nineteenth century, forcing them onto reserves that were typically geographically and culturally marginalized from the European-based Canadian culture that quickly became dominant. Aboriginal peoples' means of economic livelihood, which had sustained them for millennia, were destroyed, as were their political systems. On their reserves they were controlled by the *Indian Act* and the Indian Agent, who replaced their own forms of political organization. Attempts were made by the Canadian state to eliminate Aboriginal cultures and forms of spirituality—in some cases these were outlawed—although Aboriginal people have waged a constant 'below the radar' war of resistance aimed at keeping alive their historic cultural and spiritual ways of being. Aboriginal people were denied political rights—for example, the right of assembly and the right to vote. Perhaps most importantly, many Aboriginal children were seized by the agents of the state and forced into residential schools, where thousands died and where sickness and various forms of abuse were common (Milloy, 1999; Miller, 1996; Grant, 1996). All of these things together constitute a deliberate and systematic attempt to destroy Aboriginal cultures and ways of being. Aboriginal children in residential schools, for example, were denied the right to speak their languages and were taught to be ashamed of being Aboriginal.

These measures, this colonization, was predicated upon the *false* assumption that Aboriginal people and their cultures were inferior to European peoples and cultures. This assumption is, quite simply, not true. But many Aboriginal people themselves came to believe this false claim. They internalized this false belief in their inferiority. Many continue to do so (Adams, 1999; Hart, 2002). This manifests itself in a host of ways: a lack of self-esteem and of self-confidence; a sense of worthlessness; a lack of hope for the future. It is exceptionally difficult to navigate a complex and harshly competitive society without a sense of self-worth, without a sense of hope and optimism about the future. Colonization has eroded that positive psychological sense; it has done and continues to do deep psychological damage to Aboriginal people. This damage is less a function of personal failings than of broad structural and historical forces that can be described by use of the term colonization. And this damage is constantly reinforced by the ongoing impact of racism in its various forms and the difficulty in finding well-paid employment.

In summary, we can say that the particular form of poverty that prevails in Prairie cities is the product of the four broad socio-economic forces described in the paragraphs above. Aboriginal people began to move into Prairie cities in considerable numbers in the 1960s. Many were damaged by colonization and were consequently lacking in self-esteem and self-confidence, which was reinforced upon their arrival in urban centres by the wall of racism that they encountered. Having little money, they settled in inner-city locations, where housing was cheaper because of its age and because of suburbanization. They arrived just as the good jobs were leaving—as part of the process of suburbanization, or because of de-industrialization. The absence of good jobs, and the job discrimination they faced in attempting to find work, made it extremely difficult

to get out of poverty, and in some cases that poverty has been reproduced across generations. Because this poverty has come to be spatially
concentrated, many people only know others who are poor; because the
poverty has in some cases been reproduced across generations, in some
cases family members have always been poor. The kind of poverty that
this has produced has recently been described by the Canadian Centre
for Policy Alternatives-Manitoba by the use of two metaphors:

> One is the notion of a complex web—a web of poverty,
> racism, drugs, gangs, violence. The other is the notion of a
> cycle—people caught in a cycle of inter-related problems.
> Both suggest the idea of people who are trapped,
> immobilized, unable to escape, destined to struggle
> with forces against which they cannot win, from which
> they cannot extricate themselves. The result is despair,
> resignation, anger, hopelessness, which then reinforce
> the cycle, and wrap them tighter in the web (CCPA-Mb,
> 2005, p. 24).

This is a particularly damaging form of poverty. It is deeply-rooted.
There are no simple, nor quick, nor unidimensional solutions. This is a
form of poverty that is about much more than a shortage of income. It is
complex; it wraps people in a web, a cycle, that reproduces their problems and makes their escape extremely difficult.

A NEW FORM OF DEVELOPMENT

In response to this spatially concentrated racialized poverty, a new form
of 'development' has emerged in Winnipeg's inner city in the past 30
years, and in Saskatoon's core neighbourhoods in the last 10 years. Similar forms of development may have emerged in other Prairie cities as
well. In Winnipeg and Saskatoon this new form of development has
emerged in largely spontaneous, or unplanned, fashion. It is largely a
'bottom-up' form of development and is 'indigenous' to the inner city;
that is, it has for the most part been created by and is driven by inner-city
people as opposed to outside 'experts.' It is less a product of theory than
it is a pragmatic, locally-based response to the harsh and complex form
of poverty that has taken deep root in Winnipeg's inner city and Saskatoon's core neighbourhoods.

This form of development, or of community development, has manifested itself in a multiplicity of relatively small community-based organizations (CBOs). These CBOs, together with the highly skilled inner-city people who are their leaders, constitute an essential "infrastructure" for fighting spatially concentrated racialized poverty. These CBOs are, for the most part, creative and innovative. They have maintained a form of operation that keeps them in close touch with inner-city people. These skilled, creative CBOs, and the people who lead and work in them, are the living embodiment of the phrase "passion for action."

These CBOs have taken a wide variety of forms. They include community development corporations, or neighbourhood renewal corporations, as they are called in Winnipeg. Examples are the North End Community Renewal Corporation, the Spence Neighbourhood Association and the West Broadway Development Corporation in Winnipeg's inner city, and Quint Development Corporation in Saskatoon's core neighbourhoods. They include women's organizations, like the North End Women's Resource Centre and the North Point Douglas Women's Centre and the West Central Women's Resource Centre; and family and youth centres such as the Andrews Street Family Centre, Rossbrook House and Wolseley Family Place. There is a wide range of alternative, inner-city educational initiatives: adult learning centres (located throughout Manitoba and not just in Winnipeg's inner city); community schools (which exist also in Saskatoon's core neighbourhoods); community development and community economic development training initiatives; and the University of Winnipeg's new Urban and Inner-City Studies degree program. These are but the tip of the iceberg of a rich array of such CBOs.

In Winnipeg's inner city in particular there has emerged alongside of, and often working in cooperation with, the kinds of CBOs mentioned above, a distinctly Aboriginal form of community development, represented by some 70 Aboriginal CBOs in the city, most in the inner city. Many of these practice a "holistic" form of community development that can be described briefly as follows (for a fuller description, see Silver, 2006a, ch. 5). First, Aboriginal community development starts with the individual, and the need to heal—to heal from the ongoing damage of colonization and racism. This is the starting point because healthy communities cannot be built unless individuals are healthy. But individuals cannot heal and be made healthy unless there are strong and healthy communities in which to do so, and so an Aboriginal form of community development focuses on building such communities, and does so especially by incorporating into their work a knowledge and appreciation of Aboriginal cultures. This in turn cannot be done unless there are Aboriginal organizations in place, by which is meant organizations created by, and run by and for, Aboriginal people themselves, and run in a fashion consistent with Aboriginal cultural values. Finally, this Aboriginal form of community development is rooted in an ideological understanding of the impact of colonization, and the need to de-colonize. De-colonizing means making Aboriginal people who suffer from the complex form of poverty described above aware that the root of their problems is less their own personal failings than it is the broad historical forces described by the term colonization. Knowing that this is the case is not intended to produce victims who feel sorry for themselves because of the historical injustices to which they were subjected. Rather, it is intended to liberate them, by making them aware that they are not the problem, and that they can make their way in life, and do so as Aboriginal people who are aware of their history and culture and who are proud of who they are. Among the many Aboriginal organizations working in this way, or some variant of this way, are, for example: the Ma Mawi Wi Chi Itata Centre; the Native Women's Transition Centre; and the Urban Circle Training Centre. In Saskatoon the Saskatchewan Native Theatre Company operates in a similar fashion. These are remarkably creative and effective organizations, led by a cadre of Aboriginal people most of whom were raised poor and who experienced many poverty- and racism-related difficulties, but who have become what I have elsewhere described as "organic intellectuals" (Silver, 2006a)—people deeply knowledgeable about who they are and about how they came to be constructed as they have been by broad historical forces.

The inner cities of Winnipeg and Saskatoon have been, in recent decades, "social laboratories" (Diamantopoulos & Findlay, 2007; Silver, 2008), in which people poor in income but rich in imagination and creativity and passion for action, have built the infrastructure that has the capacity to make a major contribution to the alleviation and elimination of the kind of poverty that prevails in Prairie cities.

Governments have played a key role in supporting the emergence of this community-based anti-poverty infrastructure. In Winnipeg, for example, there have been four tri-level (civic, provincial and federal) urban development agreements since 1980, and despite many weaknesses (Urban Futures Group, 1990; Silver, 2002), these have contributed much of the start-up money for these bottom-up initiatives. Such government support has been necessary because the private sector has largely abandoned these inner cities. It is fair to say that the market has failed inner cities and that creative inner-city people, supported financially by some governments, have emerged to fill the void.

A large proportion of the CBOs described above operate according to a set of principles often called the Neechi Principles—the principles were systematized by workers at an Aboriginal worker co-op grocery store called Neechi Foods in Winnipeg's inner city (see sidebar). These principles include, among others, the notions of hiring, purchasing and investing locally (Rothney, 1991; Silver & Loxley, 2007).

The principles are sometimes expressed in the form of the 'leaky bucket' metaphor: a great deal of money goes into the inner city in various forms, but most of it leaks out again—in the form of rent paid to absentee landlords or grocery bills paid at suburban supermarkets, for example—and so the inner city does not get the full benefit of the money that comes in and just as quickly leaks out. Thus a community economic development strategy involves plugging the holes in the leaky bucket: hiring local people wherever possible and training them if necessary; renovating inner-city housing and making it available to inner-city residents; hiring and training inner-city people to do the renovating; and building inner-city grocery stores that enable people to shop locally and that incorporate local hiring. These principles are remarkably widely spread in Winnipeg's inner city and Saskatoon's core neighbourhoods. They are clearly the guiding force

---

NEECHI COMMUNITY ECONOMIC DEVELOPMENT PRINCIPLES

1. Use of locally produced goods and services.
2. Production of goods and services for local use.
3. Local re-investment of profits.
4. Long-term employment of local residents.
5. Local skill development.
6. Local decision-making.
7. Promotion of public health.
8. Improvement of the physical environment.
9. Promotion of neighbourhood stability.
10. Promotion of human dignity.
11. Mutual aid support among organizations adhering to these principles.

Source: Neechi, 1993.

behind, for example, Saskatoon's Station 20 West, an ambitious and creative example of community economic development.

Other principles that are widely used, although perhaps not as consciously articulated as the Neechi Principles, are the following: creating *opportunities* for inner-city people, as opposed to providing charity; providing *supports* to inner-city people to enable them to take advantage of those opportunities; *tailoring* those opportunities and supports to the day-to-day experiences of the people who will be using them, a notion predicated upon the assumption that many of the standardized, 'one-size-fits-all' systems do not work for the particular circumstances of inner-city people; and *laddering* those opportunities, so that people can move one step at a time, gaining their confidence as they go.

WHAT ELSE IS NEEDED?

As valuable and impressive and innovative and effective as these CBOs and people are, spatially concentrated racialized poverty persists and, in fact, worsens. This is the perplexing contradiction: a great deal that is creative and positive is being done and is proving effective, but for every step taken forward another is taken back. The depth and tenacity of this form of poverty are such that all the good efforts described above are not enough to be transformative—not enough, that is, to transform inner-city communities and their people in positive ways of their choosing. Thus the question becomes: what more is needed to enable the good work that is now being done to *become transformative*?

What follows are some thoughts on this dilemma.

First, we need more of the same. We have to persist, over time, with these innovative, community-based efforts. Spatially concentrated racialized poverty has emerged and taken root over many decades. The problems are now deeply entrenched, multi-faceted and complex. Their character is such that they *cannot* be solved quickly. The efforts described above have to be persisted in over a long period of time—time measured in decades—if success is to be achieved. That being said, we have some evidence that these efforts do make a difference. In Winnipeg's Spence neighbourhood, for example, where the Spence Neighbourhood Association has been working for approximately a decade, the differences are visible and tangible—renovated housing, community gardens, new youth programs, for example—and the long-term population decline has recently been reversed (Lewys, 2007).

But also, we need to persist over a long period of time because of the nature of the development being described here. This form of development builds on the strengths of inner-city people. It has a capacity-building character. It is rooted in the belief that people can solve their own problems, given opportunities that are tailored, supported and laddered, and given a deep experiential knowledge of the barriers such people face. This takes time. People mired in decades of racialized poverty, having experienced the damage that comes with racialized poverty, cannot *instantly* take charge of their lives. But this strategy only works if inner-city people themselves, and not outside 'experts,' are the agents of their development. In other words, there are no quick fixes. The form of development described above builds cumulatively, as people develop confidence and skills—a process that of necessity takes time and persistence.

Second, the role of the state is central to the success or otherwise of this form of development. Governments have, for the most part, funded this form of development to date. This has included the tri-level (federal/provincial/municipal) urban development agreements in Winnipeg since 1980; the currently very successful Neighbourhoods Alive! program, which funds inner-city revitalization in Manitoba urban centres, and its counterpart, the Neighbourhood Development Organization Initiative in Saskatchewan; and recent large financial commitments to inner-city initiatives in Saskatoon (Government of Saskatchewan, September 4, 2007). This form of development is dependent upon government support, and this should not be seen negatively, any more than we see government support for healthcare or education negatively.

But this government funding has been limited. Dollars invested in inner cities have been modest, relative to the huge scale and deep complexity of the problems. This has been the case even in provinces governed in recent years by New Democratic Party (NDP) governments, which might have been thought to be more sympathetic to low-income inner-city people. While it is undoubtedly true that NDP governments have invested more in community-based inner-city organizations than other governments would have done, they have not invested enough to be transformative (Silver, 2008). What is more, these governments continue to cut taxes, thus removing resources that could otherwise be invested in the inner city. For example, one study has estimated that by 2010, combined tax cuts by Gary Doer's NDP government in Manitoba will amount to $900 million, and that a family of four earning $20,000 per year will have saved $150 per year as a result of the cuts, while a family of four earning $100,000 per year will have saved $1,700 per year (MacKinnon & Hudson, 2007). Similarly, in Saskatchewan, income tax rates were cut by close to one-third between 2000 and 2006, and as in Manitoba, those earning higher incomes benefitted more than those earning lower incomes (Hunter & Douglas, 2006). These tax cuts remove money from the public sector that might otherwise have been invested in the work of inner-city CBOs, putting it instead into the private hands of higher-income individuals, where it will not benefit the inner city.

Finally, with respect to government investment in inner-city/core neighbourhoods, those investments that have been made have *not* been undertaken in a deliberate, systematic and strategic fashion. Instead, they have, for the most part, been responses to competing requests from a multiplicity of CBOs for limited funds, and thus have been partial, ad hoc and too limited. What is needed is a shift in thinking about public investment in inner cities, to a more proactive, more strategic way of thinking and a way of thinking more focused on being transformative.

CONCLUDING THOUGHTS:
WHERE DO WE GO FROM HERE?

What follows are four suggestions that arise from the argument developed above, that would, I believe, contribute to moving us gradually toward the goal of eliminating spatially concentrated racialized poverty in Prairie cities like Winnipeg and Saskatoon. Although these suggestions are not especially radical, to implement them would require a shift in public attitudes and government policies. While Canada is not moving in this direction at the moment—witness the March 2008 decision by the new Saskatchewan government of Premier Brad Wall to cancel $8 million of previously committed funding to Station 20 West in Saskatoon's core neighbourhoods, a decision that, if not reversed, will deepen the complex poverty that prevails in these neighbourhoods—shifts of this magnitude and more *have* happened often in the past and are distinctly possible in the future.

First, governments must stop cutting taxes, and citizens must individually and collectively insist that they stop cutting taxes. The tax cut approach is a powerful, Right-wing strategy aimed at significantly weakening the role of government and turning still more decisions over to the market. Continued tax cuts will make it impossible to do the work that needs to be done to solve the problem of spatially concentrated racialized poverty. At the Passion for Action conference from which this book arose, the then Minister of Social Services was asked a question, the preamble to which was that we have often heard positive statements before from government ministers, but when are we going to see real action to tackle these poverty-related problems? The Minister responded by saying that the government was trying, and he knows more is needed, but there are limits to what they can do because "it comes down to funding" (author's notes, September 13, 2007). He said that the provincial government does not have enough money to do all that needs to be done. But the more accurate answer would have been: "It comes down to priorities, and we have chosen to cut taxes that benefit higher-income individuals rather than investing seriously in a strategy aimed at transforming spatially concentrated racialized poverty." Continued tax cuts will make such a strategy impossible and should therefore be opposed.

Second, I take for granted and therefore have said little about, the need for higher minimum wages, higher social assistance rates, and national, universal social programs such as a national childcare program. The provinces of Manitoba and Saskatchewan have recently begun to move in a more positive direction on minimum wages and deserve full credit for the steps they have taken in that regard. Saskatchewan's minimum wage will move in stages, starting in January 2008, to the level of the LICO by 2010, and will then be indexed to the growth of the Consumer Price Index, while Manitoba has made gains in recent years in the provision of childcare spaces. But social assistance rates remain woefully inadequate, the housing allowance component in particular is completely inadequate, and childcare spaces do not come close to meeting the need, although Manitoba has taken important steps in that regard (Silver, 2008). Higher minimum wages and the provision of childcare, for example, are important components in creating *opportunities* for people to solve their own problems and in providing the *supports* needed to enable them to seize those opportunities.

Third, we need to confront the problem of racism in a more direct fashion. Poverty in Canada is racialized. This has been set out extremely clearly by Grace-Edward Galabuzi (2006) in his important book, *Canada's*

Economic Apartheid: The Social Exclusion of Racialized Groups in the New Century. This is the reality in Prairie cities like Winnipeg and Saskatoon: the poverty is spatially concentrated and racialized. Poverty will be misunderstood, and therefore anti-poverty strategies will be less effective, if we do not acknowledge the intimate ties between poverty and racism.

Finally, we need to invest more, and to do so consistently over time and in a more deliberate and strategic fashion, in the infrastructure of community-based organizations that has grown up to combat spatially concentrated racialized poverty. These CBOs are close to the people with whom they work and are highly creative and effective. A patient, long-term strategy by which governments work closely with and invest heavily in these CBOs will produce the kinds of changes that inner-city people say they want.

Can we solve the problem of spatially concentrated racialized poverty? Yes, we can. Can we do so quickly? No, we cannot. Can we do so using the broad government policy framework of the past 25 years that features significant reductions in the role of governments? No, we cannot. To solve the problem of spatially concentrated racialized poverty we need reforms that are, by today's standards, somewhat radical: stop cutting taxes; invest in national social programs; acknowledge and combat racism; and invest patiently, consistently, and systematically over time, in the infrastructure of community-based organizations that can produce transformative change.

REFERENCES

Adams, H. (1999). *Tortured People: The Politics of Colonization* (Revised ed.). Penticton, BC: Theytus Books.

Anderson, A. B. (2005). *Socio-Demographic Study of Aboriginal Population in Saskatoon.* Saskatoon: Bridges and Foundations Project, University of Saskatchewan.

Berdahl, L. (2007). *Caring Cities? Public Opinion and Urban Social Issues in Western Canadian Cities.* Calgary: Canada West Foundation.

Blackstock, C., & Trocmé, N. (2005). Community-Based Child Welfare for Aboriginal Children: Supporting Resilience Through Structural Change. *Social Policy Journal of New Zealand, 24* (March), 12-33.

Broad, D. (2006). *Capitalism Rebooted? Work, Welfare and the New Economy.* Halifax: Fernwood Publishing.

Brownell, M., Roos, N., Fransoo, R., Guèvremont, A., MacWilliam, L., Derksen, S., Dik, N., Bogdanovic, B., & Sirski, M. (2004). *How Do Educational Outcomes Vary With Socioeconomic Status? Key Findings From the Manitoba Child Health Atlas 2004.* Winnipeg: Manitoba Centre for Health Policy.

CCPA-Mb (Canadian Centre for Policy Alternatives-Manitoba). (2005). *Promise of Investment in Community-Led Renewal. State of the Inner City Report 2005, Part Two: A View From the Neighbourhoods.* Winnipeg: Canadian Centre for Policy Alternatives-Manitoba.

Clatworthy, S. (2000). *Factors Influencing the Migration of Registered Indians Between On and Off Reserve Locations in Canada.* Ottawa: Research and Analysis Directorate, Indian and Northern Affairs Canada.

Clatworthy, S. (1996). The Migration and Mobility Patterns of Canada's Aboriginal Population. *Royal Commission on Aboriginal Peoples: People to People, Nation to Nation.* Ottawa: Minister of Supply and Services Canada.

Diamantopoulos, M., & Findlay, I. M. (2007). *Growing Pains: Social Enterprise in Saskatoon's Core Neighbourhoods.* Saskatoon: Community-University Institute for Social Research and Centre for the Study of Co-operatives.

Distasio, J., Dudley, M., Johnson, M., & Sargent, K. (2005). *Neighbourhoods Alive!: Community Outcomes Final Report.* Winnipeg: Institute of Urban Studies.

Galabuzi, G. (2006). *Canada's Economic Apartheid: The Social Exclusion of Racialized Groups in the New Century.* Toronto: Canadian Scholars' Press.

Government of Saskatchewan. (2007, September 4). Station 20 West Project Proceeds. Retrieved December 20, 2007, from http://www.gov.sk.ca/news?newsId=5069d48e-2a47-44c3-9e99-018e7d046d0f

Grant, A. (1996). *No End of Grief: Indian Residential Schools in Canada.* Winnipeg: Pemmican Publications Inc.

Hart, M. (2002). *Seeking Mino-Pimatisiwin: An Aboriginal Approach to Helping.* Halifax: Fernwood Publishing.

Hunter, G., & Donovan, K. (2005). Poor Need More Than T.E.A.: Saskatchewan's Building Independence Program Forces People Into 'Low Wage' Traps. *Saskatchewan Notes.* Regina: Canadian Centre for Policy Alternatives- Saskatchewan.

Hunter, G., & Douglas, F. (2006). Report Card on Child Poverty in Saskatchewan. *Saskatchewan Notes.* Regina: Canadian Centre for Policy Alternatives-Saskatchewan.

Jackson, K. (1985). *Crabgrass Frontier: The Suburbanization of the United States.* New York: Oxford University Press.

Lewys, T. (2007). Core Rising: How Spence Beat the Odds to Become a Model for Treating Urban Decay. *Winnipeg Free Press,* March 25, F1.

Lezubski, D., Silver, J., & Black, E. (2000). High and Rising: The Growth of Poverty in Winnipeg's Inner City. In J. Silver (Ed.), *Solutions That Work: Fighting Poverty in Winnipeg* (pp. 26-51). Halifax: Fernwood Publishing.

MacKinnon, S., & Hudson, P. (2007) Manitoba Budget 2007: A Budget Without Courage. *Fast Facts.* Winnipeg: Canadian Centre for Policy Alternatives-Manitoba.

Manitoba Health. (1995). *The Health of Manitoba's Children* (by Brian Postl). Winnipeg: Queen's Printer.

Miller, J. R. (1996). *Shingwauk's Vision: A History of Native Residential Schools.* Toronto: University of Toronto Press.

Milloy, J. (1999). *A National Crime: The Canadian Government and the Residential School System, 1879-1986.* Winnipeg: University of Manitoba Press.

National Council of Welfare. (2006). *Welfare Incomes 2005.* Ottawa: National Council of Welfare.

Neechi Foods Co-op Ltd. (1993). *It's Up To All Of Us.* Winnipeg: Neechi Foods.

Peters, E. (n.d.) *Atlas of Urban Aboriginal Peoples.* Retrieved June 22, 2007, from http://gismap.usask.ca/website/Web%5FAtlas/AOUAP/cities.htm

Ross, D., & Roberts, P. (1999). *Income and Child Well-Being: A New Perspective on the Poverty Debate.* Ottawa: Canadian Council on Social Development.

Rothney, R. (1991). Neechi Foods Cooperative Limited: 1991 Original Study. Retrieved December 20, 2007, from http://www.ainc.inac.ca/pr/ra/coo/neec1991_e.html

Schissel, Bernard. (1997). *Blaming Children: Youth Crime, Moral Panics and the Politics of Hate.* Halifax: Fernwood Publishing.

Silver, J. (2002). *Building on our Strengths: Inner-City Priorities for a Renewed Tri-Level Development Agreement.* Winnipeg: Canadian Centre for Policy Alternatives-Manitoba and Urban Futures Group.

Silver, J. (2006a). *In Their Own Voices: Building Urban Aboriginal Communities.* Halifax: Fernwood Publishing.

Silver, J. (2006b). *North End Winnipeg's Lord Selkirk Park Public Housing Developments: History, Problems and Prospects.* Winnipeg: Canadian Centre for Policy Alternatives-Manitoba.

Silver, J. (2008). *The Inner Cities of Winnipeg and Saskatoon: A New Form of Development.* Winnipeg and Saskatoon: CCPA-Manitoba and CCPA-Saskatchewan.

Silver, J., & Loxley, J. (2007). Community Economic Development: An Introduction. In J. Loxley, J. Silver, & K. Sexsmith (Eds.), *Doing Community Economic Development* (pp. 2-13). Halifax: Fernwood Publishing.

Skelton, Ian. (2002). "Residential Mobility of Aboriginal Single Mothers in Winnipeg: an Exploratory Study of Chronic Moving." *Journal of Housing and the Built Environment, 17,* 127-144.

Social Planning Council of Winnipeg. (2006). *Manitoba Child and Family Poverty Report Card 2006.* Winnipeg: Social Planning Council of Winnipeg.

Statistics Canada. (2008). *Aboriginal Peoples in Canada in 2006: Inuit, Metis and First Nations, 2006 Census.* Catalogue No. 97-558-X1E. Ottawa: Minister of Industry.

Teeple, G. (2000). *Globalization and the Decline of Social Reform: Into the Twenty-First Century.* Toronto: Garamond Press.

Trocmé, N., Fallon, B., MacLaurin, B., & Neves, T. (2005). What is Driving Increasing Child Welfare Caseloads in Ontario? Analysis of the 1993 and 1998 Ontario Incidence Studies. *Child Welfare, 84*(3), 341-359.

Urban Futures Group. (1990). *Community Enquiry Into Inner City Revitalization.* Winnipeg: Urban Futures Group.

Wilson, W. J. (1987). *The Truly Disadvantaged: The Inner City, the Underclass and Public Policy.* Chicago: University of Chicago Press.

ABSTRACTS

Passion, Action, Strength and Innovative Change: The Experience of the Saskatchewan Children's Advocate's Office in Establishing Rights-based "Children and Youth First" Principles

Marvin M. Bernstein, Roxane A. Schury

Passion, Action, Strengths and Innovative Change—this is the exact terminology needed when considering purposeful changes in child welfare. It is the contention of this chapter's authors that child welfare services—and the children and families they serve—would greatly benefit from a change that would entrench child rights as a foundation for services and put children and youth at the centre of the circle of this work. The United Nations *Convention on the Rights of the Child* (UNCRC) and the Saskatchewan Children's Advocate Office (CAO) "Children and Youth First" Principles are two rights-based documents that are core to this needed paradigm shift in child welfare.

This chapter explores the importance and relevance of child rights, as articulated within the United Nations *Convention on the Rights of the Child*, the definitive international treaty regarding child rights. The connection between the *Convention* and the Saskatchewan Children's Advocate is clarified, and the work of the Office is described. Actual children's case studies that exemplify a lack of child rights and child-centred legislation, policy and practice in child welfare are provided to illustrate the strong need for such principles and the action that should follow from them. A list of user-friendly child rights-based child welfare practice points is also provided, leading into the Saskatchewan Children's Advocate "Children and Youth First" Principles. A call to action is followed by the conclusion supporting the necessity of moving from children's "paper rights" to "lived rights."

From Longing to Belonging: Attachment Theory, Connectedness and Indigenous Children in Canada

Jeannine Carriere and Cathy Richardson

In this article, the Metis authors document some of the historical, colonizing influences on Indigenous children and their families. The massive state-supported transfer of Indigenous children into Euro-Canadian homes can be attributed both to culturally-deprived child welfare practice and the ongoing colonial move to assimilate Indigenous Canadians. The authors discuss attachment theory and how it has been used, along with other western psychological theories, to facilitate child removal; they also make suggestions about how ideas of attachment and connection may influence practice positively. Responding appropriately to the current high rates of Indigenous child removal, rates currently three times higher than during the peak of residential schools, may mean attending to issues of ongoing child connection to the natural family, to the nation, and to non-European cultural traditions. This approach to helping and strengthening children is based on promoting a sense of belonging and continuity in their lives.

Jumping through Hoops: A Manitoba Study Examining Experiences and Reflections of Aboriginal Mothers Involved with Child Welfare in Manitoba

Marlyn Bennett

Ka Ni Kanichihk Inc., an urban Aboriginal organization in Winnipeg, undertook to conduct a review into the experiences of Aboriginal mothers involved with the child welfare system and family courts regarding child protection matters. This paper describes some of those experiences and reflections. The findings draw from in-depth recorded interviews conducted with 32 Aboriginal mothers during March to June of 2007. Each interview was transcribed and thematically analyzed; collectively, the mothers' stories about their experience with the child welfare and legal profession revealed a number of predominant themes. The paper highlights a number of solutions identified by mothers about how child welfare and family court systems can be improved to work better for Aboriginal mothers and their children.

Rehearsing with Reality: Exploring Health Issues with Aboriginal Youth through Drama

Linda Goulet, Jo-Ann Episkenew, Warren Linds, and Karen Arnason

This chapter examines a research project that was undertaken as a partnership between the File Hills Qu'Appelle Tribal Council (FHQTC), the First Nations University of Canada, and Concordia University. Our research project, Developing Healthy Decision-Making with Aboriginal Youth through Drama, used Forum Theatre workshops to help First Nations youth critically examine the choices they make that affect their health and to utilize the power of theatre to explore other choices and their potential consequences. We believed that by engaging youth in an examination of the factors that affect their decision-making, we could help them develop healthy lifestyles, which would, in turn, prevent their and their subsequent children's involvement in the child welfare and judicial systems.

The research is situated in the historical and present-day realities of the effects of colonization on First Nations people using "post-colonial" traumatic stress response. We also explore the theory and application of drama and Forum Theatre to First Nations communities. After describing the drama workshops central to the research, we examine the effects of colonization evident in the youth's dramatic portrayal of their lives. We conclude that drama is one way to engage Aboriginal youth in the investigation of the health issues in their lives as its form and process gives space for youth to voice their perspectives. The chapter ends by outlining how important it is to work with Aboriginal youth to identify and create places in their lives where different choices, and, consequently, different realities, are possible.

Making the Connection: Strategies for Working with High-risk Youth

Peter Smyth and Arlene Eaton-Erickson

High-risk youth are "the disconnected." These youth speak of negative experiences in the child welfare system, saying that their needs were not met and that their relationships with social workers and service providers were generally distant and problematic. Many youth have been labeled "manipulative" and/or "defiant," leaving them unable to access services they require. These youth typically struggle with authority and have few, if any, people they can trust. They live risk-filled lifestyles involving drugs, sexual exploitation, violence, living on the streets and family breakdown. Despite this, all youth have strengths to build on; they demonstrate resilience. A number of strategies offer direction and ideas to those who have a passion for working with high-risk youth. These strategies encourage a practice that strives to be anti-oppressive, flexible, responsive and harm reducing. It is non-traditional and creative and, according to youth, a better way to meet their needs.

The Moving Forward Project: Working with Refugee Children, Youth and their Families

Judy White and collaborators Dawn Franklin, Klaus Gruber, Cody Hanke, Bernadette Holzer, Nayyar Javed, Pat Keyser, Ashraf Mir, Ijeoma Udemgba, Micheline Veszi, and Clive Weighill.

The Moving Forward project was developed in 2004 to respond to the needs of refugee children, youth, and families coming from war-affected regions and situations of extreme violence. The primary components of this project were education, intervention, resource development and dissemination. The team, in consultation with an advisory committee, set up an orientation program for everyone involved in the project, and facilitated group sessions for parents and for youth. Major challenges included the lack of strong English language and literacy skills among participants in the program. The project emphasized the importance of creating a safe space where parents could meet, build new relationships (especially relationships of trust), feel safe, laugh, cry, and begin to build community. While one might approach working with children and youth differently from working with adults, the overall goals of prevention and empowerment remain the same. This project exposed the strong influence of Western ways of "doing and thinking," and challenged the team as a whole to rethink how one might provide programs and services in contexts where populations are becoming increasingly culturally diverse and where migration has been a strong influence on these changes. Services to address the child welfare needs of refugee children would reflect a commitment to prevention, and to creating the kinds of strong community supports and infrastructures that would enhance access and utilization by refugee children, youth, and their families.

Children with FASD Involved with the Manitoba Child Welfare System: The Need for Passionate Action

Don Fuchs, Linda Burnside, Shelagh Marchenski, and Andria Mudry

Meeting the needs of children with disabilities creates significant challenges for child welfare agencies. In Manitoba, it has been shown that one-third of children in care fall within a broad definition of disability and that 17 percent of children in care were affected by diagnosed or suspected Fetal Alcohol Spectrum Disorder (FASD). FASD encompasses a range of conditions that are caused by maternal alcohol consumption during pregnancy. Children with a diagnosis of FASD present agencies with an array of complex and variable needs. Both the significant proportion of children with FASD in care and the nature of their needs make it important to understand the relationship of this population to child welfare agencies. This chapter reports on the results of a study that was aimed at gathering information on the placement and legal status histories of children with FASD in care, comparing those histories to the histories of children with other disabilities and of children with no disabilities. Specifically it reports that children with FASD come into care at a younger age than any other group of children, became permanent wards more quickly and spent a greater proportion of lives in care of an agency than other children. Further, the chapter discusses the implications of the research findings for policy makers, administrators, service providers, and trainers and for further research in this area.

Passion for Those Who Care: What Foster Carers Need

Robert Twigg

Those researching and writing about child and family services generally focus on the needs of the children coming into care. Some expand that focus to include the children's families, and others include the social systems that impact on them. The needs of those who provide services to these children and their families are rarely the focus of research, writing, or policy. This chapter looks at the needs of one group of service providers: foster carers and their own children. The thesis of this chapter is that fostering can and must become a service that successfully meets the needs of both those who need the service (foster children and their families) and those who provide the care, including foster carers and their families. The chapter focuses on the implications of the needs identified, and on how child and family services agencies could modify the way in which they work with foster carers for the improvement of the system.

Physical Punishment in Childhood: A Human Rights and Child Protection Issue

Ailsa M. Watkinson

The physical punishment of children in Canada has been a topic widely discussed for decades. A recent United Nations' global study on violence against children found that physical punishment is one of the most extensive forms of violence experienced by children worldwide. In 2004, the Supreme Court of Canada considered the first major children's rights case under the Canadian Charter of Rights and Freedoms, which challenged the use of physical punishment on children. The decision has important implications for social workers, parents, educators and others. But how well do people know and understand the decision? This paper reviews the Supreme Court's decision and considers the current social and legal positioning of children in Canada regarding the use of physical punishment, and reports on findings of a study into the public's knowledge, understanding and needs arising from the Supreme Court decision. It raises questions concerning the intersection of child protection and children's rights and challenges social workers to take action to reduce the detrimental impact of child physical punishment and support initiatives that affirm a child's inherent rights and dignity.

Complex Poverty and Home-grown Solutions in Two Prairie Cities

Jim Silver

This chapter describes a particular form of poverty—spatially concentrated racialized poverty—that has emerged in recent decades in many western Canadian inner cities. This poverty is about much more than a shortage of income; it damages people in many ways. It is a form of poverty that is deeply entrenched and resistant to quick or easy solutions. The chapter argues that despite the complexity and tenacity of this form of poverty, out of its midst are emerging community-based solutions that are innovative and effective, and that have significant potential for overcoming poverty. The chapter will argue that in order for these community-based solutions to become truly transformative in communities plagued by spatially concentrated racialized poverty, additional policy measures are needed. The chapter concludes by offering some thoughts on what these might be.

RÉSUMÉS

La passion, l'action, la force et les changements novateurs : l'expérience du Bureau d'assistance à l'enfance de la Saskatchewan dans l'établissement de la vision *Les enfants et les jeunes d'abord* ancrée par un ensemble de huit principes connexes

Coauteurs : Marvin M. Bernstein et Roxane A. Schury

La passion, l'action, la force et les changements novateurs… Voilà la terminologie exacte requise lorsqu'on envisage des transformations d'envergure dans les services de protection de l'enfance. Les auteurs de ce chapitre soutiennent que les services de protection de l'enfance, ainsi que les enfants et les familles recevant ces services, bénéficieraient grandement d'un changement qui garantirait que les droits des enfants servent de fondement pour les services et qui placerait les enfants et les jeunes au centre de ce cercle d'intervention. *La Convention relative aux droits de l'enfant* des Nations Unies et les principes *Les enfants et les jeunes d'abord* du Bureau d'assistance à l'enfance de la Saskatchewan sont deux documents fondés sur les droits qui sont au cœur du changement de paradigme requis en protection de l'enfance.

Ce chapitre explore l'importance et la pertinence des droits des enfants, comme stipulé par la *Convention relative aux droits de l'enfant* des Nations Unies, le traité international définitif en matière de droits des enfants. Le lien entre la Convention et le rôle de l'intervenant en faveur des

enfants de la Saskatchewan est clarifié, et le travail du Bureau est également décrit. On y trouve des cas réels d'enfants qui illustrent le peu de
reconnaissance des droits des enfants ainsi que l'absence de législation,
de politiques et de pratiques centrées sur les enfants. Ces cas servent donc
à souligner le grand besoin de tels principes, ainsi que l'action devant y
découler. Les auteurs présentent également une liste conviviale de points
sur les pratiques en matière de protection de l'enfance axés sur les droits
des enfants. Y sont ensuite présentés les principes *Les enfants et les jeunes
d'abord* de l'intervenant en faveur des enfants de la Saskatchewan. Une
invitation à passer à l'action est lancée, suivie d'une conclusion soulignant la nécessité de passer de droits théoriques à des droits concrets.

De l'envie à l'appartenance : la théorie de l'attachement, l'interdépendance et les enfants autochtones du Canada

Coauteures : Jeannine Carriere et Cathy Richardson

Dans ce chapitre, les auteures métisses présentent quelques influences
historiques de la colonisation sur les enfants autochtones et leurs familles.
On peut attribuer le transfert massif d'enfants autochtones appuyé par
l'État à des familles euro-canadiennes à des pratiques de protection de
l'enfance culturellement tendancieuses ainsi qu'à la pression coloniale
continue d'assimiler les Autochtones du Canada. Les auteures traitent
de la théorie de l'attachement et de la façon dont elle a été interprétée,
de pair avec d'autres théories psychologiques occidentales, pour faciliter
le retrait d'enfants. Elles présentent également des suggestions sur les
façons dont les notions d'attachement et d'appartenance peuvent influer
positivement sur les pratiques. Une réaction appropriée à l'égard du taux
élevé de retrait d'enfants autochtones qui sévit actuellement—un taux
de prise en charge trois fois plus élevé qu'à l'époque des pensionnats—
pourrait nécessiter qu'on se penche sur les enjeux liés au sentiment
d'appartenance à la famille biologique, à la nation et aux traditions cul-
turelles non européennes. Les auteures soutiennent que, pour appuyer les
enfants, il faut nourrir leurs sentiments d'appartenance et de continuité.

Course à obstacles : une étude manitobaine concernant les expériences et les réflexions de mères autochtones recevant des services du système de protection de l'enfance

Auteure : Marlyn Bennett

Ka Ni Kanichihk Inc., un organisme autochtone urbain de Winnipeg au Manitoba, a examiné les expériences de mères autochtones impliquées avec les services de protection de l'enfance et avec les tribunaux de la famille en raison de problèmes de protection de l'enfance. Ce chapitre décrit certaines de ces expériences et réflexions. Les données sont tirées d'entrevues approfondies enregistrées sur bande qui ont été effectuées auprès de 32 mères autochtones entre mars et juin 2007. Chaque entrevue a été transcrite et analysée thématiquement, et six thèmes prédominants se sont dégagés des expériences des mères au chapitre de la protection de l'enfance et des professions juridiques. Ce chapitre présente diverses solutions formulées par les mères pour améliorer leurs expériences avec les services de protection et les tribunaux de la famille.

Mise en scène de la réalité : les jeunes autochtones, l'art dramatique et la santé

Coauteurs : Linda Goulet, Jo-Ann Episkenew, Warren Linds et Karen Arnason

Ce chapitre traite d'un projet de recherche entrepris grâce à un partenariat entre File Hills Qu'Appelle Tribal Council, l'Université des Premières nations du Canada et l'Université Concordia. Notre projet de recherche, intitulé *Promouvoir la prise de décisions saines chez les jeunes autochtones par l'entremise de l'art dramatique*, s'est appuyé sur des ateliers de théâtre forum visant à aider des jeunes des Premières nations à examiner d'un œil critique les choix qu'ils ayant un impact sur leur santé. Ils sont encouragés à utiliser le pouvoir du théâtre pour explorer d'autres choix, ainsi que leurs conséquences potentielles. Nous considérons qu'en incitant les jeunes à examiner les facteurs influant sur leur prise de décisions, nous pouvons les aider à choisir un style de vie sain. Cela aura pour effet de prévenir les démêlés avec les services de protection de l'enfance et les tribunaux, tant maintenant que lorsqu'ils seront eux-mêmes parents.

La recherche s'appuie sur les conséquences actuelles et historiques de la colonisation sur les Premières nations selon l'optique du trouble de stress traumatique « postcolonisation ». Nous explorons également la théorie et l'application des principes de l'art dramatique et du théâtre forum à l'égard des communautés des Premières nations. À la suite d'une description des ateliers de théâtre au cœur de cette recherche, nous examinons les effets évidents de la colonisation sur la mise en scène dramatique que font les jeunes de leur vie. Nous aboutissons à la conclusion que l'art dramatique est une façon d'inciter les jeunes autochtones à examiner la façon dont ils abordent leur santé, puisque la forme et le processus théâtraux permettent aux jeunes de verbaliser leurs perceptions. Le chapitre se termine en soulignant l'importance de travailler avec des jeunes autochtones de façon à ce qu'ils identifient et créent des occasions pour effectuer différents choix en vue de construire des réalités différentes.

Faire alliance : des stratégies pour intervenir auprès de jeunes à haut risque

Coauteurs : Peter Smyth et Arlene Eaton-Erickson

Les jeunes à haut risque se sentent mis à l'écart de la société. Ces jeunes parlent d'expériences négatives vécues dans le système de protection de l'enfance et ils relatent comment leurs besoins n'ont pas été répondus et que leurs relations avec les travailleurs sociaux et les prestateurs de services étaient habituellement froides et posaient problèmes. Plusieurs de ces jeunes ont été étiquetés comme étant « manipulateurs » et/ou « rebelles », ce qui les empêche d'obtenir les services dont ils ont besoin. Ces jeunes sont habituellement réfractaires à l'autorité et ils ont peu de personnes à qui ils peuvent faire confiance. Leur vie est remplie de risques comprenant la toxicomanie, l'exploitation sexuelle, la violence, l'itinérance et la détérioration familiale. Malgré cela, ces jeunes ont tous des forces pouvant appuyer leur résilience. De nombreuses stratégies sont présentées en vue d'offrir de la direction et des idées aux personnes ayant la passion de travailler avec les jeunes à haut risque. Ces stratégies s'appuient sur une pratique axée sur l'anti-oppression, la souplesse, la sensibilité et la réduction des méfaits. Ce type de pratique est non traditionnel et créatif, et, selon les jeunes, il consiste en une meilleure façon de répondre à leurs besoins.

Le projet *Allons de l'avant* : intervenir auprès d'enfants et de jeunes réfugiés et leurs familles

Auteure : Judy White et ses collaborateurs Dawn Franklin, Klaus Gruber, Cody Hanke, Bernadette Holzer, Nayyar Javed, Pat Keyser, Ashraf Mir, Ijeoma Udemgba, Mechilene Veszi, Clive Weighill

Le projet Allons de l'avant a été mis sur pied en 2004 afin de répondre aux besoins d'enfants et de jeunes réfugiés et de leurs familles provenant de régions touchées par la guerre et par la violence extrême. Les principales composantes du projet étaient l'éducation, l'intervention, la création de ressources et la diffusion. L'équipe, en consultation avec un comité consultatif, a conçu un programme d'orientation pour toutes les personnes consacrées au projet, et a animé des séances de groupes de parents et de jeunes. Parmi les principales embûches, il y avait les difficultés sur les plans de l'expression orale et de la compréhension écrite de l'anglais chez les participants du programme. Dans le cadre du projet, l'accent a été placé sur la création d'un lieu sécuritaire où les parents pouvaient se rencontrer, créer de nouvelles relations (particulièrement des relations de confiance), se sentir en sécurité, rire, pleurer et laisser naître un sentiment d'appartenance. Même si les approches diffèrent dans le travail avec les enfants et les jeunes comparativement à celui avec les adultes, les objectifs généraux de prévention et d'autonomisation demeurent les mêmes. Ce projet a permis d'exposer l'influence marquée des façons de faire et de penser occidentales et a incité l'équipe à revoir comment fournir des programmes et des services dans des contextes de plus en plus diversifiés sur le plan culturel où la migration influe grandement sur ces changements. Les services conçus pour répondre aux besoins de protection et de bien-être d'enfants réfugiés doivent refléter un engagement à l'égard de la prévention, notamment par la création de ressources et d'infrastructures communautaires très présentes conçues pour assurer l'accès et l'utilisation par des enfants et des jeunes réfugiés et leurs familles.

Les enfants atteints de l'ensemble des troubles causés par l'alcoolisation foetale recevant des services de protection de l'enfance au Manitoba

Coauteurs : Don Fuchs, Linda Burnside, Shelagh Marchenski et Andria Mudry

Répondre aux besoins d'enfants ayant des handicaps représente un défi de taille pour les organismes de protection de l'enfance. Au Manitoba, il a été constaté qu'un tiers des enfants pris en charge font partie de la catégorie générale d'enfants atteints d'un handicap, et 17 % des enfants pris en charge sont diagnostiqués ou soupçonnés comme ayant l'ensemble des troubles causés par l'alcoolisation foetale (ETCAF). L'ETCAF regroupe une vaste gamme de conditions causées par la consommation d'alcool par la mère durant la grossesse. Les organismes desservant les enfants atteints de l'ETCAF doivent répondre à leur éventail de besoins tant complexes que variables. En raison du nombre important d'enfants pris en charge atteints de l'ETCAF et de la nature de leurs besoins, il est important de comprendre les liens unissant cette population aux organismes de protection de l'enfance. Ce chapitre présente les résultats d'une étude visant à recueillir de l'information sur le placement et le statut juridique d'enfants atteints de l'ETCAF afin de comparer leurs antécédents à ceux d'enfants atteints d'autres handicaps ou d'enfants n'ayant aucun handicap. On y constate que les enfants atteints de l'ETCAF sont pris en charge plus jeunes que tout autre groupe d'enfants, qu'ils deviennent des pupilles de l'État plus rapidement et qu'ils sont pris en charge pendant une plus longue période que les autres enfants. De plus, on y traite des implications des résultats de recherche pour les décideurs, les administrateurs, les prestateurs de services et les formateurs, tout en soulignant le besoin d'approfondir les recherches dans ce domaine.

De la passion pour ceux qui s'occupent des autres : ce dont les familles d'accueil ont besoin

Auteur : Robert Twigg

Les personnes effectuant de la recherche ou écrivant sur les services offerts aux enfants et aux familles se concentrent habituellement sur les besoins des enfants pris en charge. Quelques-uns élargissent leur portée pour inclure les familles des enfants, tandis que d'autres incorporent les systèmes sociaux ayant un impact sur ces usagers. Toutefois, la recherche, les écrits et les politiques traitent peu des besoins des personnes fournissant des services à ces enfants et familles. Ce chapitre est consacré aux besoins d'un groupe de ces prestateurs de services, les parents d'accueil et leurs propres enfants. Le chapitre présente la thèse que l'accueil familial peut et doit devenir un service qui répond avec succès aux besoins des personnes nécessitant le service (c.-à-d. les enfants et leurs familles) et aux besoins des personnes fournissant les soins (c.-à-d. les parents d'accueil et leurs familles). On y traite des implications liées aux besoins identifiés et les façons dont les organismes de services aux enfants et aux familles peuvent modifier leur approche avec les parents d'accueil de façon à améliorer le système.

Les punitions corporelles et les enfants

Auteure : Ailsa Watkinson

Depuis des décennies, le sujet des punitions corporelles infligées aux enfants a été largement débattu au Canada. Une récente étude mondiale des Nations Unies sur la violence contre les enfants a démontré que les punitions corporelles sont l'une des formes les plus courantes de violence vécues par les enfants de partout au monde. En 2004, la Cour suprême du Canada s'est penchée sur le premier cas d'importance en matière de droits des enfants, interprété en fonction de la *Charte canadienne des droits et libertés*, qui contestait le recours aux punitions corporelles infligées aux enfants. La décision a eu d'importantes implications pour les travailleurs sociaux, les parents et les éducateurs, entre autres. À quel point cette décision est-elle connue et bien comprise? Ce chapitre examine la décision de la Cour suprême ainsi que le statut social et juridique actuel des enfants canadiens quant à l'utilisation de punitions corporelles. On y traite également des résultats d'une étude sur les connaissances, la compréhension et les besoins du public quant à cette décision de la Cour suprême. Des questions sont soulevées sur les liens entre la protection de l'enfance et les droits des enfants. De plus, l'auteure incite les travailleurs sociaux à agir de façon à réduire les effets néfastes des punitions corporelles et à appuyer les initiatives visant à maintenir la dignité et les droits inhérents des enfants.

Réflexion sur la pauvreté complexe et les solutions locales de deux ville des Prairies

Auteur : Jim Silver

Dans ce chapitre, on décrit une forme particulière de pauvreté, soit la pauvreté racialisée concentrée dans l'espace, qui a fait son apparition au cours des dernières décennies dans de nombreuses grandes villes de l'ouest du Canada. Beaucoup plus qu'une absence de revenus, cette pauvreté affecte les gens à bien des égards. Il s'agit d'une forme de pauvreté qui est profondément enracinée et résistante aux solutions rapides ou faciles. Dans ce chapitre, on fait remarquer que malgré la complexité et la ténacité de cette forme de pauvreté, on voit émerger de cet abîme des solutions communautaires innovatrices et efficaces qui présentent un potentiel important pour surmonter la pauvreté. L'auteur indique que, afin que ces solutions communautaires puissent véritablement transformer les collectivités assaillies par la pauvreté racialisée concentrée dans l'espace, de nouvelles politiques devront être mises en œuvre. En conclusion, il propose quelques idées sur ce que pourraient être ces politiques.

CONTRIBUTORS

KAREN ARNASON is the health educator for the File Hills Qu'Appelle Tribal Council in Fort Qu'Appelle. She has experience teaching in the public school system, as well as in a post-secondary teacher education program. As a health educator, Karen provides information to schools and communities for topics such as FASD, HIV/Aids, Anti-bullying, and Youth Peer Leadership. She is the driving force behind the Healthy Communities: Healthy Youth Project where a committee of youth and adults gather monthly to address issues of healthy living for youth.

MARLYN BENNETT is an Ojibway woman employed by the First Nations Child & Family Caring Society of Canada and is an interdisciplinary student at the University of Manitoba. She works and lives in Winnipeg with her fourteen-year-old daughter, her partner Mike, and their furry canine (Zak) and feline (Smokey).

MARVIN BERNSTEIN took office as Saskatchewan's second Children's Advocate on September 6, 2005. At the time, Marv had 28 years of senior leadership and child welfare experience in Ontario. Marv is an independent officer of the Legislative Assembly of Saskatchewan and was awarded the Saskatchewan Centennial Medal in February 2006. Marv has a Bachelor of Arts, a Juris Doctor and a Master of Laws in Alternative Dispute Resolution. He has been called to the Bar in both Saskatchewan and Ontario. He has provided legal representation in child welfare cases at all court levels and has acted as counsel in the Supreme Court of Canada on two occasions. He is also a widely published author, having written extensively in the areas of children's rights, child welfare, child and youth access to justice, permanency planning, adoption, adoption disclosure, alternative dispute resolution, mediation, privacy legislation, inquests and social worker liability.

IVAN BROWN is the manager of the Centre of Excellence for Child Welfare, a national body supporting dissemination, research, and policy in child welfare. He is an internationally recognized expert in child and family issues, particularly with regard to disability and quality of life. He has published widely in the academic literature and has written or edited nine scholarly books. He has initiated several major quality of life studies, including an international initiative in family quality of life in seventeen countries, and has demonstrated active leadership in international organizations in the field of intellectual disabilities. Dr. Brown is semi-retired, but is active in teaching and providing research support at the Factor-Inwentash Faculty of Social Work, University of Toronto.

LINDA BURNSIDE is currently the acting director of Disability Programs, Manitoba Family Services and Housing. She is a social worker and certified counselor (with the Canadian Counseling Association). She has recently completed her Ph.D. in social work at the University of Manitoba. Much of her work experience is in the field of child welfare: she has worked as a child protection social worker, a therapist in sexual abuse treatment, an assistant program manager with Winnipeg Child and Family Services and as authority relations director with Child Protection Branch of Manitoba Family Services and Housing.

JEANNINE CARRIERE is a Metis woman originally from the Red River area of Manitoba. Her educational background includes a Ph.D. in Human Ecology Family Studies, an M.S.W. and a B.S.W. Jeannine is an associate professor at the University of Victoria School of Social Work in the Indigenous Specialization. Her research interests include child and family services, mental health, and ways of knowing and knowledge transfer. Dr. Carriere has several publications in these research areas and serves on a number of volunteer committees related to Aboriginal child welfare. She has recently received the Adoption Activist award from the North American Council on Adoptable Children (NACAC).

ARLENE EATON-ERICKSON is an advocate at the Office of the Child and Youth Advocate (Alberta). She has been a social worker for twelve years and was with Child and Youth Services, Region 6 (Edmonton and Area Child and Family Services) as a front-line worker and a supervisor from 1996 to 2004. During this time, Arlene was the case worker attached to a high-risk youth caseload from 1999 to 2003, and was involved in founding the Old Strathcona Youth Society. Arlene was instrumental in producing the report *The Word on the Street: How Youth View Services Aimed at Them*, released in March 2005.

JO-ANN EPISKENEW teaches classes on Aboriginal Literature and Theatre that examine the effects of historical trauma on Aboriginal communities. Her research examines the application of Aboriginal literatures, including theatre, and its applications in improving the socio-cultural health of Aboriginal people and communities. Along with Renate Eigenbrod, she is co-editor of *Creating Community: A Roundtable on Aboriginal Literatures* (Theytus, 2002). Her recent articles include "Living and Dying with the Madness of Colonial Policies: The Aesthetics of Resistance in Daniel David Moses' *Almighty Voice and His Wife*," published this year in H. Lutz (Ed.), *What is Your Place? Indigeneity and Immigration in Canada* (Shriftenreihe der Gesselschaft für Kanada-Studien, 2007).

DAWN FRANKLIN is a settlement worker in schools. She is employed with the Saskatoon Open Door Society.

DON FUCHS is a full professor at the Faculty of Social Work at the University of Manitoba. He has conducted extensive research on the role of social network and social support in strengthening the parenting abilities of families and in preventing child maltreatment. His current research focuses on creating profiles of children with disability in the care of the state, and examining the determinants which result in children with disabilities coming into care. He has also done extensive international social development work for ten years in Russia as part of a CIDA-funded project. He has served as Dean of the Faculty of Social Work at the University of Manitoba for eleven years, and was a founding participant in the development of the Prairie Child Welfare Consortium. He has been instrumental in the development of a B.S.W. option in Child and Family Services at the University of Manitoba.

LINDA GOULET is an associate professor at the Department of Indigenous Education, First Nations University of Canada, where she teaches classes in culturally relevant pedagogy. Her work in drama grew out of her interest in effective teaching practices for Aboriginal students. She works in community with students and educators, using drama to examine health issues, as well as racism and discrimination in schools. This work is reflected in her most recent publication, co-written with Warren Linds, "Performing praxis: Exploring anti-racism through drama" in S. Moore & R. Mitchell (Eds.), *Power, pedagogy and praxis: Social justice in the globalized classroom* (Sense Publishers, 2008).

KLAUS GRUBER is the executive director of Family Service Saskatoon and former executive director of Saskatchewan Association of Social Workers. Klaus has often taught as a sessional instructor for the Faculty of Social Work and has been a volunteer in the area of refugee settlement for many years. Klaus and his family have been sponsors for numerous refugees families.

CODY HANKE is the vice principal of Walter Murray Collegiate, one of the Saskatoon high schools with a large English as an Additional Language population.

BERNADETTE (BERNIE) HOLZER is the program manager at Family Service Saskatoon. She retired from the Department of Social Services as a regional director and has worked as a faculty field liaison with the Faculty of Social Work, University of Regina. Bernie supervises social work practicum students.

NAYYAR JAVED is a psychologist with Saskatoon Community Clinic. Prior to this position, Nayyar worked for several years with Saskatoon Adult Mental Health Services. Nayyar is an avid community activist and is the president of Saskatchewan Intercultural Association.

PAT KEYSER is a counsellor with Family Service Saskatoon. Pat's role at Family Service Saskatoon includes individual counselling and domestic abuse group work. Pat has played a lead role facilitating groups with the Moving Forward project. Pat is a sessional instructor with the Faculty of Social Work, University of Regina, and supervises social work practicum students.

DEXTER KINEQUON is the executive director of the Lac La Ronge Indian Band Indian Child & Family Services Agency. A member of the Daystar First Nations Cree Band of Treaty Four, he earned his Bachelor of Indian Social Work in 1994 from the First Nations University of Canada. Dexter has been involved extensively in the development of First Nations child welfare in Saskatchewan and is the past chairman of the newly established Saskatchewan First Nations Family and Community Institute. Additionally, Dexter represents Saskatchewan at the Child Welfare League of Canada Board of Directors and is registered with the Child Welfare League's National Roster of Experts for special child welfare investigations. Dexter also represents First Nations' interests in his role as Commissioner for the Saskatchewan Legal Aid Commission. In 2004, Dexter participated as a member of the Governor General's Canadian Leadership Conference, which brings together high potential individuals expected to achieve senior leadership positions in their organizations and communities.

WARREN LINDS is assistant professor in the Department of Applied Human Sciences, Concordia University, Montreal, and has over twenty-five years of experience in popular education and Forum Theatre. He has published "Theatre of the Oppressed: Developing a Pedagogy of Solidarity?" in *Theatre Research in Canada* (1998); "Metaxis: Dancing (in) the in-between" in J. Cohen-

Cruz & M. Schutzman (Eds.), *A Boal Companion* (Routledge, 2006); and, with E. Vettraino, "Collective Imagining: Collaborative Story Telling through Image Theater" in *Forum: Qualitative Social Research* (2008). Warren works with Linda Goulet, using Forum Theatre in urban schools to help students examine issues such as racism and violence. Together they co-authored the chapter, "Performing praxis: Exploring anti-racism through drama" in S. Moore & R. Mitchell (Eds.), *Power, pedagogy and praxis: Social justice in the globalized classroom* (Sense Publishers, 2008).

SHELAGH MARCHENSKI is a social worker who practiced for many years in northern Manitoba. Her experience includes direct service provision in the child welfare, family services, education and non-profit sectors. Since 2004, she has worked as a researcher with the Faculty of Social Work, University of Manitoba, and the Child Protection Branch, Manitoba Family Services and Housing, on projects related to children with disabilities. She is presently seconded to the Office of the Children's Advocate.

SHARON MCKAY is professor emerita, Faculty of Social Work, University of Regina. Her teaching career began at Lakehead University School of Social Work, following ten years full- and part-time practice in the fields of child and family services and mental health. She served as Dean of the Faculty of Social Work, University of Regina, from 1990-2000, and is a founding member and steering committee chair of the Prairie Child Welfare Consortium (1999-present). She served as president, Canadian Association of Schools of Social Work (now Canadian Association of Social Work Education) from 2002-2004. In earlier years, she served as president, Ontario Association of Professional Social Workers from 1985-87 (now Ontario Association of Social Workers); and national director for Ontario, Canadian Association of Social Workers (1987-90). She is an active member of current provincial and national child welfare initiatives.

ASHRAF MIR is currently employed with the Government of Saskatchewan's Department of Immigration. Ashraf was the first co-ordinator with the Moving Forward project and worked as executive director with International Women of Saskatoon prior to current employment.

ANDRIA MUDRY is currently a business analyst with the Child Protection Branch, Manitoba Family Services and Housing. She is also a research associate with the Children in Care with Disabilities Research Project, Faculty of Social Work, University of Manitoba. Andria has over ten years of experience working with children, families and seniors in a variety of social and health programs. She has also been involved with research projects on cardiac rehabilitation, legal aid and children with disabilities.

She has her M.S.W. (Policy and Planning), a B.H.Ec. (Foods and Nutrition) and a Counseling Certificate. Over the years she has developed an interest in children, health promotion, and evaluation. She is also a member of the Winnipeg Regional Health Authority Advisory Board.

CATHY RICHARDSON is a Metis woman with a long history of social activism and engagement in the helping professions. She has a doctorate in child and youth psychology with a specialty in Aboriginal wellness. Cathy has a work history involving education, counselling and family therapy, child welfare, and alternative dispute resolution. Based on principles of human dignity and social safety, her work has focused on issues of violence prevention and recovery from violence and mistreatment. She is an assistant professor in the School of Social Work, Indigenous Specialization, at the University of Victoria.

ROXANE SCHURY has worked as a social worker with children and families in many capacities ranging from child welfare to clinical work. Roxane joined the Saskatchewan Children's Advocate Office (CAO) in 1998, working in both advocacy and investigations. Roxane collaborated in the development of the CAO investigation process, carried the Systemic file on Sexual Exploitation and co-authored a submission to the United Nations *Convention on the Rights of the Child (CRC)* Committee Day of General Discussion. Roxane's academic focus has been on Indigenous studies and child rights. In 2005 she worked with the NGO Group for the *CRC* in the Liaison Unit with the United Nations *CRC* Committee. She also contributed to a report conducted by the NGO Group, which was submitted to the UN Violence against Children Study. Roxane was the recipient of the International Studentship Award, University of Calgary, and the Distinguished Alumni Award – Humanitarian/ Community Service, University of Regina, both in 2005.

JIM SILVER is chair of the Politics Department and co-director of the Urban and Inner-City Studies program at the University of Winnipeg. He has written extensively on inner-city issues. His latest book is *In Their Own Voices: Building Urban Aboriginal Communities* (Halifax: Fernwood Publishing, 2006).

PETER SMYTH is a supervisor with Child and Youth Services, Region 6 (Edmonton and Area Child and Family Services). Currently he is supervising the High Risk Youth Unit. Peter has been a social worker with Children's Services for over 20 years, 12 of those as a supervisor. He has much experience working with youth, particularly high-risk youth, and has represented Region 6 on innovative multi-disciplinary community projects, including Partners for Youth and Inner City Connections, over the past 14 years. He helped found the Old Strathcona Youth Co-op starting in 1997, and developed a high-risk youth caseload in his unit in 1999. Peter spearheaded a study released in March 2005 titled *The Word on the Street: How Youth View Services Aimed at Them.*

MARY ELLEN TURPEL-LAFOND was appointed British Columbia's first Representative for Children and Youth in November 2006, for a five-year term. The Representative for Children and Youth is an independent officer of the Legislature, and works to support vulnerable children, particularly Aboriginal children and youth. Ms Turpel-Lafond, who took a five-year leave from the Saskatchewan Provincial Court, was appointed to the bench in 1998. She was the Administrative Judge for Saskatoon, involved in the administration of the Provincial Court of Saskatchewan in relation to access to justice, Aboriginal justice and healing, and public outreach. She has also worked as a criminal law judge in youth and adult courts, which led her to work at developing partnerships to better serve the needs of young people in the justice system, particularly sexually exploited children and youth, and children and youth with disabilities, such as fetal alcohol spectrum disorder. Prior to her judicial appointment, Ms Turpel-Lafond was a lawyer in Nova Scotia and Saskatchewan and a tenured professor of law at Dalhousie University Faculty of Law. She taught law at the University of Toronto, the University of Notre Dame and other universities, and held the position of Aboriginal Scholar at the University of Saskatchewan. She has been a visiting professor at the University of British Columbia and the University of Victoria law schools. Ms Turpel-Lafond is Cree and Scottish. She is a member of the Muskeg Lake Cree Nation in Saskatchewan and the mother of four children, which she considers her greatest opportunity for learning and growth as a person.

ROB TWIGG is retired as associate professor, Faculty of Social Work, University of Regina, and is currently engaged in teaching and private practice in Winnipeg. His areas of interest include clinical practice and child welfare with a special interest in foster care. Prior to entering academia he worked for 10 years in a Treatment Foster Care program in southern Ontario. He has researched, published and presented workshops on the topic of how foster carers' children experience fostering. He is currently a member of the research committee of the Foster Family Based Treatment Association. The FFTA published his monograph *Withstanding the Test of Time: What We Know about Treatment Foster Care* in 2006.

IJEOMA UDEMGBA began her employment with International Women of Saskatoon as co-ordinator of the Moving Forward project and later became the executive director of that agency. Ijeoma worked as a lawyer prior to coming to Saskatchewan.

MICHELINE VESZI is a settlement worker in schools. She has been employed with the Saskatoon Open Door Society for many years.

AILSA WATKINSON is a professor with the Faculty of Social Work, University of Regina. She received her Ph.D. in educational administration from the University of Saskatchewan. Her research was on the Courts' interpretation of the *Canadian Charter of Rights and Freedoms* and its implications for administrators. In 1995 Ailsa began the legal process of challenging the use of corporal punishment on children. She argued that section 43 of the *Criminal Code* was a violation of children's rights under the *Charter of Rights and Freedoms*. Section 43 provides a defence from charges of assault for parents, teachers and others acting in their place when they use physical force on children to correct their behaviour. The case was eventually heard by the Supreme Court of Canada in 2004. The Court ruled that s. 43 did not violate the rights of children; however, the Court also imposed limits on its use. Ailsa is co-editor of *Contesting Fundamentalisms*. She is also the author of *Education, Student Rights and the Charter* and co-editor of two books on systemic violence. She has published a number of articles on such topics as sexual harassment, women's and children's equality rights, employment equity, religion in public spaces, the Charter as policy advocate and the administration of equality rights.

CLIVE WEIGHILL is the chief of police with the Saskatoon Police Services.

JUDY WHITE is an associate professor at the Faculty of Social Work, University of Regina. She is a board member of International Women of Saskatoon, Canadian Research Institute for the Advancement of Women, the Vanier Institute of the Family, and also a member of the board of governors for Prairie Metropolis. Judy is past chair of the Saskatoon Settlement and Integration Coordinating Committee, and has been a commissioner with the Saskatchewan Human Rights Committee since 2005. The primary focus of Judy's volunteer work has been on the issues affecting immigrant and refugee peoples, and on immigrant and refugee women and their families living in Saskatchewan. Judy has also been involved in the Moving Forward project which has focused on responding to the needs of children and youth coming from regions of war and extreme violence. Judy has presented locally and nationally on topics related to racism, post traumatic stress responses, and women's mental health.

Subject Index

Author Index

NOTE: The lowercase letter "n" following a page number indicates that the citation is in a footnote. For example 40n.15 indicates foonote 15 on page 40.